Ancient Rome's Provinces: The History of Roman Empire in

By Charles Rive

Lionel Royer's painting, *Vercingetorix throws down his arms at the feet of Julius Caesar*

About Charles River Editors

Charles River Editors provides superior editing and original writing services across the digital publishing industry, with the expertise to create digital content for publishers across a vast range of subject matter. In addition to providing original digital content for third party publishers, we also republish civilization's greatest literary works, bringing them to new generations of readers via ebooks.

Sign up here to receive updates about free books as we publish them, and visit Our Kindle Author Page to browse today's free promotions and our most recently published Kindle titles.

Introduction

Roman Provinces

A bronze statue of Caesar

"Caesar, having stationed his army on both sides of the fortifications, in order that, if occasion should arise, each should hold and know his own post, orders the cavalry to issue forth from the camp and commence action. There was a commanding view from the entire camp, which occupied a ridge of hills; and the minds of all the soldiers anxiously awaited the issue of the battle. The Gauls had scattered archers and light-armed infantry here and there, among their cavalry, to give relief to their retreating troops, and sustain the impetuosity of our cavalry. Several of our soldiers were unexpectedly wounded by these, and left the battle. When the Gauls were confident that their countrymen were the conquerors in the action, and beheld our men hard pressed by numbers, both those who were hemmed in by the line of circumvallation and those who had come to aid them, supported the spirits of their men by shouts and yells from every quarter. As the action was carried on in sight of all, neither a brave nor cowardly act could be concealed; both the desire of praise and the fear of ignominy, urged on each party to valor. After fighting from noon almost to sunset, without victory inclining in favor of either, the Germans, on one side, made a charge against the enemy in a compact body, and drove them back; and, when they were put to flight, the archers were surrounded and cut to pieces. In other parts, likewise, our men pursued to the camp the retreating enemy, and did not give them an opportunity of rallying…" – Julius Caesar, *De Bello Gallico*

Graeco-Roman relations in the ancient world are normally assumed to date, essentially, from 146 B.C., when Rome organized its supervision of Greece through its Governors in Macedonia. In fact, the first direct interactions of any note between the two come about during the first Illyrian War in 229 B.C, although, of course there had been contacts of numerous kinds even prior to this date. Phillip V of Macedon had allied himself with Hannibal and that, in itself, guaranteed, at some point, that the Romans would turn their full attention to the eastern Mediterranean area, if for no other reason than to settle that outstanding score once and for all. Phillip was defeated in 197 B.C. at the Battle of Cynoscephalae and his son Perseus, at Pydna in 168 B.C. Following these defeats, Macedonia was divided into four republics under Roman governorship, but the rest of Greece was left relatively free from direct Roman rule. In due course, opposition to Rome's increasing domination of the region led to the establishment of the Achaean League, comprising a number of city states, headed by Corinth, to oppose the Romans. The whole endeavour failed miserably and in 146 B.C. Corinth was totally destroyed in the process. Rome's treatment of Corinth was particularly brutal; all the men were killed, and all women and children sold into slavery. The city was razed to the ground as an example and warning to all others that might think of opposing Rome.

Notwithstanding these dire examples of how Rome treated its defeated enemies, opposition to the Republic grew steadily in the years that followed and in 88 B.C. a number of Greek cities, particularly Athens, took the opportunity provided by Mithradates V's war against Rome, to ally itself with him in the hope of ending Roman exploitation of Greece. Sulla's campaign was waged with the same savage intensity that Rome had shown in its previous dealings with the Greeks. He quickly eliminated all resistance and Athens, which had so ardently supported Mithradates, was singled out for especially vicious treatment. Sulla's troops occupied the city, destroyed the walls and systematically looted the most valuable of the city's sculptures.

It is from this period until the Battle of Actium in 31 B.C. that Greece became a theatre for internecine Roman warfare and Greek cities were constantly "milked" of resources, both in terms of direct taxes and materials, by their Roman masters. Cities that could not meet the huge, and constant, demands were subjected to severe punishments, including the selling of entire populations into slavery. Gytheum in 71 B.C. is an example of a *polis* that learned the hard way that inability to pay was no excuse in the eyes of the Romans. However, it was after Actium, and Octavian's victory over Antony and Cleopatra, that the Pax-Romana imposed by Rome, provided Greece with the longest period of peace in its entire history, a period that lasted three hundred years. The starting point for this period of peace was, in many ways, Augustus' re-organisation of the system of governance which saw the foundation of the new Roman province of Achaea with the rebuilt Corinth as its capital.

In the early years of the Principate[1] despite growing Philhellenism in the Empire, the vast majority of Greeks, with the notable exception of Sparta, were very unwilling subjects of Rome. There was unrest in the Augustan period (27 B.C. - AD 14), particularly in Athens, and the imperial cult made little or no headway until the time of Nero (AD54 - 68), who, along with Hadrian much later (AD117 - 138), took a special interest in Greece and all things Greek. Nero, for example began the work on the Corinth canal, using slave labour, of course, and Hadrian completed a number of projects that are dealt with later in some detail. The antagonism that the majority of Greeks felt towards Rome was not helped by Caesar's foundation of a Roman colony at Corinth in 44 B.C. and another by Augustus at Nicopolis in 31 B.C. In both cases the establishment of the colonies had led to the forcible removal of the indigenous populations to make room for the colonists.

What was, however, even more resented was what the Greeks considered to be the pillage of their culture and heritage. Various emperors systematically looted Greek temples and public buildings of their sculptures and other priceless works of art, taking them back to adorn the homes of the rich or public buildings in Rome. The pillage of Greek heritage extended to attempts to absorb Greek cults and Suetonius[2] records the ultimately failed attempt to transfer the whole Eleusinian mystery cult to Rome. However, despite the ravages wrought on the Greek cities and their populations by Roman rule, in the end the Hellenism that came to be such a feature of the Roman Empire actually did more to secure the continuation of Greek culture and heritage than anything the Greeks themselves could have done.

It can be argued that Roman culture was, indeed, Graeco-Roman rather than Roman. It was the Greek language that served as the *lingua franca* in the Eastern Empire and much of the west including Italy. Many Greek intellectuals, including Galen, were based in Rome and the Roman aristocracy more and more came to embrace Greek literature and philosophy. Homer's epics inspired Virgil's *Aeneid* and Seneca wrote in Greek. Earlier, Scipio Africanus (236 – 183 B.C.), the epitome of the Roman martial hero, studied Greek philosophy and regarded Greek culture as the benchmark against which all others had to be judged. The Roman poet and philosopher Horace studied in Athens during the Principate and, in common with many of his class, saw that city as the intellectual centre of the world.

In the minds of most people today, Gaul equates to modern France. However, the vast geographical area that Caesar named Gaul, in fact, was made up of a number of very distinct regions and covered, in addition to modern-day France, Belgium, Luxembourg, parts of the Netherlands, Germany, Switzerland and Northern Italy. The Romans called the northern area of

---

[1] The Principate was the name given to the period from Augustus to Caligula when Roman Emperors maintained the fallacy of a Republic with the Senate in theory holding ultimate authority.
[2] Suetonius, *Caligula,* 22; *Claudius,* 23.

the Italian peninsula, which is now part of modern Italy, Cisalpine Gaul, or Gaul on this side of the Alps. Early Romans did not even consider this region as part of Italy and repeated incursions southwards, and the sacking of Rome itself in 390 B.C., resulted in Rome taking full control of the area in 221 B.C. and thoroughly Romanizing it to the extent that even the Celtic language totally disappeared and was replaced by Latin. The region was initially a province but by the beginning of the 1st century B.C., it had become fully integrated into the Roman heartland and became an administrative region of Italy rather than a province.

Ironically, the Roman Republic's development from a city state into a world power that controlled large swathes of modern Italy, Gaul and Spain, as well as other parts of Europe is seen by many as being the direct result of Roman fear of the "Celtic Threat." The sacking of Rome by the Gauls in 386 B.C. became indelibly imprinted into the Roman psyche, and with this fear came a desire to put as much distance as possible between the city of Rome and any potential enemy. The result was the gradual acquisition of buffer zones that became provinces of an empire that grew without any particular thought out or deliberate strategy of expansion.

Narbonensis was the first area in what might be termed Gaul proper to fall under Roman rule, in 120 B.C., a conquest that was largely the result of the need to secure a land route to the new provinces in Iberia that had been acquired three years earlier at the end of the Punic Wars. The need to protect this area from the northern Gauls, including the Helvetii, gave Julius Caesar the excuse he needed to push further into Celtica and then on into Belgica and Aquitania.

The Gallic Wars, the series of campaigns waged by Caesar on behalf of the Roman Senate between 58-50 B.C., were among the defining conflicts of the Roman era. Not only was the expansion of the Republic's domains unprecedented (especially when considering it was undertaken under the auspices of a single general), it had a profound cultural impact on Rome itself as well. The Roman Republic, so dynamic in the wake of the destruction of their ancient enemy, Carthage, had recently suffered a series of dramatic upheavals; from the great slave rebellion of Spartacus to the brutal and bloody struggle for power of Marius and Sulla. Rome had been shaken to its very core, and a victory was essential both to replenish the dwindling national coffers and to instill in the people a sense of civic pride and a certainty in the supremacy of the Republic.

Quite simply, in terms of scale, the Gallic Wars were unmatched by anything the Roman Republic had witnessed since the Punic Wars. By the end of the campaigns, ancient historians estimated that more than a million people had died, and still more were displaced or enslaved. Even by the more conservative estimates of modern historians, a casualty count in the hundreds of thousands appears possible. Either way, the war was a cataclysm, involving tens of thousands of combatants, and it also marked the greatest displays of skill by one of the greatest battlefield generals history has ever known.

Caesar's successful campaigns in Gaul have become the stuff of military legend on their merits, but it helped that he had the foresight to document them himself. Caesar himself wrote a famous firsthand account of the Gallic Wars, apparently from notes he had kept during the campaigns, and he wrote *Commentarii de Bello Gallico* (*Commentaries on the Gallic War*) in the third person. Caesar's account described the campaigning and the battles, all as part of a propaganda campaign to win the approval of the Roman people. As a result, he left out inconvenient facts, including how much of a fortune he made plundering, but the work still remains popular today, and it is still used to teach Latin.

Augustus and his successors then began a program of Romanization that, in a remarkably short period of time, transformed Gaul into four provinces. All of these locales added enormously to the Roman Empire in terms of manpower, material goods and wealth. Even today, historians are amazed at how such a large population that was not without its own systems of administration and vibrant culture and tradition could so easily succumb to Rome's pacification process, and to such an extent that, within short periods of time, the indigenous language and traditions of the Celtic peoples of Gaul were totally supplanted. The reasons why Rome was able to subjugate and then transform what was for that time an immense population of over 10 million people lie not only in its military superiority but its system of organization and its conscious program of Romanization.

Although Alexander never lived to rule over Egypt, one of his generals, Ptolemy I, did, and it was he who established the last great pharaonic dynasty in Egypt, known as the Ptolemaic Dynasty. The Ptolemies gave ancient Egypt an injection of vitality that had not been seen in the Nile Valley for centuries, preserving many aspects of native Egyptian culture while adding their own layer of Hellenic culture. The first few Ptolemaic rulers proved as able as any of their Egyptian predecessors as they worked to make Egypt a first-rate power in the world once again. Unfortunately, these able rulers were followed by a succession of corrupt and greedy kings, more concerned with personal wealth and power than the stability and greatness of their kingdom. Eventually, Ptolemaic Egypt collapsed due to weak rulers, internal social problems, and the rising power of Rome, but before the Ptolemaic Dynasty was extinguished, it proved to be one of the most impressive royal houses in ancient Egyptian history.

The end of the Ptolemies also happened to coincide with the most famous period of Roman history. In the latter 1st century B.C., men like Julius Caesar, Mark Antony, and Octavian participated in two civil wars that would spell the end of the Roman Republic and determine who would become the Roman emperor. In the middle of it all was history's most famous woman, Cleopatra, who famously seduced both Caesar and Antony and thereby positioned herself as one of the most influential people in a world of powerful men. Cleopatra was a legendary figure even to contemporary Romans and the ancient world, and she was a controversial figure who was equally reviled and praised through the years, depicted both as a benevolent ruler and an evil seductress (occasionally at the same time). Over 2,000 years after her death, everything about Cleopatra continues to fascinate people around the world, from her lineage as a Ptolemaic pharaoh, her physical features, the manner in which she seduced Caesar, her departure during the Battle of Actium, and her famous suicide. And despite being one of the most famous figures in history, there is still much mystery surrounding her and the end of the Ptolemies, leading historians and archaeologists scouring Alexandria, Egypt for clues about her life and Egypt's transition to Roman rule.

As for Roman Egypt, the period from 30 B.C. until the Roman Empire was split into two halves in the 4th century A.D. It is scarcely mentioned, yet, it was a time when Egypt, if no longer a great power in its own right, was a pivotal province in the Roman Empire. It could also be argued it was a power without which the Roman Empire would not have survived. Its wealth, especially its fertility, was the key for any Roman emperor hoping to feed and entertain Rome's ever-demanding masses and was particularly vital to Augustus as he established himself as the first emperor of Egypt. The institution of imperial, as opposed to senatorial, provinces proved crucial in the consolidation of imperial power. Moreover, how Egypt in this period was administered and exploited provides invaluable information as to how Rome manipulated and controlled large populations for its benefit in the rest of its empire. Tactics used again and again throughout the Roman world were honed in this, the most valuable of Rome's provinces.

Egypt's key role in imperial politics was crucial, but so was its role in the rise of Christianity. For many years, the belief that Christianity had spread from Jerusalem to engulf the Roman Empire has been largely unchallenged, but more recent scholarship suggests the codification of Christian doctrine and success of missionaries from Alexandria and not Jerusalem, were instrumental in Christianity becoming the state religion of the empire. Given the importance of Christianity to both European and world history, this issue is of a real significance.

Judea is one of the most important regions in the modern world. It is the center of two of the world's great religions and extremely important to a 3rd. Politically, the whole area is the focus of conflict between Jews and Arabs, as well as different Muslim sects. Its history is littered with wars, insurrections, and religious revolutions. To say that it has had a turbulent past is to understate the case in the extreme.

The history of Judea is, of course, inextricably linked to the history of the Jewish people, their dispersal throughout the Mediterranean world, and their reestablishment of the modern state of Israel in the wake of the horrors of the Holocaust. And among all the tumultuous events associated with Jewish history, few can rival the period of Roman rule during the 1st century A.D., when Roman attempts to suppress Jewish nationalism met with violent resistance. Ultimately, the Romans forcibly removed much of the Jewish population from the region, setting the scene for later events that have impacted so directly on world history. Events in the region during the 1st century A.D. also brought about the birth of Christianity, a religious movement that has been at the forefront of European history ever since.

Over 1,100 years before William the Conqueror became the King of England after the Battle of

Hastings, Julius Caesar came, saw, and conquered part of "Britannia," setting up a Roman province with a puppet king in 54 B.C. In the new province, the Romans eventually constructed a military outpost overlooking a bridge across the River Thames. The new outpost was named Londinium, and it covered just over two dozen acres.

For most of the past 1,000 years, London has been the most dominant city in the world, ruling over so much land that it was said the Sun never set on the British Empire. With the possible exception of Rome, no city has ever been more important or influential than London in human history. Thus, it was only fitting that it was the Romans who established London as a prominent city.

Londinium was initially little more than a small military outpost near the northern boundary of the Roman province of Britannia, but its access to the River Thames and the North Sea made it a valuable location for a port. During the middle of the 1st century A.D., the Romans conducted another invasion of the British Isles, after which Londinium began to grow rapidly. As the Romans stationed legions there to defend against the Britons, Londinium became a thriving international port, allowing trade with Rome and other cities across the empire.

By the 2nd century A.D., Londinium was a large Roman city, with tens of thousands of inhabitants using villas, palaces, a forum, temples, and baths. The Roman governor ruled from the city in a basilica that served as the seat of government. What was once a 30 acre outpost now spanned 300 acres and was home to nearly 15,000 people, including Roman soldiers, officials and foreign merchants. The Romans also built heavy defenses for the city, constructing several forts and the massive London Wall, parts of which are still scattered across the city today. Ancient Roman remains continue to dot London's landscape today, reminding everyone that almost a millennium before it became the home of royalty, London was already a center of power.

The Romans were master builders, and much of what they built has stood the test of time. Throughout their vast empire they have left grand structures, from the Forum and Pantheon in Rome to the theatres and hippodromes of North Africa and the triumphal gates in Anatolia and France. Wherever they went, the Romans built imposing structures to show their power and ability, and one of their most impressive constructions was built on the northernmost fringe of the empire. Shortly after the emperor Hadrian came to power in the early 2nd century A.D., he decided to seal off Scotland from Roman Britain with an ambitious wall stretching from sea to sea. To accomplish this, the wall had to be built from the mouth of the River Tyne – where Newcastle stands today – 80 Roman miles (76 miles or 122 kilometers) west to Bowness-on-Solway. The sheer scale of the job still impresses people today, and Hadrian's Wall has the advantage of being systematically studied and partially restored.

Spain's geographical position has made it a focus of attention throughout history for numerous migrants, traders, colonizers, and conquerors alike. Iberia, also known as Hispaniola or Hispania, is in the southwestern corner of Europe and is separated from Africa by a mere eight miles, the point at which the Mediterranean meets the Atlantic. The whole of the Iberian Peninsula, which today incorporates the modern nation states of Spain and Portugal, was known to the Romans and Greeks as Hispania.

Over the centuries, before Roman involvement in the Iberian Peninsula, it had been settled by different waves of eastern tribes: Celts, Phoenicians, Greeks, Africans, and Carthaginians. It was the settlement in the south of Spain by the last of these that led to Roman interest in the area, and ultimately to its conquest and integration into the Roman Empire, though the complete process was to take over 200 years.

Once the Carthaginian territories had been taken, those parts of Hispania became the two provinces of Hispania Citerior and Hispania Ulterior, which in turn were later subdivided into further provinces. They became some of the wealthiest and most Romanized of the empire's provinces, but the process by which the whole of Spain came under Roman rule was both violent and complex. Given that the Iberian Peninsula is Europe's second largest peninsula, maintaining control required vigorous efforts, including Roman-sponsored migrations by the Sueves, Alani, Vandals, Visigoths, and other tribes. For example, the Visigoths first set foot on the peninsula in the year 416, where they were tasked with forcefully re-instituting Roman authority upon other Germanic invaders who had occupied the land. Initially, the Visigoths followed instructions to a tee, but as time progressed, it appeared that there may have been reason to have been suspicious of the Visigoths after all. In 418, they were relocated to France, where they established a makeshift kingdom of their own in Toulouse. When they inevitably wizened up to their employer's increasingly fragile authority, they realized it would not take much to squeeze the disintegrating empire out of the picture.

The ramifications of 600 years of Roman rule had significant consequences for the rest of the ancient world, and it had a profound impact on subsequent European history. In fact, it can be argued that those consequences are still being felt in Spain today, in terms of language, culture and political complications.

Ancient Rome's Provinces: The History of the Foreign Lands Ruled by the Roman Empire in Antiquity looks at Rome's famous conquests, and the importance of the provinces to history's most famous empire. Along with pictures depicting important people, places, and events, you will learn about the various Roman provinces like never before.

Ancient Rome's Provinces: The History of the Foreign Lands Ruled by the Roman Empire in Antiquity

About Charles River Editors

Introduction

   The Romans and Gauls

   The Decline of Ancient Greece

   Hispania and the Carthaginians

   Roman Consolidation of Gaul

   The Hellenization of Rome

   Judea and Herod

   Caesar's Invasions of Britannia

   The Gallic Wars

   The Collapse of the Egyptian Empire

   Incorporating Egypt as a Province

   The Final Subjugation of Britannica

   Londinium

   The Jewish Wars

   The Romanization of Gaul

   The Romanization of Hispania

   Online Resources

   Further Reading

Free Books by Charles River Editors

Discounted Books by Charles River Editors

The Romans and Gauls

Gaul, or Gallia as the Roman's called it, covered a huge area of Western Europe that today comprises modern day northern Italy, France, Belgium, parts of the Netherlands, Switzerland and parts of Germany on the west bank of the Rhine. Caesar estimated the population of Gaul in the mid-1st century B.C. as approximately 10 million, an enormous number for that time.

As for Gaul itself, it was comprised of a few regions that were gradually conquered by the Romans. Gallia Cisalpina was conquered by 203 B.C., while Gallia Transalpina was brought under Roman control by 123 B.C. The remainder of Gaul, Gallia Comata or the land of the Longhaired Gauls, made up of Belgium, Celtica and Aquitaine, fell to the Romans in 51 B.C. when Caesar defeated Vercingetorix. This whole area covered approximately 190,000 square miles. Both the Greek and Latin names for the area derived from a Celtic word for a clan, but in fact they called themselves Celtae. While there are various theories about the origin of the term Gaul apart from this, one that is supported by modern research is that it is linked to the Welsh and Cornish words meaning power, hence the definition of Gaul as the land of the powerful people.

The Gauls were a group of mainly, but not entirely, Celtic peoples who inhabited the area of Europe that came to be known as Gaul. The Gallic, or La Tene, culture emerged as a distinct entity somewhere around the 5th century B.C. north of the Alps and spread in the 4th century B.C. throughout what is now France, Belgium, Spain, Portugal, Switzerland, Southern Germany, Austria, the Czech Republic and Slovakia. They also expanded into northern Italy, the Balkans and Galatia in the 3rd century B.C., when they reached the height of their power.[3] They were never a united people under one king or founded anything remotely akin to a nation state, but they were capable of combining for short periods to achieve short term objectives.

There were numerous individual tribes and prior to the Roman conquest, to the extent that the numbers of separate tribes ran into the hundreds, but following the conquest by Rome they were grouped into 60 tribes. Their expansion came to an abrupt halt in 225 B.C. when the Romans resoundingly defeated them at the Battle of Telamon, and, thereafter, Rome's preoccupation with the Punic Wars brought them into closer and closer contact with the Gauls. When, as part of the settlement of the Punic Wars, Rome gained territory in Iberia, the Romans actively looked to secure a land route to the new provinces, and this led them to acquire, initially, a small section of land from the city of Massilia and from that point on Rome gradually expanded in Gaul.

The Gauls called themselves Celtae, and their culture developed out of the Celtic culture that had developed from the Urnfield culture, which existed between 1300 and 750 B.C. The development of iron working proved to be the major turning point in the development of the Celts, and the Hallstatt culture developed through the use of this metal in the 8th century B.C.

---

[3] 'Gaul', *Encyclopaedia Britannica* (2009).

From the Hallstatt culture came the La Tene culture around the 5th century B.C., at about the same time the Greeks were beginning to have an influence on southern Gaul. Indeed, the Gauls had working and profitable gold mines well before the Roman conquest, with possibly as many as 200 in the Pyrenees. In conjunction with that, they had developed their own unique type of settlement that Caesar named *oppida*, a combination of a small town and a fort. Archaeological evidence proves that the many different areas of Gaul were wealthy and enjoyed a much higher level of civilization than that attributed to them by the contemporary Roman writers. Their merchants traded throughout the Mediterranean world and beyond, and their artifacts revealed a sophistication that matched any people at that time.

The Celts have fascinated people for centuries, and the biggest fascination of all has been over the Druids, a religious class at the heart of Celtic society that wielded great power. Naturally, people have been interested in Druids for centuries mostly because they don't understand much about the Druids or their practices. The earliest meaning of the word comes from the Ancient Romans, who labeled them "Druidae" in reference to the white robed order of Celtic priests living in Gaul, Britain and Ireland. They were a well-organized, secretive group who kept no written records and performed their rituals - allegedly including human sacrifice - in oaken groves, all of which interested and horrified Roman writers. As Pliny wrote in the 1st century A.D., "Barbarous rites were found in Gaul even within my own memory. For it was then that the emperor Tiberius passed a decree through the senate outlawing their Druids and these types of diviners and physicians. But why do I mention this about a practice which has crossed the sea and reached the ends of the earth? For even today Britain performs rites with such ceremony that you would think they were the source for the extravagant Persians. It is amazing how distant people are so similar in such practices. But at least we can be glad that the Romans have wiped out the murderous cult of the Druids, who thought human sacrifice and ritual cannibalism were the greatest kind of piety."

Caesar himself mentioned them, writing, "Throughout all of Gaul there are two classes of people who are treated with dignity and honor. This does not include the common people, who are little better than slaves and never have a voice in councils. Many of these align themselves with a patron voluntarily, whether because of debt or heavy tribute or out of fear of retribution by some other powerful person. Once they do this, they have given up all rights and are scarcely better than servants. The two powerful classes mentioned above are the Druids and the warriors. Druids are concerned with religious matters, public and private sacrifices, and divination."

The order was eventually crushed under the weight of first Roman conquest and then the imposition of Christianity, and from the remains, centuries of myths, imaginings and dreams were superimposed over the little that was known about the Druids. Not surprisingly, people have come to associate the Druids with what have been imposed. Even today, there is a revived Druidic religious movement that fuses this skeleton of knowledge about the ancient Druids with ideas such as rituals at standing stones (like Stonehenge), nature and sun worship, the carrying of ornate staves, and Arthuriana.

Britain was the center of Druidism and there is significant evidence that Gallic Druids traveled to Anglesey, in particular, to undergo rigorous training that would take up to 20 years to complete. The Druids did not allow any of their beliefs to be written down and, consequently, many of these beliefs have been lost. However, it is clear that they did have a concept of an afterlife and the Druids held enormous sway over all aspects of everyday daily life, as well as political matters, including decisions on war. They were also the only real source of education for the aristocracy. The power to excommunicate was a particularly potent weapon in their armoury and they used it to control and guide the clan.[4] The Druids seemed to be particularly conscious of issues relating to agriculture, and given the population, it is likely that overuse of land for agricultural purposes would have caused major problems for their management of the Celtic system.

There were numerous gods and goddesses, some worshipped by all or most Gauls, while others were just local deities. Many of these deities were related to the Greek pantheon, and again this plethora of divine beings may have made the acceptance of Roman deities relatively easy. The origin of the Druids themselves is unclear but by Roman times their right to determine major issues such as peace and war was unquestioned. Their monopoly of education was another tool in their armoury for securing the loyalty of the Gallic aristocracy and once again the Druidical practices, taking the children of the elite to be educated by Druids and the acceptance that a power other than the tribal leader or leaders could ultimately make the most important decisions, all paved the way for the Romans to slip into those positions previously occupied by the Druidical Order.

The Gauls practised animism and gave human characteristics to most naturally occurring geographical features, such as rivers and mountains. Indeed, the worship of animals was not uncommon throughout Celtic regions, with the boar being the most sacred, occupying a position in the minds of the Gauls similar to that of the Roman eagle.[5] In terms of gods, there were a few worshipped by all Gauls, but in addition there were numerous deities worshipped only by one or two clans, and individual family gods. Even some of the gods themselves were related to Greek deities, the most important of which was Teutates,[6] who equated to Hermes. The god associated with the land of the Gauls as a people was identified by Caesar as equivalent to the Roman god Dis Pater, a god that was subsumed into the god Pluto.[7]

Many Celtic clans sought new lands to farm beyond the normal confines of Gaul. Early forays into northern Italy began in the 6th century B.C., but it was in the 4th and 3rd centuries B.C. that the Gallic clans spread beyond what would today be continental Roman Gaul, Pannonia, Illyria,

---

[4] P. 78, *The Druids: a study in Celtic prehistory* by T. Kendrick (1966). New York.
[5] P. 22 *The Religion of the Ancient Celts* by J. A. MacCulloch (1911). Edinburgh.
[6] Can also be spelt "Toutais" and "Toutates."
[7] *World of Myths: The Legendary Past* Ed. M. Warner (2003). University of Texas.

Transylvania, and Asia Minor and migrated in significant numbers into northern Italy.

Caesar defined three distinct ethnic subdivisions within Gaul: the Belgae in the north; the Celtae, in a central position; and the Aquitani, situated in the southwest. The other major groups of people living within the confines of Gaul at this time included the Greeks and Phoenicians who had established thriving trading centers such as Massilia, modern day Marseilles.

The basic social unit was the tribe and within each tribe there were sub divisions into what Caesar termed *pagi*. Each tribe was governed by a Council of Elders and initially all the tribes tended to have a king. This came to change over the course of time to an elected leader who often served only for one year. The tribes at the macro level were organised into groups that the Romans referred to as *civitates* and it was these groupings that the Romans used, as did the Catholic Church in later years, to organise their own administrative system. Despite the groupings, there was no cohesive way of ensuring unity in times of a real emergency and the Romans were able to exploit that fact during the Gallic Wars. It is quite easy to imagine a much different outcome to the Gallic Wars if Vercingetorix had had the authority to call all the Gauls together right from the start of the Roman incursion into their lands. That disunity ultimately proved to be a key factor in ensuring Roman success.

That disunity was also reflected in the languages spoken within Gaul. Caesar identified three main languages in his *Gallic Wars* - Celtic, Aquitanian and Belgic - but within each there were further branches making Gaul a linguistically very diverse region. The fact that there were so many variations spoken may well account for the success of Latin in supplanting all other languages so quickly. The need and benefits of a common language and the means of spreading it relatively easily meant that Latin was adopted throughout Gaul within one or two generations. Pockets of indigenous language speakers did continue to exist until the end of Roman rule but their numbers and influence was minimal. However, the local languages did play their part in shaping the Vulgar Latin that was spoken in Gaul.[8]

Brennus led a major campaign into Italy around 390 B.C. and the Etruscans, fearing that they would be totally overrun, asked Rome for help against the invaders. Rome responded, which began the long period of hostilities between the two sides. It was at this time that the city of Rome itself was sacked by the Gauls, initiating a centuries-long fear and loathing by the Romans of the Gauls. Brennus unsuccessfully tried to push into the Balkans, but his force was largely exterminated by the Greeks. Nonetheless, the Gauls were able to establish themselves in Illyria and Thrace, as well as in Galatia in modern Turkey. During these unsuccessful attempts to invade mainland Greece, the Gauls defeated a Greek army at Thermopylae by using the same pass as the Persians had used to encircle the Greeks. Despite some successes against the Macedonians and the Spartans, the Gauls were not able to secure a base and moved on after

---

[8] P. 106, 'Insular Celtic as a Language Area' by R. Matasovic (2007). *International Conference of Celtic Studies* XIII.

Brennus died at Delphi.

Celtic Gaul itself had been invaded by Gauls from the Rhine Valley, and many Gauls of both Celtic and German origin fought as mercenaries on behalf of Carthage in the Punic Wars, only adding to Rome's hatred of their northern neighbors.[9] As mercenaries, the Gauls were well regarded because they were considered to be physically very strong. Ammianus Marcellinus and Diodorus Siculus both provided descriptions of the average warrior: "The Gauls are tall of body with rippling muscles and white of skin and their hair is blond and not only naturally so but they make it their practice to increase the distinguishing color by which nature has given it.[10]"

The Gauls also had a custom of shaving the chin while maintaining a moustache and shaving the front of the head. Marcellinus seemed to confirm his description, writing, "Almost all Gauls are tall and fair skinned with reddish hair. Their savage eyes make them fearful objects; they are eager to quarrel and excessively truculent."[11] His description of female Gauls was unflattering to say the least. He compared them to "missiles launched by the twisted strings of a catapult" and pointed to their "swollen necks and gnashing teeth" with "great white arms."[12]

By the time Rome seriously turned its attention to the Gauls, they were a populous, wealthy, civilized, and by all accounts bellicose group of tribes whose women were believed to be as fearsome as their men. They had a functioning social system and the military capacity, on the face of it, to ward off any attempt to conquer them. Their problem was that they were not united or cohesive enough to really mount an effective defense against a foe that was, in contrast, highly organized and had tried and tested strategies for pacifying conquered territories.

As a result, when Caesar fought them in the 1st century B.C., the Gauls at the time were not a single nation but a loose confederation of tribes sharing a common language, customs and ethnic origin. As such, they were in a constant flux of alliances, double-crossings and wars, both among themselves and with the neighboring Germans of the Rhineland. Some of the tribes of southern Gallia enjoyed a large degree of close contact with Rome, to the point of having Roman tradesmen and diplomats living among them, and were more similar to the Romans in dress, habits and other behavior than to their Gaulish brethren to the north. Caesar began his commentaries on the Gallic Wars by describing "Gaul": "All Gaul is divided into three parts, one of which the Belgae inhabit, the Aquitani another, those who in their own language are called Celts, in our Gauls, the third. All these differ from each other in language, customs and laws. The river Garonne separates the Gauls from the Aquitani; the Marne and the Seine separate them

---

[9] 'Gaul', *Encyclopaedia Britannica* (2009).

[10] Diodorus Siculus, *Bibliotheca Historica*, 5.28, 1-3, in J.Bromwich *The Roman Remains of Northern and Eastern France A Guidebook* (2003), p.341. Routledge.

[11] P. 80, *The Roman History of Amminianus Marcellinus during the reigns of the Emperors Constantius, Julian, Jovianus, Valentinian and Valens,* by Marcellinus Ammianus, trans. C.D. Yonge (2011).

[12] *The Roman History of Amminianus Marcellinus during the reigns of the Emperors Constantius, Julian, Jovianus, Valentinian and Valens,* by Marcellinus Ammianus, trans. C.D. Yonge (2011).

from the Belgae. Of all these, the Belgae are the bravest, because they are furthest from the civilization and refinement of [our] Province, and merchants least frequently resort to them, and import those things which tend to effeminate the mind; and they are the nearest to the Germans, who dwell beyond the Rhine, with whom they are continually waging war; for which reason the Helvetii also surpass the rest of the Gauls in valor, as they contend with the Germans in almost daily battles, when they either repel them from their own territories, or themselves wage war on their frontiers. One part of these, which it has been said that the Gauls occupy, takes its beginning at the river Rhone; it is bounded by the river Garonne, the ocean, and the territories of the Belgae; it borders, too, on the side of the Sequani and the Helvetii, upon the river Rhine, and stretches toward the north. The Belgae rises from the extreme frontier of Gaul, extend to the lower part of the river Rhine; and look toward the north and the rising sun. Aquitania extends from the river Garonne to the Pyrenaean mountains and to that part of the ocean which is near Spain: it looks between the setting of the sun, and the north star."

At the present time, there is little archaeological evidence available to shed any light on the details of how these people lived their daily lives before the Roman conquest. These Celtic tribes were part of the La Tène culture that had spread throughout Gaul in the 5th and 4th centuries B.C., which was, itself, profoundly influenced by the Hellenistic culture of the preceding centuries. Each clan consisted of at least one, but normally more, *pagi,* a Council of Elders, and in the earlier years a king. It is from this word, *pagi,* that the French word *pays* derives. In later years, the clan developed a position with the title *Vergobret* that was very similar to a king but whose powers were restricted by the Council of Elders. The clans were organized into *civitates* for administrative purposes, and the Romans eventually took over the entire system for themselves. In turn, this regionally based structure was the foundation for the division into ecclesiastical bishoprics and dioceses, a system that survived virtually intact until the French Revolution at the end of the 18th century.

The Decline of Ancient Greece

The period between 479 B.C. and 431 B.C. (known as the *Pentacoetia*) and to some extent the decades that followed, although they were marred by the harrow of the Peloponnesian War, were the golden age of Athens. The victory over the Persians ushered in an era of burgeoning confidence and dynamism that made the Athenians feel invincible, as well as ushering in a fresh wave of democratization. Salamis, Athens's most dazzling triumph, had not been the product of the gentlemen-rankers of the heavy infantry but of the lowest of the working classes, the oarsmen and marines of the Athenian fleet, and they reveled in their status as preservers of Hellenic freedom and spoke forth with unprecedented vigour in the *Ecclesia*. The Acropolis, which had been destroyed by Xerxes, was rebuilt into the dazzling spectacle that still stands to this day, while under the auspices of the great sculptor Phidias the mighty buildings were decorated with sculpture of unprecedented grace and beauty. At the same time, colossal walls miles long were built to link Athens to the port of the Piraeus, meaning that Athens could never be besieged by land forces alone.

The Battle of Salamis, by Wilhelm von Kaulbach

Under the leadership of Pericles, the great statesman who took power in Athens in 461 B.C. and held it largely without interruption until his death thirty years later, the city flourished. The arts, including theater, poetry and philosophy, blossomed like in no other city in Greece, as did science, including architecture, medicine, natural philosophy and mathematics. Athens could boast, and with good cause, that all of Greece looked to them for its knowledge, but there was trouble in paradise. The dynamism and expansion hid the reality of oppression of other fellow members of the Delian League, whose lavish tribute was needed to fund Athens's public works and its various schools. Many of the Delian allies were resentful, and the Spartans were downright hostile. And throughout it all, the politicians of Athens relentlessly schemed and betrayed each other in a constant quest for power and influence. A crisis was coming, but Athens rushed blissfully unaware towards it. Indeed, there is even some indication that Pericles deliberately orchestrated it to preserve himself from political issues at home.

Bust of Pericles

The inevitable war broke out in 460 B.C., splitting Greece down the middle and forcing most of the great *poleis* to align themselves with Sparta or Athens. At the time, however, Sparta itself was unable to field a significant force due to being occupied at home with mopping up the helot revolt. That also required leaving much of the Spartan army on standby in case of further uprisings.

The main Spartan achievement in what became later known as the First Peloponnesian War (the prelude to the far more devastating Second Peloponnesian War which followed shortly thereafter) was a victory over Athens at Tanagra in 457 B.C. At that battle, the Spartan army had supported the Boeotians in preserving their independence, but after the victory they decamped, allowing Athens to take over the region anyway. This caused a scandal in Sparta, ending with the exile of the two kings for supineness, and Sparta was forced to call for a somewhat embarrassing five-year treaty with Athens to recover its strength in the wake of the revolt. It has been suggested that it was around this time that some elements of the *perioikoi* were incorporated into the Spartan line infantry to make up for manpower shortage, although this is an issue of some contention. More importantly, Sparta signed a 30 year peace with its old rival Argos, ensuring it was free to pursue hostilities with Athens when the time came.

That time came quickly. The Thirty Years Peace was quickly threatened by Athens's cavalier treatment of Corinth, a Spartan ally: Athens allied with Corcyra, a rival of the Corinthians, supported them in a naval battle, and then ordered its Delian ally Potidea, which had close ties to Corinth, to tear down its walls and sever all connections with their mother city. In 433 B.C. the Athenians also established a virtual trade embargo against the Megarans, leaving them bereft of the economic ability to survive. In response to this continued Athenian aggravation, in 432 B.C. the Spartans summoned the states of the Peloponnesian League to assembly and returned with the verdict: war. Athens had broken the peace and must pay the price.

In 431 B.C., war broke out again. Sparta had made no secret of its hostility to Athens in the years following the First Peloponnesian War and had only narrowly been stopped from engaging in another showdown some years before by the intervention of Corinth. Ostensibly due to the Peloponnesian League's desire to support Korkyra and Potidea against rampant Athenian imperialism, the war was chiefly fought because Sparta feared Athenian imperialism, which threatened to overshadow Sparta altogether.

After decades of war, the victorious Spartans installed a pro-Spartan regime in Athens known as the Thirty (or Thirty Tyrants), but they were so universally hated that they were soon driven from the city. Democracy was restored by Thrasybulus, with the Spartans' grudging blessing. Still, Athens never truly recovered from the shattering blow it had received as a result of its defeat in the Peloponnesian War, a defeat which was largely due to the short-sightedness and greedy desire for personal gain of its politicians. No general or admiral, no matter how stellar their record, could be safe from prosecution if they lost even one minor battle, meaning that brilliant leaders were often stripped of their command.

In the wake of the Peloponnesian War, the Spartans began to harbor imperialistic ambitions again. They openly supported Cyrus, who had enjoyed a friendly relationship with Lysander, in his attempt to seize the throne of Persia from his older brother Artaxerxes, and even though he was killed at Cunaxa the Spartans used an appeal for help from the Ionians (so often previously rebuffed) and invaded Anatolia. However, their army was crushed by Artaxerxes at Cnidus in 394 B.C., apparently causing a sigh of relief from the Ionian cities who felt Spartan rule would be even more oppressive than subjugation to Persia.

In 370 B.C. Sparta attempted to preserve a toehold of influence in Arkadia by invading, but the

Arkadians, knowing which way the wind blew, promptly asked for assistance from Thebes. A Theban army under Epaminondas was promptly sent to the Arkadians' aid and, after having liberated the region, began marching toward Sparta proper. For reasons unknown, Epaminondas decided not to march toward the city itself, perhaps realizing that such an unprecedented threat to their very city would drive the Spartans to feats of Herculean desperation. Instead, he diverted his army toward the helot capital of Messene and began liberating vast tracts of Messenia, ensuring an all-out helot uprising and then fortifying the city so the Spartans could not retake it.

Though Thebes had long been an important city, it had never been predominant militarily. Once it did, however, the main city-states of Greece now turned against Thebes. Worried by the newly ascendant power of Thebes, several of Sparta's erstwhile enemies, including Mantinea and Athens, made common cause with the Spartans. In 362 the Boeotian League, led by Theban forces, faced this impromptu coalition at the Battle of Mantinea. Though the Spartans were once again defeated, Epaminondas himself was killed in the hour of victory. A peace was sought, but Sparta snubbed the negotiations, which decreed Messenia independent. Hemmed in by enemies – Argos, Messenia, Arkadia – on all sides, Sparta was in no position to pursue imperialistic policies, and indeed the city's very survival was threatened.

A semblance of balance was established, with each of the great *poleis,* Athens included, sitting back and catching their breath. For several years it even seemed as though peace might be an option, but just outside the borders of Greece a new enemy was stirring.

In the years following Mantinea, Macedon, a previously unregarded and marginalized political entity on the border of Greece, began a military revolution under King Philip. Philip, with a mighty and apparently invincible army at his back, began to take an active interest in Greek affairs. When the Social War broke out between Athens and its erstwhile League allies Cos, Chios and Rhodes over Athens's pre-eminence in the Athenian League, Philip took advantage of the chaos to seize the silver mines at Amphipolis and convinced the Athenians he would return them in exchange for the port of Pydna and Potidaea. The Athenians ceded those ports to him, only to find that Philip had hoodwinked them and had no intention of returning Amphipolis. Between 356 and 346 B.C. Athens fought a bitter, inconclusive and largely unsuccessful war against Philip, but they eventually realized the futility of taking on Macedon. Disappointed by a lack of any substantial gains, they allowed the orator Demosthenes to establish a peace between Macedon and Athens. However, Demosthenes found the peace to be inexpedient and, certain that Philip would eventually use an excuse and invade, began to campaign in Athens for a resumption of hostilities against Macedon.

Demosthenes

After several years of continual provocations, including alliances with Philip's enemies and attacks on his allies, Philip tired of the belligerence. In 338 B.C. the Macedonian army, including as a cavalry commander Philip's young son Alexander, marched on Greece using a flimsy pretext. He was opposed by a loose coalition of Greek *poleis*, Athens and Thebes chief among them, with the backbone of the army provided by the Theban elite units, including their vaunted Sacred Band. The two armies met at Cheaeronea in August of 338 B.C., and the Greek forces were badly beaten. Spartan warriors might well have helped turn the tide, but they were ringed by enemies and none could march to battle. Philip spared Athens and the other Greek city-states, but he dissolved the various federations in favor of a new one, to which all save Sparta subscribed, known as the League of Corinth. And though the Spartans refused to join the League of Corinth, an anti-Persian Hellenic coalition with Philip as *hegemon*. Sparta might have been humbled, but she was hardly broken. When Philip decided to threaten the Spartans, warning them that if he were forced to enter Laconia in arms he would raze Sparta to the ground, the Spartan envoys replied simply, "If". Alone among the Greek city-states, Sparta refused to join the expedition that Alexander, in the wake of his father's death, launched to destroy the Persian empire, a snub Alexander never forgot.

The League of Corinth's purpose was an attack on Persia, for which Philip needed the Athenian fleet, but before he could realize that dream Philip was murdered in 336 B.C. The throne of Macedon passed to Alexander, whose position was far from stable. This led Demosthenes to persuade the Athenians to rebel, as did many other city-states. However, when Alexander led his army through Thermopylae with the intention of crushing the rebellious cities, Athens sensibly sued for peace. Thebes, which remained defiant, was destroyed. Athenian troops and naval forces would go on to serve with distinction as Alexander's allies in his conquest of the Persian empire, but it galled Athenian pride to be subservient even to someone as brilliant as Alexander.

Seven years later, while Alexander (now *hegemon* of the League of Corinth in addition to a host of recently-acquired titles, including Emperor of Persia) was warring in the East, Greece rose up in all-out rebellion. A coalition, headed by Sparta itself, marched against the Macedonian garrisons scattered throughout the country, overthrowing several before laying siege to Megalopolis in 331 B.C. Battle was joined before the city's walls between the Macedonian army left behind by Alexander, commanded by the veteran general Antipater, and the Greek forces under the Spartan King Agis III. As at Chaeronea, however, the Greek hoplites found themselves hopelessly incapable of confronting the relentless machine of the Macedonian phalanx, whose soldiers employed pikes three times as long as the hoplite spears. More than 3,000 Spartans, in the thickest part of the fighting, were killed. The mortally wounded Agis, in the grand tradition of Leonidas and the Three Hundred, ordered his men to abandon him during the retreat so he could buy them some time, and he slayed several of the enemy before he was finally brought down. In the wake of their defeat, Alexander, mindful of their proud history, was merciful to the Spartans, his only condition being that they join the League of Corinth like the other great *poleis.* Even still, during the Lamian War, a renewed Greek uprising against Macedonian rule which followed the conflict at Megalopolis, Sparta remained aloof and continued to do so until Alexander's death.

When Alexander died prematurely in 323 B.C., his vast empire rapidly fell apart. The Athenian assembly, inflamed by Demosthenes and the demagogue Hypereides, clamored for Athens to throw off the Macedonian yoke. An army of 10,000 Athenian hoplites, 12,000 Aetolians and other Greek contingents assembled, while Antipater, Alexander's regent of Greece and Macedon, prepared his own forces to offer battle. Antipater was outnumbered and sought refuge within the walls of Lamia, where the Athenians and allies besieged him unsuccessfully for the better part of a year. An Athenian naval defeat at Amorgos in 322 B.C. allowed reinforcements to reach Antipater, and he was able to defeat the Greeks at the Battle of Crannon later that year. Despite the rebellion, Antipater was generous with Athens. Though Demosthenes was forced to kill himself and Hypereides was condemned to death, Athens itself was left untouched, except for the establishment of a plutocratic government which gave citizenship rights only to the wealthy, ostensibly to prevent demagogues spurring the mob into a frenzy.

Like Athens, Sparta recognized Alexander's death was an opportunity to reassert its independence. When Demetrius the Besieger, one of the most successful *diadochii,* set about conquering the Peloponnese in 294 B.C. the Spartans attempted to resist. Due to their antiquated equipment and tactics, however, they were defeated twice, and Sparta itself was spared only due to Demetrius's apparent lack of interest and the fact that Sparta did not possess any valuable plunder, since they had no currency or a citadel worthy of that name.

For the following 20 years, Sparta engaged in a series of scrappy internecine wars against other Greek cities in an attempt to re-establish some form of Peloponnesian ascendancy, but their magic had long since vanished and they were defeated repeatedly, even by an undistinguished military power such as the Aetolians. In 272 B.C. Sparta faced an all-out catastrophe when, abetted by the exiled King Cleonymus, Pyrrhus of Epirus invaded the Peloponnese and marched on Sparta itself. The city was only saved thanks to a last-ditch defense in which even the women, children and elderly of the city are said to have taken part.

Bust of Pyrrhus of Epirus

Macedonian rule also did not sit well with Athens, and in 267 B.C., the Athenians revolted once again, this time rising up against the Antigonid dynasty established in Macedon with the aid of other Greek *poleis* and the Antigonids' rivals the Ptolemies of Egypt. The Greek *poleis*, led by

Athens and Sparta, had some initial successes but were eventually crushed by Antigonus Gonatas near Corinth in 265 B.C. Athens was besieged by Antigonus for three years, until he succeeded in starving it into submission in 261 B.C. Where Philip, Alexander and Antipater had been inclined to be generous, Antigonus was not so gentle. He erased all Athenian claims of independence and garrisoned the city with Macedonian troops, which remained there until 229 B.C. at least.

Meanwhile, Sparta entered a period of flux. Between 264 B.C. and 244 B.C. it fought in a number of skirmishes and small wars in an attempt both to cast off Macedon's yoke and to establish itself as the dominant power in the Peloponnese in the face of growing Aetolian and Achaean opposition. Sparta's woes – and its destiny as an irrelevant former power – seemed to be cemented when the Aetolians raided Laconia and made off with captives which supposedly numbered in the tens of thousands.

Sparta did not take this increasing marginalisation and loss of power lying down, however. In 229 B.C. the Spartan King Cleomenes III besieged Megalopolis, leading to a war with the Achaean League. Despite being outnumbered four to one by the troops of his rival Aratus, Cleomenes succeeded in defeating the Achaeans before leaving most of his army in the field and hurrying back to Sparta with a handful of loyalist troops, where he promptly seized absolute power in a coup, putting four of the five Ephors to death and abolishing the office altogether. Cleomenes then enacted land distribution reforms and conferred the title of Spartiate on new candidates to help beef up the dwindling numbers (now significantly less than a thousand) of full citizens. He also ensured that the land barons, a bare two or three hundred of which possessed the majority of land in Sparta, were stripped of their wealth in favor of a more democratic system. Cleomenes urged a renewal of strict adherence to the Laws of Lycurgus, under the tutelage of his advisor Sphaerus (who was not himself Spartan but, like Alcibiades before him, had made himself "more Spartan than the Spartans"). However, Cleomenes weakened his position by refusing to institute social reform outside of Sparta – instead, he subjugated ruthlessly many newly enfranchised cities which had previously been under Spartan rule.

Cleomenes then turned his attention on Achaea, inflicting a number of defeats upon the Achaean League thanks to financial backing from the Ptolemys of Egypt. Ultimately, however, Aratus allied himself with Macedon and, at the Battle of Sellasia in 222 B.C., crushed Cleomenes and his army. That same year, the King of Macedon, Antigonus III, entered Sparta in arms, a calamity which the city had never experienced throughout its entire history, which led to the re-establishment of the ephorate and the temporary abolishment of the kingship.

Spartan decline continued despite Cleomenes's efforts at reform. Sparta continued to be involved in petty squabbles with neighboring states and coalitions until 207 B.C., when Nabis took power in Sparta. Nabis, who was regarded with loathing by many of his (Roman) biographers, was something of a pirate and a bandit, but also a reformer in the vein of

Cleomenes. Like his forebear he attempted to promote a measure of social equality and made changes in the political establishment, but to little avail.

During his reign, the Achaeans abandoned their alliance with Macedon to side with the rising power of Rome, and the Spartans – by default – chose to support Rome's rival, Macedon. In order to keep Argos under more direct control, Philip V, then King of Macedon, ceded it to his newfound ally. This left Nabis, once the Romans had roundly defeated Philip, in the unenviable position of being in contravention of the Roman law that stipulated that all Greek cities should be free. The Romans invaded, besieged Sparta, and forced Nabis to submit to humiliating peace terms which snuffed out Sparta's brief period of ascendancy. Nabis himself was murdered in 192 B.C., and Sparta was forced to endure the humiliation of being forcibly enrolled in the Achaean League.

Athens had one more fight left in it near the end of the 3rd century B.C., this time supporting Attalus of Pergamum against Philip V of Macedon in the Cretan War of 205 B.C. In response to this, Philip invested Athens by land and sea, but in so doing provided the burgeoning power of Rome with a long-awaited *casus belli*. They warned Philip that if he continued to attack Athens he would face dire consequences, and the result was that when Philip refused to withdraw the Romans went to war with him, eventually turning Macedonia into a vassal state.

Even after the fall of Macedonia, Athens and other Greek cities retained their independence, but it would only take a few decades before Rome came for them as well.

Hispania and the Carthaginians

With the introduction of bronze-working by one of the many migrant tribes, around 1900-1600 B.C., Almeria and Andalusia reached a peak in terms of early civilization. The capital was Tartessus, known in the Bible as Tarshish, and is thought to have been located in the Guadalquivir Valley. It was the silver that was mined in the region that brought traders, especially the Phoenicians, to Iberia. The Phoenicians founded their own city along the coast from Tartessus around 800 B.C. and named it Gadir, modern day Cadiz. In the years that followed, they built further centers of trade along the south and east coasts, as well as on the Balearic Islands.

The Phoenicians were primarily merchants and not interested in colonization, but they inevitably had an impact on the local populations with whom they traded, including sharing technological innovations and business practices which were readily adopted by the indigenous population. The Phoenicians were also responsible for bringing the Peninsula to the attention of the Mediterranean states and for bringing it out of the relative isolation from the rest of the world that it had found itself in, prior to the Phoenician settlements.

In the 6th century B.C., the Greeks were enticed westwards by the tales of the silver of

Cartagena, the gold of the Sierra Morena, and the copper of Rio Tinto. They founded a settlement at Emporion, modern day Ampurias in Catalonia, and it quickly surpassed Massilia (modern day Marseilles) as the Greeks' most important port in the western Mediterranean. Like the Phoenicians before them, the Greeks built additional settlements along the south and east coasts, and they brought new ideas and culture to those with whom they traded. Their particular gifts to the local population were the introduction of the olive tree and the grapevine, gifts that featured ever larger in the economy of the region as the years went by.

By the time the Greeks arrived, the peoples living there had come to be known as Iberians. It is now accepted that this was a generic term for all the various ethnic groups living in the coastal areas stretching from Catalonia to Andalusia, not the name of any specific race or group. As a people, these Iberians were quite distinct from those living in the interior. In fact, in the years during which the Phoenicians and the Greeks were developing their trade in the east and south, the lands in the interior, from 900 B.C. until approximately 600 B.C., had witnessed invasions by successive waves of Celtic tribes. These warrior Indo-European groups integrated remarkably easily with the existing populations of the north and west, and they opened up what had previously been unpopulated lands.

It was unavoidable that the Celts and Iberians would come into contact, especially on the Central Plain, and ultimately, they interbred and formed a new group known as the Celtiberians. The general cliché seemed to view the Celts as violent, rustic shepherds while the Iberians were the pacifist farmers and town dwellers, but these are rather simplistic stereotypes. The Celts had a more specific identity than the Iberians and brought with them metallurgy, the broad sword, and trousers to Spain. There is little archaeological evidence of their way of life, and since they burned their dead, there are no burial sites that have often been valuable sources of information about other civilizations.

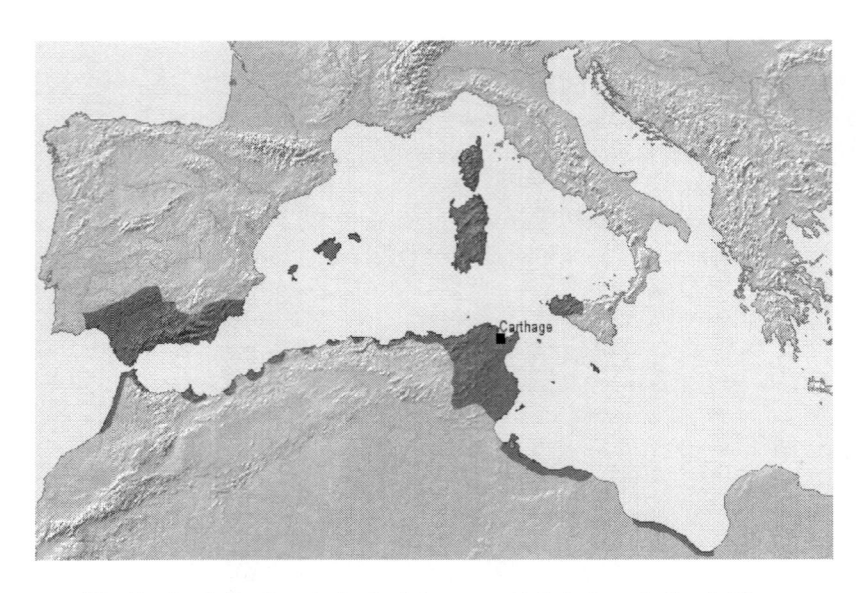

The Carthaginian Empire in the 3rd century B.C., before the Punic Wars

Carthage was almost certainly founded during the colonization boom of the Phoenician Empire. This was a movement which took advantage of the relative collapse in the fortunes of Greece, Crete and the Hittite Empire to establish a string of up to 3,000 colonies between Asia Minor and Spain, and Carthage was conveniently positioned smack in the middle of the extremely lucrative Iberia–Asia Minor raw metals route. Although it was a convenient position, Carthage itself was apparently not intended to be anything special in terms of colonizing efforts, particularly because the Phoenician colonial method differed radically from the Greek variant. While the Hellenes would create a settlement that was self-sustaining and almost always self-governing, while still retaining ties of alliance and friendship with the so-called "Mother City" on mainland Greece, the Phoenicians, both for administrative control reasons and due to population constraints, did not as a rule create self-sufficient colonies. Instead, the Phoenicians exerted more control over the settlements, particularly when it came to trade regulations. Thus, the settlement which gradually spread upon the hill of Byrsa was very low in the food chain. Initially, Carthage paid tribute to the local Lybian tribes to avoid being attacked and had a governor (sometimes incorrectly labeled "King" by ancient Greek sources) who had most likely been imposed upon them from Tyre. Carthage, however, was fortunate in having a larger neighbor, the Phoenician city of Utica, which provided them with significant economic and trade assistance during the colony's early years. That was a decision Utica would later regret when Carthage grew in size and eclipsed it entirely.

From 850–650 B.C., Carthage gradually became more and more wealthy thanks to her privileged position straddling the major land and sea trade routes of the Mediterranean. These two centuries saw the emergence of what would later become known as "Punic" (Carthaginian) culture, a distinctly West African Phoenician identity which differed noticeably from its predecessor. The growth of this culture indicated a rise in influence on Carthage's part, and that rise manifested itself in 650 B.C. when Carthage founded its own independent colony, a settlement on Ibiza, without assistance from Tyre. As the fortunes of Tyre and the Phoenician Empire waned, first with the loss of Sicily to the ever-expanding Greeks and then with Nebuchadnezzar of Babylon's great siege of Tyre in 585 B.C., Carthage's fortunes continued to rise. More settlements were founded, more cities of the North African seaboard were brought under direct Carthaginian control rather than paying their dues to Tyre, and a large colony was established in Syrtis, between Tunisia and Lybia. Additionally, Carthage's rise was bolstered by the influx of a large number of immigrants of both wealth and high political status from Tyre itself, as many of the elite fled the conflicts which enveloped the Phoenician capital.

After Babylonian Emperor Nebuchadnezzar II successfully besieged Tyre in 586 B.C., Carthage all but inherited the Phoenician commercial empire. As before, the mineral wealth of Hispaniola attracted envious predators, and the Carthaginians soon dominated the western Mediterranean. The Greeks continued limited trading along Spain's east coast, but Carthage acquired a commercial hegemony in the Iberian Peninsula that they were able to maintain for nearly 300 years. Greek artifacts such as bronze statues found in the Sierra Morena and Corinthian helmets like those found near Huelva gradually gave way to Carthaginian sculptures, jewelry, and ceramics, and the Carthaginians brought new skills, including fish curing and the production of esparto grass.

It was around this time that the name Hispaniola first came to be used. Some scholars have suggested that it derives directly from a Punic cognate of the Hebrew *ishfania*, meaning island of the hyrax, island of the hare, or possibly even island of the rabbit, which may account for the use of a rabbit on Roman coins minted in Spain.[13] Another theory is that the name is of Iberian origin, and that evidence for this can be found in the pre-Roman name for Seville, which was Hispalis. An ancient name for the area was Hispa, but its root is now lost. Hispalis might derive either from the Greek Heliopolis, the city of the sun, or from the Phoenician word for lowland, *spal*, though this explanation is less popular.[14] There are other theories suggesting that the word came from the Basque for border or edge, or even from an eponymous hero named Hispan. Whatever the origin, the terms Hispaniola and Hispania was widely used throughout the Mediterranean world by the 6th century B.C. to denote this geographical area.

For centuries, Carthage's expansion progressed relatively smoothly, with no one challenging their dominion over the Mediterranean. Even the Etruscans, whose heyday coincided with Carthage's rise to prominence, had not vied with the Punic Empire for supremacy. In fact, the Etruscans had become valued trading partners and then allies, despite several incidents involving

---

[13] P. 106, *Carthage, The Maritime Empire* by Z. Herman (1963). Massadah Ltd.
[14] P. 93, *SPAL: Revista de prehistoria y arqueologia de la Universidad de Sevilla* (1998). Publicaciones de la Universidad de Sevilla.

pirates.

However, all that changed with the colonial drive that suddenly propelled the Greek *poleis* westwards. From approximately 600 B.C. and onward, Carthage, whose citizens had been watching with growing concern as superior Greek products flooded its commercial lifelines and colonies sprang up in its backyard from Sicily to Southern Italy all the way to the invaluable mining regions of Iberia, shifted to an overtly aggressive stance. However, the Greeks were not the Lybians, and Carthage suffered several notable reverses, particularly in the scramble for Sicily. Despite their best efforts to curb the tide, pirate havens and independent Greek settlements were fast springing up all over Italy, much to the Carthaginians' chagrin.

In 550 B.C., Carthage witnessed the rise of Mago I, founder of the Magonid dynasty. Mago was an able general who held the title of King at various points for the next two decades, while his two sons, Hasdrubal and Hamilcar, also shared this honor. According to sources, Hasdrubal, who served as King over 10 times in the late 6th century B.C., was awarded a triumph by the elders of Carthage no less than four times, apparently making him the only general in recorded Carthaginian history to merit such an honor.

Under the guidance of the Magonids, Carthage went on the offensive. Following the founding of Alalia by Phokian Greeks on Corsica and its subsequent degeneration into a pirate stronghold which preyed upon northern Mediterranean shipping, the Carthaginian-Etruscan alliance launched an attack on the city. The naval Battle of Alalia in 540 B.C. was a catastrophic defeat for the Greeks, and over the next few years the alliance succeeded in expelling them from Corsica altogether. A treaty was ratified with the Etruscans, who took over control of Corsican affairs while giving Carthage free rein to engage in the conquest of Sardinia. In the ensuing wars, the Sardinian tribes, bolstered with gold and arms from the Greek *poleis*, managed to hold out against Carthage for a quarter of a century. Mighty Hasdrubal himself died of wounds sustained in the Sardinian campaign, which exhausted vast supplies of troops and gold with relatively little return.

Those troops and that gold were sorely needed, for shortly after the Battle of Alalia a new Greek threat emerged. The *polis* of Massalia launched an attack against Phoenician Iberia in an attempt to muscle into the Carthaginian sphere of influence and wrest away control of the rich mines of the Iberian Peninsula. Despite several notable reverses, the Carthaginians were ultimately able to blockade Gibraltar against Greek incursions and deny the Massalians a foothold in the south, even though they were unable to prevent them from establishing settlements in Eastern Iberia. Taking advantage of the fact they had troops in the region, Carthage also successfully wrested the colony of Tartessos away from the Greeks and also subjugated several notionally independent Phoenician cities, bringing them directly into the Carthaginian orbit.

Once the struggle for Iberia was over, Carthage barely had time to gather itself before being embroiled in a battle in her very heartland. Although successful campaigns against the Lybians had enlarged Carthage's North African domains, tribute to the Lybian King still continued on a yearly basis. However, a new threat emerged in the shape of the Spartan Doreius in 514. Doreius and his forces invaded Leptis Magna, Carthage's backyard, and for the next three years engaged in a vicious struggle with Hamilcar, Hasdrubal's brother, until he was eventually driven out of North Africa. Doreius next moved to Sicily, where in 510 B.C. he was killed attempting to create a fortress near Eryx on the island's western coast. After Doreius's death and the crushing of a Sardinian uprising in 509 B.C., Carthage could at last afford to breathe easier. Although Sicily was vast, wealthy, and crawling with hostile Greeks right on Carthage's doorstep, Carthage could rest secure in the knowledge that virtually all of Iberia was under their direct or indirect control, along with Sardinia and large swathes of the North African seaboard.

Nevertheless, near the end of the 6th century, a new power was emerging on the Mediterranean with hitherto unseen forcefulness, swallowing up the Etruscan cities and pursuing a policy of ruthless military expansion which threatened to upset the balance of power for good. The Carthaginian elite felt nervous enough watching the rapid growth of Rome that in 509 B.C., a treaty, the first of several, was signed between Carthage and Rome. Although at the time Carthage was far more significant both politically and militarily, an ally on the Italian mainland who would be both belligerent and at odds with the Greeks was certainly useful. The treaty itself was similar to others that the Carthaginians had signed with various states throughout the Mediterranean, and it served to limit the sphere of influence and commercial enterprise each power was meant to abide by. This initially cordial relationship, however, would prove to be far from lasting. Inevitably, Carthage and Rome would be locked in a mortal struggle that would define one city and ruin the other.

In 348, Carthage signed a treaty with Rome, which was now quickly becoming the dominant power in Italy. Rome gained trade access (but not settlement rights) to Sicily, while Carthage maintained a monopoly on trade in Iberia and Sardinia. Rome also gained valuable Latin possessions from the treaty, further cementing its position as a dominant Italian power.

By 264 B.C., Carthage was rich, had a large navy, and was commercially organized. Essentially, the city was more interested in trade than territorial expansion, though it did maintain and defend its trading centers throughout the Mediterranean world. Meanwhile, Rome had emerged as a strong aristocratic republic and had expanded by conquering territories in southern Italy, but those acquisitions did not satisfy the Romans' growing demand for new lands to service a rapidly expanding population. Carthage had already established links with Sicily, which meant Roman conquests in the south of Italy brought the two powers into dangerous geographical proximity.

After a period of increased tensions, the inevitable war finally erupted in 264. Hiero II of Syracuse was at war with Messina, whose elders initially appealed to Carthage for help but then promptly switched sides and beseeched the Roman Senate for aid. The Carthaginian leadership was so indignant that, in a remarkable reversal of historic policy, they threw in their lot with Syracuse. Once again Sicily became a battleground, sucking in field armies from both Rome and Carthage. However, while the Carthaginian army might have learned to battle Greek hoplite heavy infantry with some success, Roman legionaries were another matter. In 262, a numerically inferior Roman force crushed the Carthaginian army at the Battle of Agrigentum, inflicting thousands of casualties and causing a shift in policy among the Carthaginian military elite. Rather than face the legions on land, they would attempt to resolve the conflict at sea, where their massive and highly proficient professional navy had the advantage.

The strategy initially paid off, and two years later the Roman navy was dealt a crushing defeat at the Battle of Lipari, but Rome did not take this defeat lying down. Instead, the Senate authorized a massive financial package for the navy, boosting wartime production to hitherto untold (and virtually unsustainable) levels so that more than 100 Roman triremes were constructed within less than two months, a monumental undertaking. Once Rome had the ships, however, the Romans still needed to find experienced captains and crews to use those ships effectively, so a stopgap solution was developed: the *corvus*. Rather than ram the enemy ships and try to sink them, the Roman galleys would close alongside the Carthaginians and then drop the *corvus*, a hook-ended bridge, onto the enemy deck, linking the ships together. Once that was in place, Roman legionaries would swarm across the bridge, effectively turning a naval battle into a land one and returning the combat to terms which were favorable to them. The Carthaginians suffered grievously at the hands of this brilliantly simple device (though it was eventually phased out of service as the Roman navy became as adept as its Punic counterpart) and soon lost sea supremacy as well as land supremacy.

Matters looked grim for Carthage when Rome, after a string of victorious naval and land battles, took the fight to North Africa, advancing into the Carthaginian heartland. Only a last-ditch defense by the mercenary general Xanthippus at the Battle of Tunis in 241, when the Roman cavalry found itself utterly outnumbered and the Roman legions were forced to face the shock of Punic war elephants, saved Carthage from a siege. Having suffered a grievous reversal, the Romans decided it was time to seek peace, but they did so from a position of utter supremacy. For the first time since they had first gotten involved in Sicilian affairs, Carthage was forced to surrender the entire island to Roman control, as well as pay a colossal war indemnity. Additionally, Rome also secured the release of 8,000 prisoners of war without paying a penny in ransom, blows which badly crippled the Carthaginian economy.

In addition to this financial burden, the Carthaginians were also suffering from the effects of decades of war, and after its defeat in the First Punic War, the Carthaginians fundamentally changed their policy with regard to the acquisition of territory. Carthage needed to replenish its coffers and that meant adopting a more exploitative approach in general, and to Hispania in particular.

At the same time, Carthage relied chiefly on mercenary armies. Thousands of mercenaries throughout the Carthaginian Empire were suddenly not getting their wages, and the result was inevitable: war. An all-out insurrection of mercenary contingents throughout the Punic Empire, including Iberia, Sardinia and Corsica, and a renewed attack from the subjugated Lybian tribes, followed. Suddenly, Carthage was fighting for her very life, and grudgingly accepting military and financial aid from her two old enemies, Syracuse and Rome. The war dragged on for two years, but by 238 Carthage was once again secure, with order restored to her dominions. Still, the cost had been heavy; taking advantage of Carthage's desperate situation, Rome had conveniently seized both Sardinia and Corsica, which had been plunged into lawlessness by the mercenary uprising, and there was nothing Carthage could do about it. The mines of Iberia, with their vast amounts of as yet untapped wealth, were still secure, but control of them was dubious.

While the Carthaginians had been so involved in the First Punic War, the Iberians had taken much greater control of their country, but Carthage's desperate needs following the war led Hamilcar Barca to set about re-asserting and increasing Carthaginian influence on the Iberian Peninsula. What had begun as commercial settlement started to look something more like the establishment of an empire.

A coin believed to depict Hamilcar and a man riding on an elephant

Initially, Hamilcar found it difficult to transport his army to Hispania because of Roman control of the Mediterranean. His solution was to march his army along the North African coast to the Straits of Gibraltar and ferry his troops across to Spain. He made his base in Gades in 236 B.C. and from there advanced eastwards, defeating the Iberian tribes as he went. After each victory, he took great pains to make allies of those he had conquered, and in this way he soon consolidated his hold on the whole southern part of the Iberian Peninsula. On the east coast, near Alicante, he established an advanced base at Lucentum, but in 228 B.C., while leading this campaign, he drowned crossing a river. He was succeeded as leader of the Carthaginians by his son-in-law, Hasdrubal the Handsome, who carried on with Hamilcar Barca's plan and extended

Carthaginian influence as far north as the River Ebro.

The Carthaginians up to this point not only exploited Spanish resources under the noses of the Romans, on the pretext that this was the only way that Carthage could pay the indemnity demanded by Rome, but they also began to recruit Spaniards for their army, especially Celtiberian infantry and Balearic slingers. Hamilcar had realized early on that Rome was virtually safe from any seaborne attack due to its naval superiority, but Spain could serve as a base from which to launch a land-based attack on Rome.

Spain quickly became almost a personal fiefdom of Hamilcar's family and Carthage found it increasingly difficult to control him, but when Hasdrubal went so far as to establish a capital in Hispania at Carthago Nuevo (modern Cartagena), the Romans finally became suspicious of his intentions. As Carthago Nuevo became a thriving city with its own fortifications, palaces, mint, docks, and an arsenal, the Greek colonies along the eastern coast were also increasingly alarmed at the Carthaginian advance. Eventually, Massalia, then an ally of Rome, raised these concerns with the Romans.[15]

At the time, Rome had no territory in either Gaul or Spain, which meant their concerns were primarily economic and related to the possibility that Carthage could regain the pre-eminent position it had held prior to the First Punic War. A very specific problem was tin, which was a highly strategic material because a mixture of 10% tin to 90% copper was needed to make bronze, the essential alloy used to make non-rusting weapons. Copper was readily available but tin, for Massalia, came almost exclusively from Cornwall. The route from Cornwall was via Brittany and then down the west coast of Gaul, skirting the Pyrenees, then around Carcassonne before reaching its destination. Both the Massalians and the Romans were concerned that any Carthaginian advance beyond the Ebro would put this vital trade route at considerable risk.

In 226 B.C., a Roman delegation met with Hasdrubal to negotiate a settlement of the issue. At that meeting, it was agreed that the Roman sphere of influence would extend as far as the northern bank of the Ebro, while Carthaginian influence was to stop at the southern bank. However, there was one problem, in the form of Zakynthos (later Saguntum). This Greek city lay south of the Ebro, putting it within the Carthaginian sphere of influence, but it would prove pivotal in leading the Carthaginians and Romans to renew their hostilities in what became the Second Punic War.

Hasdrubal was looking for a way to strike back at Rome in retaliation for the First Punic War and the blatant land grab in the chaos that followed. It appears likely that around 225, Hasdrubal began plotting with the Gauls of the Po Valley in the north of Italy (the only as yet unconquered area in the Italian Peninsula) to launch an attack on Rome with Carthaginian backing, but the Senate got wind of the plan and ordered a pre-emptive strike of their own, leading to a five-year

---

[15] Livy, *History of Rome* 21.2.7 and 21.5.

war which eventually led to the annexation of the Po Valley. Hasdrubal himself was assassinated in 221, possibly with Roman collusion.

Rather than solve the Romans' problems, Hasdrubal's death brought about the rise of the most famous Carthaginian of all. Hasdrubal was succeeded by his brother-in-law and Hamilcar's son, Hannibal. In the history of war, only a select few men always make the list of greatest generals, and one of them is Hannibal, who has the distinction of being the only man who nearly brought Rome to its knees before its decline almost 700 years after his time.

In 237 B.C., legend has it that when Hamilcar was about to set off to Spain, Hannibal, then nine years old, begged his father to take him with him. Hamilcar was about to offer a sacrifice to the gods to ensure the success of his campaign and although he refused his son's request, he did place Hannibal's hand on the animal to be sacrificed and asked him to swear that he would never forget that Rome was the enemy. The story is recounted by Livy, but there are reasons to suppose that there is some truth in it.[16]

The Barca family felt Carthaginian humiliation at the hands of the Romans very deeply and all the brothers honoured the oath throughout their lives.[17] Hannibal proved to be a natural military genius and a leader who inspired his men with his personal bravery and his willingness to share all their day to day hardships. He was elected as leader by the troops without the permission of the Carthaginian Senate but they could not do anything other than endorse their choice. This method of choosing their own leader re-enforces the idea that leadership in Spain was a kind of personal dictatorship vested in the Barca family. Cornelius Nepos claimed that Hannibal was a scholar as well as a soldier and this assertion ties in with the level of statesmanship that he exhibited in the latter part of his career.[18] He was taught Greek by Sosilos and it is said he wrote books in Greek.

---

[16] Livy, *The History of Rome*, XXI
[17] Livy, *The History of Rome*, XXI, I.
[18] Cornelius Nepos, *Lives of the Eminent Commanders: Hannibal.*

A bust believed to depict Hannibal

For two years, Hannibal bided his time, consolidating his position in the Iberian peninsula and massing his forces, abiding by one of the greatest military truths and one which doubtless his tutors and his father, with their tales of Alexander and Alcibiades, had contributed to instill in him: numbers do not matter so much as concentration of force, i.e. what troops are available to fight in one single critical location, at any given time. Meanwhile, even as Hannibal was preparing to strike out against their very heart, the Romans seem to have grown unusually complacent; after all, Hannibal was new to overall command, and with both Hamilcar and

Hasdrubal dead, they must have felt themselves secure. When in 218 Hannibal resurrected his brother-in-law's plan for a joint Gaulish and Carthaginian invasion of the Italian peninsula, the Romans were caught napping, something which they would live to regret in the following years.

The troops that Hannibal commanded were professional soldiers who fought for pay and plunder rather than any particular state or political ideal. They comprised a relatively small number of Carthaginians, Gauls, Africans and Iberians. The typical Greek phalanx was the core of the army and its tactics derived from the hoplite warfare practiced in Greece. However, the most distinctive troops were the Balearic slingers. They used pebbles or leaden bullets and were accurate both over short and long range. It is said that they could hit a target at distances that archers could not match. Their overall firepower was well in excess of anything that contemporary archers could match.

The Spaniards tended to provide heavy cavalry with two men on horseback, one to fight from the horse and the other to dismount and fight on foot. The Numidians, who came mainly from Algeria and Morocco, were considered the most fearsome of the Carthaginian troops. The term Numidian stems from the word nomad and they were expert horsemen. Their light cavalry units were swift and they developed a tactic of charge and retreat, charge and retreat that heavily armed hoplite troops could not counter.

The most famous Carthaginian units were the fighting elephants. Unlike most fighting elephants previously used in war, which were Indian, the Carthaginian ones were African of the cyclotis variety known as forest elephants to distinguish them from the larger bush elephants found in central and southern Africa. They were first used by the Carthaginians in the First Punic War at Agrigentum in Sicily in 262 B.C. and thereafter were a feature of all Carthaginian armies.[19]

When Hannibal first took command of the Carthaginian forces, there was still considerable consolidation work to be done in Spain before he could turn his attention to Rome. In 221 B.C. he besieged the Oclades capital of Carteia. The Oclades tribal area was located south of the Ebro, so in the Carthaginian sphere of influence, but it had not yet been absorbed into the territory controlled by them. By taking this area, he moved right up to the agreed border of Carthaginian-Roman spheres of influence. More importantly for later relationships with Rome, this annexation meant that the city of Saguntum was now surrounded by Carthaginian territory. At the time of the agreement between Rome and Carthage that designated their respective areas, Saguntum, while south of the Ebro, was not adjacent to any Carthaginian territory. Part of the Ebro Treaty stated that "neither side should extend its dominion beyond the Ebro while Saguntum, situated between the empires of the two peoples, should be preserved in independence."[20] Saguntum, along with other Greek cities in the northern part of the east coast that were also concerned about Carthaginian ambitions, allied themselves with Rome for protection.

---

[19] P. 57, *The First Punic War: a military history* by J. F. Lazenby (1996). Stanford University Press.
[20] Livy, *History of Rome*, 21.2.7.

For the time being, however, Hannibal left Saguntum to its own devices and turned his attention to the north of Spain. He crossed the Sierra Morena, past Merida to Salamantica, modern Salamanca, which he captured. He defeated the Vaccaei, a tribe based around the River Doro, and then turned south again towards Toledo.[21] The Iberians combined to attack him as he crossed the Tagus, but Hannibal slipped past them and came up behind their lines. The Iberians were routed, and this victory brought the whole of Iberia south of the Ebro under Carthaginian control with the notable exception of Saguntum.[22]

Having secured his base, Hannibal turned his thoughts to how he might implement the plan Hamilcar had conceived to defeat Rome. It combined the elements of initiative and surprise with shock. The main feature of this audacious plan was none other than the concept that the next war with the Romans had to be fought on Italian soil, and the route to Italy had never looked as possible as it did in the first years of Hannibal's leadership. The Gauls, in northern Italy, were already in a state of ferment, and as recently as 225 B.C., an alliance of Gallic tribes had invaded Etruria, defeating a Roman army at Faesolae and going on to ravage the countryside. To prevent further invasions, the Senate had ordered the invasion of Cisalpine Gaul, but the Romans insisted on unconditional surrender and, in due course, Cisalpine Gaul became a province.

Roman colonies were established in the newly acquired territory at Placentia, now Piacenza, Cremona, and Mutina, now Modena, to act as a check on the Gauls. Hannibal knew that the Gauls felt humiliated by their defeats and the foundation of Roman colonies, and he was determined to profit from this unrest. He was also aware that the Romans had further difficulties in Illyria and Greece. It seems that the Romans never entertained the thought that the Carthaginians might launch an overland attack on Italy, an attack that would mean crossing the Ebro, the Pyrenees, Gaul, the Rhone, and the Alps to reach their target. Of course, that is precisely what Hannibal was determined to do.

Hannibal planned his operation in great secrecy, and the details were worked out meticulously. He gathered information on his intended route to Italy and assessed the fighting capabilities of all potential foes he might encounter on his march.[23] As well as gathering military intelligence, he gathered political intelligence about all the tribes he might have to deal with. He was, naturally, particularly keen to learn of any aversion to Roman rule. All of this information was crucial if he was to plan for a successful march to a destination over 1,000 miles from his base. Practical issues such as how his army was to be fed until it reached what he assumed would be the welcoming arms of the Cisalpine Gauls were thought through in minute detail. It is rumored that one of his commanders, Hannibal Monomachus, suggested that the troops should be trained in how to live off human flesh, which, if true, was quickly dismissed by Hannibal.[24]

---

[21] Polybius, *Histories*, III.14.5-8.
[22] Livy, *History of Rome*, 21.5.6-16.
[23] Livy, *History of Rome*, 21.5.
[24] Polybius, *Histories*, IX.

Although Hannibal could rely on the loyalty of his troops, he faced difficulty in persuading the Carthaginian Senate to support his plans. The Senate had numerous members who were determined to maintain the peace with Rome at any price and a number who resented the Barca family's domination of Iberia. Hannibal was reasonably certain that the Senate would never declare war on Rome, and he knew he had to manipulate the situation to achieve his goal.

Hannibal supported an Iberian tribe that had a dispute with Saguntum, and the Saguntines immediately appealed to Rome for help under the terms of the Ebro Treaty, fearing a Carthaginian attack. The Roman Senate duly sent a delegation to Hannibal to remind him that Saguntum was under Roman protection.[25] By the time the envoys arrived in Spain in 219 B.C., Hannibal had already laid siege to the city and claimed to be too busy to meet with them. His hope was that the Romans would declare war there and then, but instead the envoys withdrew and sailed to Carthage to complain about their treatment, demand a cessation of hostilities against Saguntum, and ask for Hannibal to be handed over to atone for the breach of the treaty that had ended the First Punic War.[26] Hannibal had alerted his supporters in the Carthaginian Senate of the impending arrival of the Roman delegation, and, forewarned, they ensured that when Rome's demands were made known to the whole Senate, they took immediate offense and declared that the Saguntines were the ones at fault and that it would be most unwise of Rome to side with them and render null and void the good relations that had been built up in the years following the end of the war.

While all of this diplomacy was going on, Hannibal continued with the siege and duly breached its defenses after eight months. The city was treated savagely, with the population massacred and their belongings looted. Hannibal sent the captured booty back to Carthage to bolster support for his actions.[27] The Roman envoys returned to Rome with Carthage's answer to their demands at approximately the same time news reached Rome of the fall and subsequent sacking of Saguntum. The Roman Senate was incensed and voted to declare war on Carthage, but before engaging in direct conflict, it sent new envoys to Carthage to ascertain whether Hannibal's actions at Saguntum had been carried out on his own initiative or whether they had the support of the Senate.[28]

The Carthaginians replied with a legal argument claiming that the treaty between Carthage and Rome required both parties to refrain from interfering with the allies of the other and that the treaty made no specific mention of Saguntum being an ally of Rome. They also argued that the treaty had never actually been ratified by the Roman Senate. The senior Roman envoy was Quintus Fabius Maximus, who, clearly frustrated by what he regarded as Carthaginian obfuscation, said, "Here we bring you peace or war. Choose which you prefer."[29] The

---

[25] Polybius, *Histories*, III.15.5.
[26] Livy, *History of Rome*, 21.6.
[27] Livy, *History of Rome*, 21.10-15.
[28] Polybius, *Histories*, III.21.6.
[29] Livy, *History of Rome*, 21.

Carthaginians replied that the Romans could choose. Fabius said, "War." The Carthaginians responded, "So be it."[30] Through Hannibal's machinations, the Romans declared the Second Punic War, and on that basis it could be claimed that it was the Romans who had violated the peace treaty.

In the spring of 218 B.C., at the head of approximately 50,000 infantry, 15,000 cavalry, and 50 war elephants, Hannibal began marching northeast. His plan was breathtakingly ambitious: he would march through the Pyrenees, across southern Gaul, over the Alps and into Italy proper, thereby avoiding the heavily fortified border in the northwest of Italy. It was a route no general had ever taken before, let alone a general with so many animals (including elephants). His father Hamilcar had been defeated trying to invade southern Italy and attempting to outfight the Roman navy at sea; Hannibal would not make the same mistake.

Pushing aside with contemptuous ease the stiff resistance of the Pyrenean tribes, who contested every step of the way from their strongholds of the mountain passes, Hannibal pushed forwards with remarkable speed, leaving behind a detachment of some 10,000 Iberian soldiers to keep his lines of communication open and pacify the tumultuous region. He then marched on into southern Gaul, negotiating with the local chieftains and outfighting those who had a mind to contest his advance. His speed of maneuver, and his ability to move his army across rough terrain, proved unmatched in the ancient world since the time of Alexander the Great. By that point, his army, which now numbered some 40,000 infantry, 8,000 cavalry, and around 40 war elephants, danced up the valley of the Rhone to evade a Roman force sent to bar his passage southwards through the strategically vital gap in the mountains where the Alps meet the Mediterranean. With that route closed to him, Hannibal, undaunted, struck south and east across the Alps themselves.

For the year 218 B.C., Tiberius Sempronius Longus and Publius Cornelius Scipio had been appointed Consuls. Longus received Sicily as his province and Spain was given to Scipio. The Romans now saw Spain as an important defensive bulwark against Carthaginian encroachment. However, the sacking of Saguntum had so undermined their prestige in the area that many of the Greek settlements that had sought their protection now sided with the Carthaginians. Rome sent a mission to reassure these erstwhile friends but were received with such open hostility that they quickly left and returned to Gaul. Their reception in Gaul was not much friendlier, and many of the Gallic tribes made it clear that they would remain totally neutral in the conflict with Carthage. The Roman delegates had to return to Rome with nothing but bad news, with the exception that Massalia remained loyal.

It was in this context that the Senate decided to send Scipio and an army to Spain. When he arrived at Massalia, Scipio discovered that Hannibal was no longer in Spain but was further inland and on his way to Italy. Two reconnaissance forces met near the point that Hannibal was

---

[30] Livy, *History of Rome*, 21.18.

crossing the Rhone and the Romans emerged victorious. Nonetheless, Scipio decided to return to Italy with the intention of fighting Hannibal there. He sent his brother, Gnaeus Scipio Calvus, on to Spain with the bulk of the army. The Romans landed with two legions at Emporion, near to modern day Tarragona, and routed a Carthaginian force of 11,000 at the Battle of Cissa.[31] Within two months, the Romans had secured the area north of the Ebro. Gnaeus Scipio brought all Rome's former allies back into the fold by renewing alliances, and he also succeeded in forming new ones. He gained a reputation for clemency, and this was pivotal in his drive to establishing friendly relations with the tribes further inland, from whom he recruited a number of contingents.[32] Fierce fighting throughout the region between Hasdrubal, commanding in Spain in Hannibal's absence, and Gnaeus Scipio ensued. The Celtiberians, who had allied with Rome, defeated a Carthaginian force and killed 15,000. Publius Scipio returned to Spain at this point and took command of the campaign. Leaving the Celtiberians to continue the fight against Hasdrubal, the Romans marched to Saguntum.

A large number of hostages were kept there by the Carthaginians, and this had prevented some tribes joining Rome. The Romans, with the aid of a Saguntine, freed them, and this resulted in further Iberian tribes joining the Romans. Hasdrubal was by now very much on the defensive, but after being reinforced from Carthage in 216 B.C., he had hoped to take the fight to the enemy. The Carthaginian Senate, however, ordered him to make for Italy. The news spread quickly throughout Hispania, and there was now almost universal support for the Romans amongst the local tribes. Hasdrubal argued that leaving Spain as commanded would result in Spain falling totally into the hands of the Romans, and the Carthaginian Senate, in response, sent Himilco with a small force. When he arrived in Spain, he set up a fortified camp. Hasdrubal then marched north to the Ebro. Scipio was determined to prevent any Carthaginian reinforcements reaching Italy and organized his Iberian allies to harass Hasdrubal on his march while he prepared to meet him at the Ebro. The two forces duly met, and Hasdrubal was routed and forced to flee. This victory secured the support of the few remaining wavering tribes and prevented Hannibal from adding troops to his army in Italy.[33]

In 215 B.C., the Carthaginians sent a further army of nearly 15,000 to Spain under Hannibal's brother, Mago Barca, while Hasdrubal was dispatched to Sardinia to incite revolts against Roman rule. In Spain that year, two major battles were fought in Andalusia, and on both occasions superior Carthaginian forces were defeated by smaller Roman armies. In all, the Carthaginians lost over 30,000 men in these battles. Livy commented that "the successes gained in Hispania that summer were far greater than those in Italy."[34] The Carthaginians did have some successes against Hispanic forces though, and in 214 B.C. Mago and Hasdrubal won a major victory that would have won back much of the territory south of the Ebro that had been lost had

---

[31] Livy, *History of Rome*, 21.60.
[32] Livy, *History of Rome*, 26.3.
[33] Livy, *History of Rome*, 23. 26-29.
[34] Livy, *History of Rome*, 23.32.

Scipio not acted decisively. Scipio marched south to near Alicante, and met up with forces led by his brother. The Carthaginians, too, converged in the area and three forces led by Mago, Hasdrubal, and Hasdrubal Gisgo combined with the intention of confronting the Romans. After light skirmishing during which Scipio was wounded and nearly captured, the two armies met and once again the Carthaginians suffered severe losses, this time over 12,000. The Carthaginians regrouped and another battle ensued, but the result was the same and over 8,000 Carthaginian soldiers were killed. The Romans then captured Saguntum, and the Carthaginian garrison there was expelled.[35]

As if matters were not bad enough for the Carthaginians in Hispania, in 213 B.C. the Masaesyli in Algeria revolted.[36] Scipio sent a delegation to form an alliance with them, hoping to cause as much disruption to his enemies as he could. The Romans supported the revolt with training and equipment, and the Carthaginians in Spain were forced to divert resources to quelling the rebellion at a time when they were desperately needed in Iberia.

By 212 B.C., Rome's successive victories and the problems that the revolt in North Africa had created convinced Scipio that the time was now right for a major push against the Carthaginians to end the war in Iberia. 20,000 Celtiberians were hired but were bribed by the Carthaginians to go home.[37] The Carthaginians were then reinforced by a contingent of Numidians.

Now confident of success, the Carthaginians attacked Scipio and he was killed in the fierce fighting that resulted, forcing the Romans to retreat. The Carthaginians pursued their fleeing enemy and engaged them in another battle, during which Gnaeus Scipio was killed, just 29 days after his brother. For a time, it looked like the war in Spain might indeed be brought to an end, but not in the way Scipio had envisioned.[38]

At this point, the defeat of the Romans was almost total, and there seems little doubt that they would have been forced out of the Iberian Peninsula entirely had it not been for one Roman officer, Lucius Marcius. It was Lucius Marcius who reassembled what remained of the Roman army and joined the troops who had been left to guard Scipio's camp, under the command of Tiberius Fonteius. The troops themselves elected Lucius Marcius as their leader and camped near the Ebro. When the Carthaginians, under Hasdrubal Gisgo, crossed the river, they assumed that they would find little or no opposition. They believed the Roman army had been wiped out and had no idea who was commanding the troops that they encountered.

For whatever reason, the Carthaginians were lax in defending their encampments. They had divided their force into three parts and camped in three separate locations about five miles apart. Lucius took advantage of this lapse and attacked Hasdrubal Gisgo's camp while they slept,

---

[35] Livy, *History of Rome*, 23.41.
[36] Livy, *History of Rome*, 24.48-49, 25.32.1
[37] Livy, *History of Rome*, 25.32-33.
[38] Livy, *History of Rome*, 25.36.

massacring his troops. He quickly moved on to the second camp, which was scarcely better defended, but this time the majority of the Carthaginians were able to flee. Reports as to the numbers killed vary, but it would appear that in excess of 25,000 Carthaginians perished, with virtually no losses on the Roman side. The Roman triumph was exaggerated and romanticized by Roman writers, but there is no doubt that it was a significant defeat for the Carthaginians, who had only themselves to blame for failing to follow up their victories decisively and displaying woeful arrogance in how they conducted themselves after their successes against the Romans. [39]

Gaius Nero was sent to Hispania in 211 B.C. with additional troops and took over the force commanded by Lucius Marcius. He succeeded in trapping Hasdrubal but negotiated the Carthaginian's withdrawal from the area.[40]

At this point, the Romans had yet another problem to contend with, because the Hispanic tribes that had revolted after Scipio had been killed did not seek to renew their allegiance to Rome. Thus, it was decided to send yet more troops to subdue the region again. The son of Scipio, Publius Cornelius Scipio, was elected at the unusually young age of 24. Livy offers no explanation for this appointment, and possibly because of his age, a very senior veteran, Marcus Junius Silanus, was appointed as his second-in-command. Scipio landed at Ampurias near the Pyrenees and marched to Tarraco to take command of all the Roman troops. He then set about a diplomatic onslaught, persuading tribes to return to the Roman fold.

---

[39] P.44, *Hispaniae: Spain and the Development of Roman Imperialism* by J.S. Richardson (2009). Cambridge University Press.
[40] Livy, *History of Rome,* 26.17.

A depiction of an Iberian warrior circa 200 B.C.

Having settled the area north of the Ebro, in 210 B.C., Scipio turned his attention to the south. Despite his inferior numbers, he lay siege to Cartago Nova, defended by Mago, and captured it in a daring surprise attack. This victory proved to be the turning point in the war, at least in the Iberian Peninsula, as the Romans were now fighting in lands that had been Carthaginian for a considerable time.[41] The army that the young Scipio, known in later years as Africanus, had molded into a superb fighting machine forced its way southwards and into the Guadalquivir Valley. His command was extended in 209 B.C., and Scipio's policy of winning over the local

---

[41] And, in fact, the Romans never fought on the east coast again.

tribes was continued successfully. Scipio returned hostages who had been held by the Carthaginians and this encouraged others to join him.

Miguel Hermoso Cuesta's picture of a bronze bust of Scipio Africanus

Hasdrubal realized that his allies were deserting him and concluded that he had to take action before he was left totally friendless on the peninsula. However, Polybius suggests that Hasdrubal was having difficulty with the other Carthaginian leaders at this time, and his predicament persuaded him to engage the Romans in a major battle. He had decided that if he was defeated, he would then try to retreat into Gaul and attempt to reach Hannibal in Italy.[42]

According to Livy, the battle was a disaster for Hasdrubal and he lost 8,000 men, but there is some confusion as to when this battle took place. Polybius dates it to 208 B.C., while Livy asserted it was in 209 B.C.[43] Either way, both writers mostly agreed on the scale of Carthaginian losses, and Livy claimed that in addition to the deaths, 12,000 were captured. Scipio sent all the Iberians home and sold all the Africans into slavery. He was now lauded by the great majority of the Iberian leaders.

Meanwhile, the other Carthaginian commanders rushed to aid Hasdrubal but were too late to affect the outcome of the battle. They met to decide how they should now proceed and came up with a plan that they executed without asking the Senate back in Carthage. Hasdrubal Barca, it was concluded, should proceed on to Italy, taking with him all remaining Hispanic troops to prevent further desertions, while Mago was to proceed to the Balearic Islands to recruit more troops. Hasdrubal Gisgo was to retreat to Lusitania and avoid any direct engagement with the Romans.[44]

According to Livy's dating, there was no fighting in Hispania in 208 B.C., and Scipio's command was extended once again.[45] Livy's rationalization for this hiatus was that Hasdrubal's march had changed the focus of the war from Spain to Italy. In 207 B.C., however, hostilities in Spain erupted once again. Hasdrubal Gisgo was now ensconced in Gades. Hasdrubal Barca was replaced by Hanno, who brought a fresh army from Africa and advanced to Celtiberia. His expedition was unsuccessful, and he was captured by the Romans. The Carthaginians subsequently retreated to Gades, pursued by Scipio. After pillaging the area surrounding the city and taking the town of Orongi, losing only 90 men compared to the Carthaginians losing 2,000, he then retired for the winter to Tarraco.[46]

Livy described Hasdrubal Gisgo as the "greatest and most brilliant commander who held command in this war,"[47] but in 206 B.C., despite that brilliance, he was unable to stem the Roman tide. He raised a considerable force (Livy claimed he had over 70,000 men) and went out to confront the Romans at Silpia, 10 miles north of Hispalis. Scipio had a force of approximately 55,000 men. Part of Livy's account of the ensuing battle suggests that it took place at Baecula, but that was incorrect, and he later describes encampments at Silpia over 100 miles further west.[48]

This was the decisive battle of the war in Hispania and is the subject of detailed descriptions by both Livy and Polybius. The victory, in effect, resulted in the expulsion of the Carthaginians

---

[42] Polybius, *Histories*, x.37.
[43] Livy, *History of Rome*, 27.19 & Polybius, *Histories*, x.39.
[44] Polybius, *Histories*, x.40.
[45] Livy, *History of Rome*, 27.19.
[46] Livy, *History of Rome*, 28.4.1-4.
[47] Livy, *History of Rome*, 28.12.15.
[48] Livy called this Battle Silpia (Livy, *History of Rome*, 28.12.16) while Polybius called it Ilipa (Polybius, *Histories*, xi.20.1

from Spain.

Scipio made a forced march to capture the now virtually undefended Cartago Nova, and after taking that city, he continued on to take Carthage's first and last colony in Hispania: Cadiz.

While those events took place across the peninsula, Hannibal repeatedly threatened Rome as he continued marauding throughout Italy. In the wake of the catastrophic defeat at Cannae, the Roman ruling elite reevaluated Fabius Maximus's strategy, and they began to use his tactics to harass, delay, and whittle down Hannibal's forces in the field, studiously avoiding open battle whenever they could. For years they harried Hannibal's armies, and while there were blunders that allowed Hannibal to lash out (three Roman armies were destroyed in the period between 215 and 212 B.C.) the victories were minor and ultimately meaningless. After almost half a decade of continuous warfare, the countryside was becoming incapable of sustaining an army in the field, and Hannibal was getting no supplies either from his allies or from Carthage. Moreover, his allies were proving to be hopelessly ineffective in the field, meaning he either had to lead the force himself or risk losing one of his field armies. Whenever Hannibal did take command, the results were often devastating for Rome, but decisive victory eluded him. Rome could raise far more troops than Hannibal, unsupported, could ever hope to obtain, and a war of attrition was destined to favor them in the end. The tide was finally turning against Hannibal.

In 211, Hannibal received a massive blow as, while his army was in the field, the Romans besieged and captured, with great loss, his base at Capua. Still reeling from this news, his woes were compounded when he discovered that his Syracusan allies had also been crushed, with Sicily fallen to the Romans, and Philip, the king of Macedon, also defeated and driven out of the Roman dominions. Hannibal himself continued to prove himself a great general, inflicting several notable defeats upon all the armies sent against him, but they were, in the long term, meaningless. He fought on, but continued to lose territories throughout 210 and 209 B.C., and between 208 and 207 B.C. he was pushed ever southwards, finally being forced to retire to Apulia, where he anxiously awaited reinforcements under the command of his brother, Hasdrubal. At the eleventh hour, these reinforcements might have turned the tide, for once he had the troops at his command Hannibal planned to march upon Rome once and for all. However, Hasdrubal never reached Hannibal. He got himself entangled in a battle with the Romans on the Metaurus, and his army was defeated and he himself killed. Hannibal, knowing his situation in Apulia was untenable, was forced to retreat into Bruttium, the southernmost tip of the Italian peninsula, where he was also forced to endure the horror of having his brother's severed head tossed over the walls and into his camp.

For all intents and purposes, Hannibal's campaign in Italy was over. He succeeded in holding on in Bruttium for a further four years, but was never able to push northward and his army was fast dwindling to nothing, with his veterans being killed off and his mercenaries melting away. In 206 B.C., it was reported to him that Roman armies had occupied the entirety of Iberia, driving the Carthaginian forces from the peninsula, a victory obtained by his old enemy Scipio Africanus, who had utterly crushed the Carthaginians at Ilipa. Finally, in 203 B.C., he was peremptorily recalled to Carthage, 15 years and scores of victories after he had first entered Italy in arms. The reason for his recall was simple: Rome was on the march. A massive army, under the command of Scipio Africanus was preparing to attack and destroy Carthage. Rome wanted revenge.

Hannibal can hardly have been thrilled to see the amount of trouble the Carthaginians went to in order to assemble an army that, had he had his way years before, might well have been completely unnecessary. Certainly it appears that he prepared to take the field with less than his customary ardor. At 45, he was still far from old, but ever since he had first left Carthage he had spent virtually all of his adult life fighting, and the strain was beginning to tell. By all accounts he was in poor health, and prone to sickness. Indeed, rather than seek to bring Scipio Africanus to battle, in 202 B.C. Hannibal met the Roman general and attempted to talk peace. The army the Carthaginians had succeeded in gathering, not to mention the presence of Hannibal himself, convinced Scipio that he might be well-advised to seek a diplomatic solution, and the two began negotiations, which were helped by the fact that both generals recognized a kindred spirit in the other. Through negotiations, Carthage was forced to give up much, especially considering Hannibal's roster of victories, but Rome's star was on the rise once again, and Hannibal knew he could not hope to win a protracted war.

Hannibal agreed to Scipio's terms: Carthage would lose possession of Iberia and the Mediterranean islands, renouncing all claims to overseas territories but maintaining its heartland and African possessions, with the exception of the Numidian kingdom of Masinissa, who had declared for Rome. Reparations would be made, Scipio demanded, to Rome itself and to the countless families which Carthage's wars had decimated, and the Carthaginian army and fleet must both be reduced in numbers, in order for them to never again threaten Rome's supremacy. Hannibal, who recognized these terms, though harsh, as probably the best deal Carthage was likely to achieve, acceded to them, but the proposed peace between he and Scipio never happened. While the negotiations were going on, a Roman fleet which had gotten itself stranded upon the coast of Tunisia was seized by the Carthaginian navy and ransacked of all its supplies and equipment. When Scipio heard of this, he furiously demanded reparations, but, unaccountably, the Carthaginian oligarchy high-handedly turned him down. Perhaps they felt secure enough with Hannibal at the head of an army on Carthaginian soil to defy Rome, or perhaps the terms of the treaty stung their pride. Whatever their reasons, they could not have committed a bigger diplomatic error if they had gone out of their way to do so. Scipio departed the negotiations in a rage. There would be no terms.

Engraving of the Battle of Zama

On October 19th, 202 BC, on the plain of Zama, in modern Tunisia, battle was joined. Scipio Africanus led 34,000 Roman legionary infantry, including veteran survivors of Cannae, who had a score to settle with Hannibal, and 9,000 crack Numidian cavalry (the same heavy horse which Hannibal's general Maharbal had used to such devastating effect against the Romans for two decades). Hannibal himself marched to stop him with 45,000 Italian, Iberian, Gaulish and North African infantry (both mercenary and levied), 4,000 cavalry, and around 80 war elephants. For the first time in one of the battles of the Second Punic War, Hannibal had the infantry advantage and Rome had the cavalry advantage.

Hannibal deployed his cavalry on the wings, then placed three lines of infantry, with his Italian veterans in reserve, behind his war elephants, which were to be his secret weapon. Scipio countered by placing his own infantry in three lines, with his veteran heavy infantry in reserve and his own cavalry, which outnumbered Hannibal's by more than two to one, on the flanks. Hannibal opened the battle by pushing forward his war elephants and light infantry, but Scipio checked their advance before they could smash into his battle-lines by unleashing a cloud of skirmishers who harried the elephants with storms of arrows and javelins, while the Roman cavalry blew trumpets to confuse and frighten the elephants, several of which turned the way they had come and charged into the Carthaginian left flank, creating chaos there. Scipio also intentionally opened gaps in his own line for the elephants to drive through harmlessly. Masinissa took advantage of this to charge home against the cavalry on that flank and drive it from the field, but he found himself embroiled in a chase orchestrated on the fly by Hannibal as the Carthaginian cavalry lured him away from the main battle.

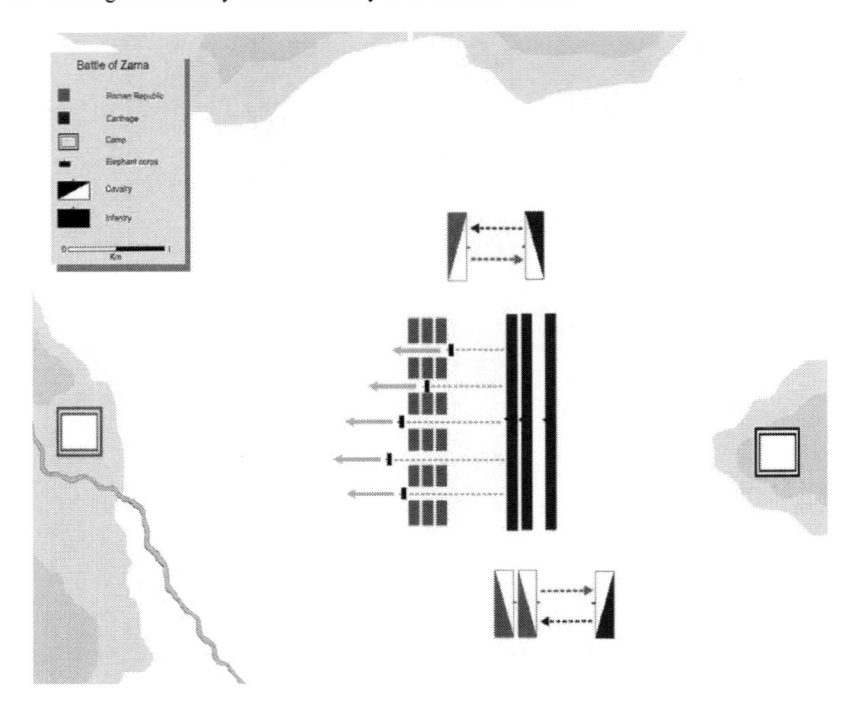

Meanwhile, the Roman and Carthaginian infantry were hammering each other in the center of the battle-line, with both sides momentarily gaining the advantage, only to be driven back in turn. The battle raged for hours, with neither side able to gain the upper hand, but eventually Masinissa, who had chased the Carthaginian cavalry clean off the field with his superior numbers, returned and charged the Carthaginian forces from behind, enveloping them. Scipio rallied his faltering and exhausted troops to one last great effort and they fell upon the Carthaginian troops, which were trapped and unable to maneuver.

Like Hannibal's masterpiece at Cannae, but this time with the roles inverted, the encircled force had nowhere to run. Thousands were cut down where they stood, with only around a tenth of Hannibal's original force, including Hannibal himself, succeeding in breaking free and escaping. For Carthage, the battle was an utter catastrophe, with over 20,000 dead and 20,000 taken prisoner, most of which were grievously wounded. Hannibal's first defeat was so dire that he lost all credibility in Carthage, and his enemies used it to blacken his reputation and forced him to surrender his generalship. With no army in the field, Carthage sued for peace, at far more costly terms than those which they could have accepted with no further loss of life.

Rome had been driven to within a hair's breadth of utter destruction, and she was not minded to be merciful. Carthage was forced to cede all of her overseas territories to Roman control and virtually all of her North African possessions became the property of Rome's Numidian ally Massinissa. What was left of the Carthaginian army was disbanded, Hannibal fled into exile to fight against Rome for foreign gold and died in exile, and Carthage was forbidden from waging wars of any sort without Roman consent. Additionally, the size of the indemnity which they were forced to pay destroyed the Carthaginian economy. Much finger-pointing and vicious recrimination inevitably ensued, with Hannibal taking a large portion of the blame, but in truth the Carthaginian oligarchy had no one to blame but themselves. If they had properly reinforced Hannibal instead of letting internal factionalism take over policy, supplying him with fresh troops and above all, a siege train, he could have sieged Rome and possibly even taken the city. Likewise, if they had provided him with enough supplies, he could have avoided antagonizing the other Italian city-states and created an anti-Roman coalition in their backyard.

Instead, Carthage now found itself mortally wounded and on the verge of collapse altogether. And in 183, Hannibal died in exile, allegedly poisoning himself to avoid being captured in battle. Roman historians speculated he had long carried the poison in a ring in case he needed to use it in battle, but poison kept that long might very well no longer be effective. In any case, Hannibal left a letter behind which dryly remarked that his death should provide some comfort to the Romans by relieving them of the fear they had felt for so long, since they apparently could not abide waiting patiently for an old man to die: "Let us relieve the Romans from the anxiety they have so long experienced, since they think it tries their patience too much to wait for an old man's death."

When the Third Punic War broke out in 149 B.C., Rome was entrenched in Hispania and Carthage could not mount any campaigns there. Carthage's final defeat and destruction in 146 B.C. confirmed Rome as the only power in the western Mediterranean and in Spain.

Roman Consolidation of Gaul

Carthage was not the only enemy that Rome had to contend with in Hispania, and while it was one of the earliest provinces to be acquired by the Romans under the Republic, it was also one of the last to be totally pacified. Hispania was, and is, extremely mountainous, and the nature of its terrain promoted the development of numerous fiercely independent tribes, particularly in the north, center, and west. This meant that the Roman conquest became something of a piecemeal affair, and in the end it took Rome 200 years to subjugate the whole peninsula as one frustrated Roman general after another discovered that it was an ideal region for guerrilla warfare.

With the Carthaginians expelled in 206 B.C., the Romans set about organizing their new territory. The well-known and wealthy areas that the Carthaginians had developed were divided into two distinct administrative areas, Nearer Spain to the east and north, and Farther Spain to the south. The first Roman town founded in Spain was Italica, near Seville, the ruins of which are a major attraction today. Under its competent conquerors, Italica swiftly evolved into a vibrant metropolis serviced by aqueducts, a 25,000-seater amphitheater, and iconic Romanesque structures. It was in this luxurious locale that the future Roman emperors Trajan and Hadrian were born.

An ancient bust of Trajan

A bust of Hadrian in Venice

In 49 B.C., Italica was renamed Hispalis by Julius Caesar, and it continued to expand under Caesar and his successors, in time encompassing a significant portion of what is now Seville today. The plot that would one day become the Alcázar, situated close to the literal heart of Seville, was turned into the grounds of the Collegium, or College of Olearians, in the 1st century A.D. *Collegia*, as defined by William Smith in *The Dictionary of Greek & Roman Antiquities,* were "civic, religious, or fraternal associations." Whether the Collegium of Olearians served specifically as a guild for businessmen, a burial society, or a social club, is uncertain; one can only assume that the association was equipped with a governing body modeled after the Senate of Rome, and that the club boasted a *curia*, or a meeting hall.

Not much, if anything, is known about the Roman establishment's appearance, but excavations conducted in recent years have given archaeologists a glimpse of its décor, as well as the construction materials the Romans might have utilized. The green hues found on 30 fragments of Romanesque wall paintings lifted from the excavation site of the Patio de Banderas, for instance, is believed to be a mix of celadonite and chlorite. "Refractive materials," such as crushed glass, and light-refracting minerals were used to create shades of Egyptian-blue.

The Romans, totally ignoring centuries of tribal tradition, labeled all the inhabitants of the Peninsula as Iberians and regarded them all as subjects of Rome. Many of these Iberians, especially those who had been more allies than conquered people, soon began to chafe at what they considered to be restrictions of Roman rule. The Romans demanded large amounts in tribute, in the form of minerals and natural products such as oil and corn. In addition, the Roman army enforced compulsory levies to supplement their auxiliary units.

On top of that, the worst indignities, as far as the Iberians were concerned, were the depredations of a series of venal governors who wrung as much as they could out of the provinces. Part of the greed displayed by various governors no doubt stemmed from the exaggerated notions of the wealth of Hispania that the Romans had. Strabo, for example, claimed that even the horses ate from mangers made of silver.[49] The history of Rome in Spain for the first few hundred years of its 600 year rule was not particularly happy, and Rome's fairly brutal regime, unsurprisingly, led to a series of revolts.

In fact, the revolts began almost immediately after the Second Punic War. On his return to Rome in 206 B.C., it had been Scipio who had recommended that Roman troops should remain in Hispania until at least the end of the war against Carthage. Having defeated Carthage, the Romans soon made it clear that they had no intention of leaving the peninsula, marking a departure from Rome's aversion to annexations. Permanent garrisons were set up in Tarraco, Cartago Nova and Gades, as well as Italica, where veterans were placed when they retired. The army in Spain became self-financing rather than funded from Rome. The first serious revolt occurred in 198 B.C. in Hispania Ulterior and spread to Hispania Citerior where a Roman army under Gaius Sempronius Tuditanus was defeated by Iberian forces.

In 196 B.C., the control of Hispania Ulterior was given to Quintus Fabius Buteo, while Quintus Minucius Thermus was made the new praetor in Hispania Citerior. Each was provided with a legion and additional cavalry from Rome's allies. They set about prosecuting a savage war against the rebels, but by the end of 196 B.C. the Senate was sufficiently concerned about the war raging on the peninsula to send a further consular army consisting of two legions and 15,000 Latin infantry under the command of Marcus Porcius Cato, commonly referred to as Cato the Elder. As his army arrived in Spain, along with two new praetors, Appius Claudius Nero and Publius Manius, news reached Cato that Quintus Minucius Thermus had defeated an Iberian force near the city of Turda, inflicting losses of over 12,000 on the rebels.[50]

The following year, Cato took Rhoda, modern day Rosas, from the Hispanic garrison. He

---

[49] Strabo, *Geography*, III. iv.
[50] Livy, *History of Rome*, 33.44.4.

adopted a scorched earth policy against any towns or cities that held out against him, spreading "terror and flight in all directions," hoping in this way to starve the rebels into submission rather than risk Roman lives in full-scale assaults.[51] In the same year, a force of 20,000 Celtiberians was defeated near Iliturgi, and when the town was subsequently sacked, the Romans massacred all males within it. Cato's campaigns became notorious for their savagery, and the Iberians came to understand that they would receive no mercy if caught in the act of rebellion. His tactics did pay dividends of sorts, and Cato proclaimed that he had pacified Hispania, but he had merely sown the seeds of further rebellions, and as soon as he left to return to Rome, the revolts broke out again.

A bust believed to depict Cato the Elder

New praetors were assigned in 194 B.C., Publius Cornelius Scipio Nasica for Hispania Ulterior and Sextus Digitus for Hispania Citerior. Digitus is described as having "fought battles, more numerous than memorable, with the tribes who had in great numbers, revolted after the departure of Marcus Cato."[52] In those many battles, he lost half of his army, and it is likely that the whole

---

[51] Livy, *History of Rome*, 34.8.6.

of the peninsula would have erupted in revolt if not for Scipio Nasica's success south of the Ebro that resulted in over 50 towns surrendering to him. In the following years a succession of new praetors all went about suppressing revolts that sprung up one after another throughout the provinces. The Romans continued to be victorious in any large engagements, such as that in 188 B.C. when the Celtiberians lost over 12,000 men,[53] and again in 186 B.C. and 184 B.C.[54] No matter how many were lost, however, the Iberians kept bouncing back and all the while maintained a hit-and-run guerrilla warfare campaign against isolated Roman garrisons and encampments.

In 182 B.C., the Celtiberians, by now exhausted and drained by constant defeats, withdrew after yet another unsuccessful campaign against the Romans who were besieging Urbicua.[55] However, 181-179 B.C. brought an even more determined effort on the part of the Celtiberians to rid themselves of the Roman yoke. The First Celtiberian War resulted in even greater losses for the rebels and the loss of numerous strategically important towns and cities.[56] The vicious circle of Roman oppression to raise money led to revolts and the loss of revenue, which led to further, more brutal, suppression to regain lost revenues.

The seemingly unbreakable cycle was, at least temporarily, broken by Tiberius Sempronius Gracchus who, with his colleague Lucius Postumius Albinus, reverted to earlier policies of seeking to win over tribes through treaties and alliances. He founded the first Roman colony in northern Hispania at Gracchurris in La Rioja and instituted a number of administrative measures, including a fairer system of taxation that ushered in a 24 year period of relative peace.[57] During this period, the Iberians tried a new tactic to try to secure fairer treatment by directly taking their grievances to Rome. There they initiated a series of lawsuits against many ex-praetors and hired prominent Romans to plead their case in court. The first of these trials was against Marcus Titinus, and after two adjournments he was acquitted of any wrongdoing. Other trials followed and these too were adjourned. There was a definite feeling amongst the Iberians that any Roman of rank would never be found guilty.

That said, they did secure valuable concessions. For example, the Senate granted their request that no Roman officer was to be allowed to set the price of grain or force local producers to sell their 5% quota at the price he determined. Moreover, they secured an agreement that no officers could directly collect money from towns.[58] These trials were the earliest known where Roman officials were accused by provincials. The Iberians also brought to the Senate's attention the issue of approximately 4,000 men who it was claimed were the sons of Romans and local women

---

[52] P. 42, *Viriathus: And the Lusitanian Resistance to Rome* by L. Silva (2013). Pen and Sword: Barnsley.
[53] Livy, *History of Rome*, 38.35.
[54] Livy, *History of Rome*, 39.8.2; 39.20.
[55] Livy, *History of Rome*, 40.16.
[56] Livy, *History of Rome*, 40.30-34.
[57] P. 58 *Viriathus: And the Lusitanians Resistance to Rome* by L. Silva (2013). Pen and Sword: Barnsley.
[58] Livy, *History of Rome*, 43.2.

who were barred from marrying legally. The Senate gave them the town of Carteia, which came to be known as the Colony of the Libertini.[59] They were also given Latin rights, and this particular tactic was one that became standard in the attempts to Romanize both the Spanish provinces and other conquered territories.[60]

Indeed, the key point that has to be kept in mind when analyzing the whole concept of Roman citizenship, whether in Spain or elsewhere throughout the empire, was that it was a privilege that granted a much sought after status and considerable benefits. Citizenship guaranteed certain rights under Roman law in relation to various aspects of life, including property and the political life of the state. Slaves, of course, could not be citizens but any free, or freed man, could aspire to one or other of the forms of citizenship allowed under Roman law. The system was hierarchical in nature, both under the Republic and the Empire, with everyone divided into different classes. At the top of the ladder, the *Cives Romani*, were the male Roman citizens who had defined and specific rights. Citizenship was not granted automatically for life, and it was not an inalienable right, but as a full citizen, the male had total legal protection. There were two subcategories, the *non optimo iure* who had property and marriage rights, and the *optio iure* who had the additional right to vote and stand for election to public office, the *ius suffragiorum* and *ius honorum* respectively.

The other main rights for the *Cives Romani* were the *ius commercii*, which gave the citizen the right to own property and be party to a contract, and *ius conubi*, which allowed the citizen to enter into a lawful marriage with a Roman citizen. This right also conferred the right of *pater familias* over all members of the family and, provided all other conditions were met, meant that the children of such a union were Roman citizens. A further right, *ius migrationis*, was the right to maintain citizenship when living away from Rome. That said, a citizen maintained his rights at the higher level only if he moved to a town or colony of similar rank to the one he held, or he would be demoted to the status of his new place of residence. All Roman citizens, of whatever class, also had rights afforded by the *ius gentium,* a set of basic human rights. Roman citizens were also immune from some taxes or local obligations and had the right to sue, and be sued, in a court of law. With this right came rights relating to defending oneself and appeal against judgements. A Roman citizen could not be tortured or crucified and even if sentenced to death, could opt for banishment instead.

There was a different, lower rung on the citizenship ladder reserved for Roman women, whose citizenship was limited in certain key respects. They did not have the right to vote or stand for public office, but the wealthiest could exert considerable political influence through the funding of religious festivities and public buildings. Most importantly, they could own property in their own right, set up their own businesses, and initiate divorce proceedings against their husbands, in

---

[59] Livy, *History of Rome*, 43.3.
[60] P. 38, *Ancient Roman* Statues, by A.C. Johnson, O. Coleman –Norton and F.C. Bourne (1961). University of Texas Press.

contrast to many other ancient societies where divorce was always at the instigation of the husband.

There were variations over time, but, generally speaking, the next class consisted of the *Latini*, who held Latin Rights. This was the form of citizenship that was relevant to the majority of those Iberians who became Romanized. Basically, this form of citizenship included those vital commercial rights and rights relating to marriage. The term was first applied to the Latins defeated in Rome's early years, and freedmen could aspire to this status and full citizens could be demoted to it if convicted of certain offences or if they moved to a Latin colony. There were other classifications for the citizens of allied states or states that were exempted from Roman taxation for whatever reason but in 90 B.C. all of these categories were rolled into one and the rights of the *Cives Romani* extended to all citizens under the *Lex Iulia de Civitate Latinis Danda*.

The benefits of citizenship were considerable and in many aspects of life in the Republic and Empire were absolutely necessary for anyone who, for example, wanted to trade or set up a viable business. A non-citizen, on the other hand, was always vulnerable and easy prey for unscrupulous officials and individuals. The trials brought by the Iberians against the corrupt officers had to be conducted by citizens, and this placed the plaintiffs, invariably, at a disadvantage. Livy's works from his *History of Rome* for the period following the trials are now lost, but it would seem that the situation remained unchanged in Spain over the next 20 years, and despite (or perhaps because of) efforts to have their grievances redressed through proper channels, the Celtiberians became increasingly disillusioned. Rebellion broke out again in 154 B.C., which came to be known as the Second Celtiberian War and was fought almost in parallel with the Lusitanian War. The wars raged on between 154 B.C. and 133 B.C., and at times it almost seemed to be a united national effort on the part of all Iberians to rid themselves of Rome.

On the Roman side, both wars were characterized by shameful examples of treachery and broken promises. For example, the war against the Lusitanians was only ended when the Romans arranged for the assassination of their chief, Viriathus, by two of his own men.[61] Viriathus is regarded as Spain's first hero. Born a shepherd, he was a military genius, and over an eight year period he dealt the Romans one blow after another. Unlike the Romans, he continuously displayed clemency towards his enemies, but to no avail; in the end, he was removed ruthlessly and without the clemency he had shown to others.[62]

The Lusitanians were not the only Iberian people who displayed extraordinary courage in their fight against oppression. The tribes in the interior displayed a dogged determination, as epitomized by Cervantes in his play *The Siege of Numantia*. From 153 B.C. onwards, the town held out against repeated attacks by the Romans. Successive Consuls came to grief trying to overcome them, and in the end the Romans bought peace with treaties that they immediately

---

[61] Appian, *Roman History: The Spanish Wars*, XV.74.
[62] Appian, *Roman History: The Spanish Wars*, XV.75.

broke. The crowning humiliation for the Romans came in 137 B.C. when a Roman force of 20,000 surrendered to a Numantian army of an estimated 8,000 men. The defeat so rocked Rome that its greatest general at the time, Scipio Aemilianus, was dispatched with an army of 60,000 to take the town once and for all. Despite overwhelming numerical superiority, Scipio did not risk an assault but instead set up 7 camps that encircled Numantia and decided to starve his enemies into submission.

The 4,000 inhabitants could not break out, and after a siege lasting six months, during which time the Romans refused to negotiate, many inhabitants committed suicide and Scipio finally took the town. He burned it to the ground and sold all but 50 into slavery. The remaining 50 were brought back to Rome to take part in his triumph. Scipio Aemilianus took the name Scipio Numantinus, a backhanded compliment to the bravery of this band of Iberians. Appian wrote, "With only 8,000 men when the war began, how many and what terrible reverses they bring upon the Romans. How many treaties did they make on equal terms with the Romans which the latter would not consent to make with any other people. How often did they challenge to open battle the last commander sent against them who had an army of 60,000 men." He went on to praise "their small numbers and great sufferings, their valiant deeds and long endurance."[63]

The fall of Numantia marked the end of the Second Celtiberian War and opened the way for further colonization of the peninsula. Iberian resistance, except for sporadic rebellions in Asturias and Cantabria, was effectively spent, and while the total subjugation of the northwest was not fully accomplished for another 100 years, all the campaigns to achieve this were more akin to police actions than actual wars. The end of the war did see some minor reforms, but, by and large, Roman rule of Spain under the Republic was still characterized by the kind of brutality that led to small outbursts of insurrection.

Some of Rome's greatest names at that time were drafted into Spain to quell any unrest. In 80 B.C., Quintus Sertorius, a former Praetor of Nearer Spain, and son of a Roman father and an Iberian mother, set up an independent government in the peninsula. Pompey was sent to deal with him, and on the way founded the city of Pamplona. Pompey's military acumen was not called into use there, however, because in 72 B.C. Sertorius was murdered at a banquet in Huesca, once again through Roman machinations.[64]

---

[63] Appian, *Roman History: The Spanish Wars*, VI. 97.
[64] Plutarch, *Parallel Lives: The Life of Sertorius*, 26.3-4.

A bust of Pompey

23 years later, the region became part of the power struggle between Pompey and Caesar. By this time, the greater part of Iberia had come to accept Roman domination, and this is evidenced by the fact that the Iberians actively supported Pompey rather than use the conflict to assert their autonomy. Caesar, however, was triumphant.

Any hope of a resurgence of some kind of Iberian nationalism finally came to an end in 19 B.C. Seven years earlier, Augustus had initiated the reduction of Cantabria, and Agrippa succeeded in finishing the emperor's work. With that, the last centers of Iberian resistance were broken, and the 200 year-long battle to subdue Hispania was over.

Gautier Poupeau's picture of a bust of Caesar

The Hellenization of Rome

The First Mithradatic War was a major challenge to Rome's rule over the Greek world and to her expanding Empire. In this war the King of Pontus, Mithradates VI, led a coalition of Greek cities against the Roman Republic. The war lasted five years and ended with Mithradates giving up all his conquests and an ignominious retreat to Pontus. The war continued with two further conflicts but it is the first that had the greatest impact on Graeco-Roman relations.

Coin of Mithradates VI of Pontus

Some of the detailed specific causes of the war, and the events of the war itself, are dealt with in this paper where they shed light on Graeco-Roman relations. However, the major issue between the antagonists was whether Pontus could expand its territory into areas in which Greek client states were determined to remain relatively free by calling upon Rome to protect them. In the summer of 90 B.C. the Senate sent Aquillius and Maltinus to restore Nicodemes of Bithynia and Ariobarzanes of Cappadocia to their respective thrones after their eviction by Mithradates and his allies.[65] Mithradates did not oppose this move on the part of the Romans but neither did he support it and he refused to co-operate in any way within Roman plans.[66]

Some have speculated that the decision to keep the Aquillian region in the area even after its purpose for being there, the restoration of Nicodemes and Ariobarzanes had been accomplished was a direct attempt to provoke Pontus into war. There is evidence to suggest that Marius had instructed Aquillius to find ways of nudging Mithradates along the path to war. If this was the case, it certainly was a very dangerous plan given Rome's other military commitments at that time.[67] Marius was Consul an unprecedented seven times and at this period was involved in a vicious battle with Sulla for the control of Rome. Control see-sawed between the two in these years and Marius may have seen the possibility of a victory over Mithradates as a way of gaining an advantage over his adversary. In the end, when war did break out, and Marius manipulated a reversal of the Senate's earlier appointment of Sulla to command the army against Mithradates, Sulla simply appealed directly to the soldiers themselves who backed him and broke all tradition by marching on Rome. The two ousted kings had taken out enormous loans in Rome to bribe Senators to support their restoration and these lenders were now anxious to capitalize on their investments. Through Aqullius, they persuaded Nicodemes and Ariobarzanes to invade Pontus in the hope of winning the booty needed to repay their loans.[68] In 89 B.C. Nicomedes invaded and plundered Mariandynia, the homeland of Mithradates, who now felt that the time was ripe for

---

[65] Livy, *Per.* 74.
[66] Apian, *Mith.*11.
[67] Appian, *Mith.* 11.
[68] Appian, *Mith.* 11.

him to challenge Rome from the position of an aggrieved party being harassed by a Roman sponsored aggressor. Initially, he tried to negotiate and his envoys took the stance that Rome would wish to honour their treaty obligations with him and punish the Bithynians who had so flagrantly flouted the peace.[69] The Bithynians, too, put their case claiming that the incursions were because of the increase in military preparations in Pontus which, in their view, could only be aimed at them and Rome.[70]

Bust of Sulla

The Pontic negotiator, Pelopidas, is acknowledged to have been extremely skilfully in the presentation of his case and the Romans found themselves embarrassed and so declared that

---

[69] Appian, *Mith*. 14.
[70] Appian, *Mith*. 13.

while they wished no harm to Mithradates, they could not allow any attacks on their Bithynian allies as to weaken him would be against Roman interests. Pelopidas was dismissed without right of reply.[71]

Mithradates could, of course, have appealed to the Senate directly but instead he sent his army into Cappadocia in late summer 89 B.C. Once again, Ariobarzanes was overthrown and Mithradates placed his son Ariarthes on the throne.[72] Mithradates knew that in taking this action he was violating the Senatus consultum that had set up Aquillius' mission and the Treaty with Rome. Mithradates could not claim in the case of Ariobarzanes, unlike Nicomedes, that he had a right to invade because of transgressions on Cappadocia's part.

By invading Cappodocia Mithradates was, de facto, declaring war on Rome and he must have been aware of this. Appian describes the preparations of both sides in considerable detail and lays the blame for the war on Pontus though in fact it was Aquillius who actually initiated direct hostilities for mainly internal Roman political reasons involving the competition between Marius and Sulla for control of the Republic.[73] The news of Mithradates' second expulsion of Ariobarzanes may well have been instrumental in Sulla's unexpected election to the Consulship in 89 B.C. Plutarch states that Sulla was fired with enthusiasm for the war against Mithradates while Marius was on the opposite side and favoured a negotiated settlement of their differences.[74]

What happened next was to have a profound effect on Graeco-Roman relations and goes a long way in explaining why Sulla was so extraordinarily vile in his treatment of the Greeks when he had defeated them. Metrodoros of Skepsis, known as ho misoromaios, the Roman hater, on account of his extreme antagonism towards Rome, was a prominent Greek adviser to Mithradates. He persuaded the king that in order to bind the communities of the Roman province together against Rome the king should exterminate all Romans, regardless of age or gender in areas under Pontic control. Most importantly he advocated that all Greek civic authorities should be made to take an active part in the suggested massacre.

In early April 88 B.C. Mithradates put the plan into action in all targeted areas at the same time, thus catching the Romans totally by surprise. Mithradates had been meticulous in his planning and all Greek civic authorities had been briefed to carry out the murders exactly one month after receipt of his letter. Appian states that 80,000 Romans and Italians were killed in what came to be known as these "Asiatic Vespers".[75] Massacres took place in Ephesus, Pergamon, Adramyttion, Caunus, Tralles, Nysa and the island of Chios. The estimates as to how many died vary from the 80,000 suggested by Appian to over 150,000 argued by Plutarch.[76]

---

[71] Appian, *Mith.* 14.
[72] Appian, *Mith.* 15.
[73] Appian, *Mith.* 17.
[74] Plutarch, *Sulla*, 7.1.
[75] Appian, *Mith.* 15 and *Memnon* 22.9.
[76] Plutarch, 24. 4.

Slaves who helped to kill their masters were spared and those who spoke languages other than Latin were also usually left unharmed. Adrienne Mayor suggests that this massacre, more than anything else, was responsible for the Senate's determination to prosecute the wars against Mithradates until he had been destroyed and his kingdom annexed.[77]

Having captured Asia Minor, Mithradates, at the instigation of some Greek cities, notably Athens, moved into Greece and Aristion was established as tyrant of Athens.[78] The Romans reacted quickly and Sulla landed in Greece in 87 B.C. and marched on Athens. His march through Greece was recorded on inscriptions that have been pieced together in recent years. From them it is known that he reached Attica by way of Boeotia where all of the cities, including Thebes, proclaimed their allegiance to Rome. Most of the cities of the Peloponnese followed suit.[79] Athens, however, remained loyal to Mithradates. Sulla placed the city under siege in the winter of 87 B.C. and the city fell on March 1st, 86 B.C. but not before the population had endured such hardships that cannibalism was reported. Sulla ordered his troops to spare no one irrespective of age or sex.

With Aristion dead, Mithradates' general Archelaus, who had been in charge of the defence of Piraeus, escaped Sulla's clutches and landed in Boeotia but was defeated at the Battle of Chaeronea in 86 B.C. and the Battle of Orchomenus which fully restored all of Greece to Roman rule.[80] The war ended following Licius Lucullus' campaign against the Pontic fleet which allowed Sulla to finally land in Asia Minor and force Mithradates to a peace settlement which, while allowing him to keep his kingdom, imposed a huge indemnity, and demands for back taxes, that left the Asian citizens saddled with a crippling debt for years to come.

The siege of Athens had proved to be a long and brutal campaign and Sulla's battle hardened troops were in no mood to show mercy to a defeated foe that had taken up arms against Rome. Both in Athens, and Piraeus, Sulla thoroughly looted the temples and civic buildings and demolished whole areas. Fire was left to burn out of control in sections of the city and in this way Philon's Arsenal was destroyed.[81] Sulla's cruelty in the aftermath of the siege was so severe that Greece remained docile for the remainder of the Mithridatic wars. The suppression of what Rome considered a revolt was not without its costs, especially in terms of Graeco- Roman relations, and the misery of the Greek states continued until the effects of Philhellenism came to

---

[77] pp. 13-24, *The Poison King; The Life and Legend of Mithradates Rome's Deadliest Enemy* by A. Mayor (2010). Princeton and Oxford University Press.
[78] Aristion had been an Athenian ambassador at the Pontic court and became a close friend of Mithradates. He was instrumental in persuading Athenians to join with Pontus to overthrow Roman rule. He was tyrant for only a very short time but according to Plutarch he behaved with extreme cruelty. When Sulla took Athens he defended the Acropolis until his water ran out. He was dragged from the altar of Athena and executed by poisoning. Plutarch, *Sulla*, 14.
[79] Pausanias, 1.20.5.
[80] Chaeronea was the site of an earlier battle where Philip II of Macedon and Alexander defeated a combined army of Thebans and Athenians to secure Macedonian hegemony in Greece.
[81] Plutarch, *Sulla*, 14.

their rescue.

Hellenism and Hellenization basically describe Greek culture and the active diffusion of that culture throughout the Mediterranean world. It has been suggested that the word Hellenization should be avoided because of the connotations of cultural imperialism[82] and the claim is that Hellenization is a modern idea reflecting modern forms of cultural domination. This argument seems to be somewhat tortuous since there can be little doubt that Alexandrian Hellenism and Hellenized Roman culture was imposed and was a form of cultural domination. Whether the word Hellenization is new or not, the concept associated with it existed and was articulated in the 3rd and 2nd Centuries B.C.

Thucydides uses the verb "Hellenize" claiming the Amphilochian Argives were "Hellenized as to their present language "by the Ambraciots.[83] The reference to "in their present language" suggests that the word had a wider meaning in a cultural sense. The historian J.G Droysen associated the word with the period between Alexander the Great and Octavian's victory at Actium, arguing that it was in this period that Greek culture was most intensely diffused. His hypothesis went on to suggest that it was the successful diffusion of Greek culture in this period that made possible the eventual rise and spread of Christianity.[84]

Plutarch, in his eulogy of Alexander, made the foundation of cities the method through which he spread Greek civilization. It is true that Alexander's policies led to Greek migration to those Middle Eastern areas he had conquered. For the Greeks the cities he founded had to be in the Greek style in terms of layout, houses public buildings and institutions. There was no attempt to incorporate any local elements in these building programmes and, consequently, they have to be seen as part of the conscious Hellenizing process instigated by Alexander.

---

[82] *Hellenism in Late antiquity* by G.W. Bowersock. (1990). Cambridge University Press: Cambridge.
[83] Thucydides, 2.68.
[84] *The German Historicist Tradition* by F.C. Beiser. (2011). Oxford University Press: Oxford.

Bust of Plutarch, by Odysses

In modern times, Hellenization has come to be associated with the post-Alexander period with Hellenism or Hellenistic used with reference to the period 336 B.C. - 31 B.C. This seems rather at odds with the most famous use of the words Hellenism and Hellenists being in Maccabees 4:13 and the Acts of the Apostles 6; 1; 9; 29.

There are two specific aspects of Philhellenism that have to be acknowledged. One of these aspects relates to culture and the positive reception and absorption of Greek language, literature and philosophy by the Roman ruling class, particularly in the 3rd and 2nd centuries B.C. The other is political and relates to Roman policy of actively encouraging behaviour and activities that were, what the Romans believed to be, respectful of, and beneficial to, the Greeks. The phenomenon is particularly associated with Flamininus Lucius Aemilus Paulus[85] and Scipio Aemilianus and his Scipionic Circle.[86] This love affair between Roman Republican aristocrats

---

[85] Flamininus was the Roman general who defeated Philip V at Cynoscephalae, he was an avowed Philhellene and even deified in some parts of Greece. He had immense influence in Rome and served as Consul as well as holding numerous posts throughout his career. He played a major part in promoting Greek culture in Rome. E. Badian 1970 Titus Quinctius Flamininus: Philhellenism and Realpolitik University of Cincinnatti).

and Greece is summed up in the word Philhellenism and there are numerous examples of the practical implications of this fascination described below.

The Encyclopaedia Britannica defines syncretism as the fusion of diverse religious beliefs and practices and notes that it was a particularly prevalent phenomenon in the Hellenistic period and immediately afterwards. The fusion of cultures that occurred under Alexander the Great brought together a variety of religious and philosophical views and the pattern established by Alexander was mirrored under the Romans. Alexander not only conquered physical areas, he displaced indigenous cultures with Greek science, religion and philosophy.[87] It can be argued that Hellenistic culture was itself syncretic, being essentially a blend of Persian, Anatolian, and Egyptian elements. The Hellenized Zeus Ammon for example, developed from the Egyptian god Amun. Such identifications of gods from other mythologies, with their own, was common in Greek history. The numerous epithets of the Olympian gods reflect this syncretic characteristic of Greek belief systems and many Olympian epithets were in relation to very specific geographical or localized myths. Zeus Molossos was only worshipped at Dodona by Molossians.

The Romans, in their turn, identified themselves as heirs to Greek civilization and identified Greek deities with figures in the Roman tradition. Rome not only absorbed explicitly Greek deities but also Hellenistic syncretic ones such as Serapis and Mithras. The correspondence varied depending on the deity: Jupiter is a more direct match for Zeus than Diana is for Artemis and differences did exist in the mythologies of Mars and Ares Bacchus and Dionysus. The Romans did not limit this syncretism to Greek or Hellenistic deities.[88]

---

[86] This was an influential group of philosophers, scholars and politicians who met regularly to indulge their passion for Greek culture and to promote a "more friendly" foreign policy towards Greece (*Oxford Companion to Classical Civilization*, p.529).

[87] Indeed many scholars see the development of Christianity as being a direct result of the syncretism of Judaism, Greek culture and philosophy and elements of Egyptian culture and can be personified in the Hellenist Saint Paul.

[88] Thor became Hercules and Odin was identified with Mercury but these tendencies were most marked in relation to Greek gods.

Marble Bust of Serapis

Roman impact on the physical aspects of Greek cities, whether through complete destruction as in the case of Corinth, or in re-shaping cities such as Athens through extensive building programmes over long periods of time, is obvious. Similarly, the rapacious looting of Greek wealth, particularly up to the Principate, had devastating impacts on the economy that could be discerned in falling standards of living and a declining population. What is less obvious is the impact Greece and Greek culture had on Rome.

Contact between Greece and Rome affected all aspects of Roman life, particularly from the 3rd century B.C. onwards. Greeks coming to Rome, whether as hostages, slaves, envoys or traders all brought with them the Greek language and Greek customs. Greek doctors and philosophers introduced the Greek way of educating the young. The incessant plundering of defeated Greek cities resulted in Greek art being brought to Rome and the luxuries associated with great Hellenistic homes were copied throughout the Roman world. Literature, too, was influenced by Greece and the earliest known Roman poet Livius Andronicus (284 B.C-204 B.C.0 was himself a Greek. Roman historians such as Fabius Pictor, Cincius Alimentus and Postumius Albinus all wrote in Greek not Latin. Even Cato whose "Otigines" was the first work in Latin prose, and who was no Philhellene, was influenced by Greek models. A further example of Hellenization can be seen in the growth of Roman theatre. Ennius wrote plays derived from those of Euripides.

The most important writers for the Roman stage were T. Maccius Plautus (254 B.C.-184 B.C.) and P. Terentius Afer (195 B.C.-159 B.C.), who both based their works on the comic writer Menander. Until comparatively recently, when some original plays on papyrus were discovered, knowledge of Menander's work was based on their adaptations. It is apparent that Romans did not just blindly copy but added to, and transformed to, create something neither Greek nor Roman but Graeco-Roman. It was Greece's classical authors that were the catalysts, and stimuli, for Roman writers to create a corpus of Roman literature. Those Roman greats, Cicero, Sallust, Horace, Virgil, Catullus and Ovid were all products of a culture that had its origins in Greece. Roman philosophy was part of Greek philosophy and Roman art developed from Greek predecessors.

The transition from Hellenistic art to Roman art was inevitably a slow process. The old styles and traditions tended to remain virtually unchanged in Greece and the Greek world but in Rome, as with the theatre, literature and philosophy, the Romans adopted, adapted and transformed Greek art over time based on new ideals and, more importantly, new patronage. These Greek-influenced developments are not surprising given that for hundreds of years after Flamininus, the average educated Roman was bilingual. This bilingualism opened up the full panoply of Greek culture to that educated group and Romans even began to fashion their history so that it merged with the Trojan cycle. As Rome became the centre of the known world in every sense that mattered, Rome coalesced all the various cultures of the Mediterranean into a Roman one and in that new culture the Hellenistic world lived on. The patronage of rich Roman Philhellenes was crucial in this whole process of Hellenization in Rome. As more and more Romans brought back art of all kinds to Rome, artists responded by producing their versions of Greek masterpieces.

During Nero's reign a specific style of painting came into vogue, called Style IV. This style is characterized by bright colours and profuse ornamentation, fusing Styles II and III. The Flavians were the great patrons of this style although the decoration of Nero's Golden Palace was the greatest example of this blending of Greek and Roman artistic tradition.[89] While Hellenistic art forms influenced Roman art heavily, purely Greek forms were modified until the time of Hadrian. Under him, art in Rome became more straightforwardly Hellenistic. The beginnings of this move away from artistic integration was noticeable in Trajan's reign and Style IV resulted in the exquisite reliefs seen on his monuments, including The Arch at Beneventum and Trajan's Column.

---

[89] p. 33, *Encyclopaedia of the Roman World* by M. Bunson (1994). New York: Facts on File.

Trajan's Column, photo courtesy of Alvesgaspar

From the mid-2nd century B.C. onwards sculptors concentrated on producing works in the classical style aimed at the Roman market that was so entranced by anything Greek. The Greeks themselves tapped into this market and in Athens the Neo-Attic school produced, almost on a mass scale, popular lines in fountains, basins, craters and garden ornaments, invariably in marble. These pieces specifically produced for the Roman market were often decorated with nymphs, maenads and satyrs. In terms of statuary, new workshops produced "pastiche" pieces again based on the perceived desires of the Romans who would purchase them. In parallel, other workshops specialised in copying famous works by the great Greek sculptors. Initially, such copies could be quite fine examples of the sculptor's art but increasingly they became mechanistic replicas with little to commend them.[90] It was not long before the copying process became more geared to the mass market through the use of plaster casts. This led to the creation of bodies moulded from copies of Greek masterpieces with different heads transplanted on to them, which did not always produce an aesthetically pleasing result.

Better results came from the later use of Greek sculptors to create totally new works based on more specifically Roman themes such as the statues found in the Temple of Neptune in Rome dating to the late 1st century B.C., and the reliefs on the Altar of Ahenobarbus. The former had both Greek and Roman themes, the Roman theme in this case being the taking of a census. This development recurred frequently in the imperial period as Roman ceremonies and events, along with attendant Roman deities, were produced in the classical style. The Ara Pacis, with its direct copies of the figures from the Caryatid porch on the Erechtheion but otherwise Roman, is an example of this new style in art.

One development occurred in sculpture involving Roman influence on Greek sculptors. Romans had long preferred portraits that concentrated on the face rather than the body, and maturity rather than good looks in these portrayals. Under Roman patronage, Greek sculptors brought their skills and quality to create the finest busts of leading Romans. These works depict "the shrewd uncompromising faces with their close cropped hair firm set mouths and deeply creviced cheeks" of those figures who masterminded Roman domination of the Mediterranean area.[91]

The austerity of early Roman sculptures was gone and was replaced by Greek embellishments. Hadrian's busts and statues had hair and beards reminiscent more of the Periclean age than the Augustan. From the time of Septmius Severus (193 A.D.-211 A.D.) until Constantine (306 A.D.-337 A.D.) official patronage of the arts was concentrated in Rome. These years saw considerable military activity and a slowly deteriorating social situation. Martial events dominated the themes in both painting and sculpture and as Rome struggled to re-assert itself there was a return to what were regarded as more Roman (but in fact, of course, Graeco-Roman) forms. However, although the forms used in the later Empire were still a fusion of Italian and Greek styles, the subjects became ever more nationalistic and Christianity, with its aversion to things Greek, also mitigated against the use of classical styles. After Constantine, Christian art dominated and overwhelmed the Graeco-Roman until the Renaissance.

---

[90] A particularly fine copy of Polyclitus' Diadumenus was found on Delos.
[91] p.521. *The Oxford History of the Classical World* by J. Boardman, J. Griffin and O. Murray (1992). Oxford University Press.

Marble Bust of Constantine, photo courtesy of Jean-Christophe Benoist

In architecture, the fashion for Greek styles led to the combination of Italian and Hellenistic features in new buildings. It became common to have a Roman atrium with Hellenistic peristyle. The aisled basilica was descended from the Greek stoa and the Roman temple and the use of Corinthian columns and other Greek decorative features became the norm in any construction work. As in Greece, marble became the preferred building material. The final evolution of the Roman temple saw the introduction of the Corinthian entablature, including modillions on the underside of the cornice. Almost in parallel with these developments came the use of concrete and with it the changes in vaulting. Though this major innovation had nothing to do with Greek influence, the Romans used the new techniques to utilise Hellenistic elements such as axial layout, open terraces and arcaded retaining walls on a totally unprecedented scale. Greek colonnades were incorporated in facades or engaged in wall schemes as decoration, especially to frame arched openings. This device became so common that it can almost be described as the epitome of the "fusion of Italian technique with Hellenistic formal vocabulary".[92] Concrete also made possible the conversion of the theatre from the Greek form, set into a hillside, to the separate structure associated with the Roman version, though over years new theatres were often combinations of both. It is no idle boast that the fusion of Hellenistic and Italian traditions spawned a golden age in architecture.[93]

---

[92] p. 517. *The Oxford History of the Classical World* by J. Boardman, J. Griffin and O. Murray (1992). Oxford University Press.

Throughout the period of the Roman Empire most Emperors retained an admiration for Greece and her culture, with several sponsoring building projects in Athens. Augustus completed the work on the Roman Agora, begun by Julius Caesar. This agora was located on the north side of the Acropolis and to the east of the existing Athenian one. The two were connected by a paved street and an inscription on the Gate of Athena Archegetis states that Caesar and Augustus provided the funding for the construction.[94] The work was completed in the 1st century B.C. and when finished it consisted of a large open courtyard with colonnades on all sides. The main entrance was through the Gate of Athena Archegetis on the west side and opposite the gate were numerous shops where a further entrance was located. On the south side there was a fountain and nearby there were public latrines. Within the precincts was the Tower of the Winds, or The Horologoin of Andronicus of Cyrrhuss, assumed to have been built in the 1st century B.C. The building was an elaborate water clock and sundial and was decorated with personifications of the eight winds, hence its nickname.[95]

The Roman Agora, rather than its ancient predecessor, became the primary marketplace for the city and the focal point for all financial and business transactions. The older Athenian Agora was relegated to something of a museum piece. Augustus was also responsible for the building of a temple, east of the Parthenon, to Roma and himself. The temple was circular with a diameter of 25 feet. It did not have a cella and the Ionic columns, nine in all, were copies of those of the Erechtheion. Another Roman building of note constructed at this time was the Agrippeaia which was constructed in the middle of the agora by Marcus Vipsanius Agrippa, the son-in-law of Augustus, who was both an architect and a general. He is credited with making a reality of Augustus' boast that he "had found Rome a city of bricks but left it a city of marble".[96] He was responsible for the design and construction of the Pantheon in Rome and was greatly influenced by what he saw in Athens.

Claudius was especially fond of the Acropolis and ordered the construction of the magnificent symmetrical stairway to the Propylaia. Nero visited Greece in 66 A.D. and despite the prohibition on anyone other than Greeks taking part in the Olympic Games, he was a contestant in a number of events, all of which, by some strange chance, he won. The following year on the 28th November, 67 A.D., at the Isthmian games, he proclaimed all Greeks to be free of Roman administration and taxation[97] but this freedom was short lived. Nero had a fascination for anything Greek and his prolonged absence in Greece may have been one of the causes of his overthrow. His overt Philhellenism made him extremely popular in the Greek world and after his assassination no fewer than three false "Neros" appeared, and were welcomed, in Greece.[98]

---

[93] p. 518. *The Oxford History of the Classical World* by J. Boardman, J. Griffin and O. Murray (1992). Oxford University Press.
[94] IG II2, 3174.
[95] S. Walker, "Athens under Augustus", in *The Romanization of Athens*, ed.s M.C. Hoff and S.I. Rotroff (1997) Oxbow: Oxford pp. 67-80.
[96] Suetonius, *The Lives of the Twelve Caesars*, Ed. J. E. Reed (1989). Philadelphia.
[97] ILS 8794 Syll. 814 Sherk, *Hadrian*, p.71.

Bust of Claudius, photo courtesy of Marie-Lan Nguyen

On an archway in Athens there are two inscriptions. On the side facing the Acropolis the inscription reads "This is Athens, the ancient city of Theseus". On the other side it reads "This is the city of Hadrian and not of Theseus".[99] Of all the Roman emperors it is Hadrian who had the greatest impact on the city of Athens, and Greece as a whole, and the sentiment expressed in the inscription is not altogether inappropriate. His full name was Publius Aelius Hadrianus and he was Emperor between 117 A.D. and 138 A.D. On the death of his father he became Trajan's ward and later his adopted heir. He was given the nickname Graeculus, little Greek, at a very early age because of his enthusiasm for studying Greek language, literature and culture. He had a lifelong interest in architectural projects and, in addition to the wall that bears his name in Athens, was responsible for many new buildings in Rome, including the Temple to Venus and Roma in the Forum Romanum. He visited Athens in 124 A.D. and was initiated into the

---

[98] p.492 *Oxford Companion to Classical Civilization* by S. Hornblower and A. Spawforth (1998). Oxford University Press.
[99] On "The Arch of Hadrian, Hadrian Street".

Eleusinian mysteries. He visited again in 128 A.D. at which time he dedicated the Olympieon[100] and assumed the name Olympus. The following year he is recorded as taking part in the mysteries once again.[101] He returned to Athens in 131 A.D. and spent the winter there, at which time he inaugurated the Olympieon.

This massive project had begun in 520 B.C. with the original intention to make it the greatest temple in the world. However, it was only completed when Hadrian took a hand and it was finally finished 638 years after work on it had begun. It was situated near to the very heart of Athens in Syntagma Square and the initial construction had been initiated by Hippias and Hipparchos, the sons of Pisistratus. They had wanted to create a monument that would outshine the Temple of Artemis at Ephesus. The architects were Antistates, Callaeschrus, Antimachides and Pornius. Work was abandoned when the tyrants were overthrown in 510 B.C. Some columns had been erected and the base had been completed. The Athenian democrats left it untouched and it lay unloved for 336 years. Aristotle claimed that the reason it had been so neglected was that the democrats viewed it as hubris to embark on works on such a scale and that the project was a device of the tyrants to keep the population without the energy to rebel.[102] When completed it was the largest temple in Greece and housed an enormous cult statue. Sadly, it was pillaged in a barbarian invasion in the 3rd century A.D.[103]

It was the Seleucid king Antiochus IV who restarted work on the temple in 174 B.C., although he employed a Roman architect, Decimus Cossutius, to oversee the project. He re-designed the columns, changing them from Doric to Corinthian, and changed the building material to Pentelic marble. However, this attempt ended in 164 B.C. when Antiochus died. Sulla's looting of Athens in 86 B.C. inflicted serious damage on the partly completed temple and he seized a number of the columns and had them transported to Rome where they were used in the Temple of Jupiter on the Capitoline Hill. Augustus made some attempts to resurrect the building work but it was not until Hadrian came on the scene that the temple was finally completed and formally dedicated in 132 A.D.

Hadrian's foundation of the Panhellenion was the culmination of his Philhellenism. He set up this institution in 131 A.D. and it was his attempt to re-create what he believed was the unified Greece of the 5Th century B.C. that had taken on and defeated the Persians. Essentially, the organization was primarily religious and admittance to membership was based on an assessment of a state's Greek credentials. In-fighting between the members after Hadrian's death led to its

---

[100] The Olympeion literally means the Columns of Olympian Zeus.
[101] p.325 *Oxford Companion to Classical Civilization* by S. Hornblower and A. Spawforth (1998). Oxford University Press.
[102] Aristotle, *Politics*, Book V, chapter 11.
[103] The Herulians sacked the city in 267 A.D. and the damage was so great that the Temple was never repaired. It is not clear whether it served any religious purpose in the years following the sacking of Athens but if there was any such use made of the building it was certainly stopped in 425 A.D. when the Christian emperor Theodosius II prohibited the worship of the old Roman and Greek gods. "Athens", *Oxford Encyclopaedia of Classical Art and Literature*. Ed. B. Hattendorf (2007). Oxford University Press.

dissolution but it did have a notable success in the creation of the Panhellenic Games in 137 A.D. which hearkened back to the Panathenaia of the 5th century B.C.[104] Hadrian was, in addition, responsible for the repair of the Parthenon, following earlier fire damage, the building of the Library of Hadrian to the east of the Agora and solving the problem of Athens' water supply by constructing a reservoir on the Lycabettus Hill which was supplied by channels from Mount Parnes. His affinity with the Greeks led him to give them rights of Roman citizenship and his sponsorship of Athens resulted in other prominent Romans also sponsoring building projects in Athens, and Greece generally. Herodus Atticus, for example, built an impressive Odeion on the west end slope of the Acropolis. The theatre could seat 50,000 and is still used today for cultural events.

Valerian (253 A.D. - 260 A.D.) had the walls of Athens rebuilt but these were insufficient to protect the city from incursions such as those of the Heruli in 267 A.D. Athens never regained the pre-eminence it had in the Classical period but it did enjoy a brief period in the late 4th and 5th centuries when her schools attracted scholars from all over the Roman world, as well as the young men of noble Roman birth. In the 2nd century A.D the Romans had endowed the University of Athens, paying teachers far more generously than was normal and exempting them from taxation. Teachers were given assurances, which were kept, that they were free to speak and teach without fear of intervention or arrest. The result was that Greek, particularly Athenian philosophy and political theory, came to be an integral part of how the Romans viewed intellectual concepts. While all of this was going on, the process of syncretism, a very clear part of the Hellenization of the Roman world, was taking place.

Judea and Herod

Evidence for Judah from the 8th century onwards is more secure and a clearer picture of the history of Judea can be formed. In 715 B.C., Hezekiah became the king. Edwin Thiele has calculated that he ruled between 715 B.C. and 686 B.C.[105] Hezekiah witnessed the destruction of the northern kingdom by the Assyrians, led by Sargon in 722 B.C., before he became king at the age of 25 when he led the resistance to Sennacherib's siege of Jerusalem in 701 B.C.[106] In the Bible, he is portrayed as a just king who consolidated Jewish monotheism and rebuilt the Temple at Jerusalem. He took advantage of the death of Sargon in 705 B.C. to attempt to throw off the Assyrian yoke and refused to pay the tribute that had been agreed by his father. He allied himself with Egypt to meet the anticipated Assyrian response. In 703 B.C., the expected invasion of Judah began, led by Sennacherib, and, in due course, as the Egyptians failed to deliver on their promise of support, Hezekiah had to try to make peace. He gave the Assyrians 300 talents of silver to lift the siege of Jerusalem.

---

[104] p.147. *Hadrian and the Cities of the Roman Empire* by M.T. Boatwright. (2003). Princeton University Press.
[105] *The Mysterious Numbers of the Hebrew Kings*, 1st edition by E. Thiele (1951). New York: MacMillan.
[106] 'Hezekiah', *Encyclopaedia Britannica* (2009).

The Bible says that after the tribute was paid, the Assyrians reneged on their promise and laid siege to the city once again. Assyrian sources say the siege ended after Hezekiah acknowledged Assyrian over-lordship and paid the required tribute. These records also include the death of Sennacherib, who was assassinated in 681 B.C.[107]

The Egyptians were led by the Nubian crown prince Taharqa and were allied with the kingdom of Judah against the Assyrians. 2 Kings 19:9 and Isaiah 37:1 both mention that "Tirhakah king of Ethiopia" led a force to help support the Judah king, Hezekiah, against the Assyrian siege, while an Egyptian source eludes to the crown prince's journey to the Levant. It states, "He (Taharqa) came Upstream to Thebes, in the midst of fine youths, his majesty, king Shebitqu, justified, went after them to Nubia, he was with him. He loved him more than all his brothers. He passed by the home of Amen Gempaaten and he worshiped before the door of the temple with the army of his majesty, sailing north together with him." (Macadam 1949, 1:14-21). Crown prince Taharqa then joined Hezekiah and his army against the Assyrians.

The confusion in the Biblical accounts concerning the correct name of the Egyptian-Nubian king can be ascribed to the fact that "the existing narrations were drawn up at a date after 690 B.C., when it was one of the current facts of life that Taharqa was king of Egypt and Nubia" (Kitchen 2003, 159-60).

The Assyrian historical annals give a more detailed account of the battle and its aftermath: "The officials, nobles and people of Ekron, who had thrown Padî, their king, bound by (treaty to) Assyria, into fetters of iron and had given him over to Hezekiah, the Jew (*Iaudai*), – he kept him in confinement like an enemy, – they (*lit.,* their heart) became afraid and called upon the Egyptian kings, the bowmen, chariots and horses of the king of Meluhha (Ethiopia), a countless host, and these came to their aid. In the neighborhood of the city of Altakû (Eltekeh), their ranks being drawn up before me, they offered battle. (Trusting) in the aid of Assur, my lord, I fought with them and brought about their defeat. The Egyptian charioteers and princes, together with the charioteers of the Ethiopian king, my hands took alive in the midst of the battle. . . I besieged Eltekeh (and) Timnah, conquered (them) and carried their spoils away. I assaulted Ekron and killed the officials and patricians who had committed the crime and hung their bodies on poles around the city . . . As to Hezekiah, the Jew, he did not submit to my yoke, I laid siege to 46 of his strong cities, walled forts and to the countless small villages in their vicinity . . . I drove out (of them) 200,150 people . . . Himself I made a prisoner in Jerusalem, his royal residence, like a bird in a cage." (Oppenheim 1992, 287-88)

Thanks to sources like that, Hezekiah's reign is the first where Biblical evidence is supported by credible documentary evidence from other sources, which include a seal bearing Hezekiah's name, a lintel from a tomb doorway believed to be that of his secretary, and store jars recording events relating to the Assyrian invasion.[108] Under Hezekiah, Judah grew in power and status.

---

[107] P. 1160, *The New Bible Dictionary* by J.D. Douglas (1965). Grand Rapids MI: Eerdmans.

Archaeological evidence suggests that there were significant increases in literacy in this period. Archaeologist Israel Finkelstein postulated, "The key phenomenon that cannot be explained solely against the background of economic prosperity, was the sudden growth the population of Jerusalem in particular and of Judah in general."[109] However, he went on to argue that this increase was probably due to Jews fleeing the Assyrian invasion of the northern kingdom.

What is not in doubt is that during the 7th century B.C. the Jewish population increased significantly and the whole area prospered under Assyrian vassalage. Manasseh ruled the kingdom from 687 B.C. until 642 B.C. and, as a vassal of Assyria, took part in the campaign against Egypt. By the time Josiah became King of Judah in 641 B.C., the whole area was in turmoil. The Assyrian Empire was collapsing, but the Neo-Babylonian Empire that would replace it had not yet emerged. Egypt was still struggling to recover from the wars against Assyria, and in the vacuum that was created, Judah was able to re-assert its independence for a short period until the Egyptians once again imposed their control of the area and Judah became a vassal, this time of Pharaoh Necho.[110]

In 605 B.C., however, the situation in the region changed dramatically when the Assyrian Empire was defeated and the area became caught up in the rivalry between the Egyptians and the Babylonians, both of whom were vying for control of the Eastern Mediterranean. The Kingdom of Judah was destroyed by the Babylonians in a series of campaigns between 597 B.C. and 582 B.C. and the elite members of the Jewish population of Judea were displaced from the homeland under the orders of Nebuchadnezzar II. Jewish revolts against the Babylonians resulted in the elimination of Judah as a kingdom, and the whole area was devastated.[111]

Jerusalem, and the surrounding area, was in effect abandoned throughout most of the 6th century B.C. This depopulation resulted in the diaspora and the scattering of the remaining Jewish population throughout the Mediterranean. Those displaced clung tenaciously to their faith, and many of their descendants would go on to play a significant role in the Jewish-Roman Wars. Jerusalem was only repopulated under Persian rule from 539 B.C.

There now followed a period of relative tranquility. The Temple was rebuilt, and the region prospered until Alexander the Great's defeat of the Persian Empire in 333 B.C. Alexander's forces occupied Judea in 332 B.C., and Alexander himself passed through on his way to Gaza and on his way back from his campaign in Egypt. There is some doubt as to whether he dealt personally with a Jewish insurrection, but for the most part, until his death in 323 B.C., he was content to leave the Jews to their own devices as long as they paid due tribute.

---

[108] 'Hezekiah' in *The Anchor Bible Dictionary Vol. II* (ed.) D.R. Hilliers (1992). New York: Doubleday.
[109] *The Quest for Historical Israel Debating Archaeology and the History of Early Israel* by I. Finkelstein (2007). Leiden: Brill.
[110] P. 142, *A History of the Jewish People* by A. H. Ben-Sasson (1976). Harvard University Press.
[111] P. 208. *A History of the Jews and Judaism in the 2nd Temple Period* by L. Grabbe (2004). T & T Clark International.

After his death, his various generals, known as the Diadochi, or successors, carved up the empire between themselves. Ptolemy took Egypt in 323 B.C. immediately following Alexander's death but was not crowned Pharaoh until 305 B.C. He succeeded, initially, in incorporating Judea within his realm, but he ultimately came into conflict with the Seleucids,[112] who had established themselves in the eastern part of Alexander's empire. Judea changed hands between the two rival Greek powers no fewer than five times in the years following Alexander's death, and the total confusion that engulfed the region enabled Judea to maintain a situation of relative independence. By 301 B.C., however, Ptolemy had asserted control over the former kingdom. Seleucid incursions did continue, and documents from the reign of Ptolemy II (r. 283-246 B.C.) give accounts of the setting up of a number of Greek cities in the area, as well as details of troops who were sent to garrison the country and information on the trade between Egypt and Judea.[113]

While evidence about these matters is quite plentiful, information about how the internal affairs of the kingdom were conducted are scant. It is clear that the High Priest became the focal point of local governance and in 242 B.C. it is known that Joseph was appointed as tax collector for the whole country.[114]

In 221 B.C., Antiochus III unsuccessfully launched a full scale invasion of Judea. When he was repulsed, he bided his time until the death of Ptolemy IV in 203 B.C. gave him the opportunity to try again. In 201 B.C., the Seleucids invaded again and on this occasion were successful. By 198 B.C., they had established complete control, which would be maintained until the Maccabean Revolt in 168 B.C.

The years of Ptolemaic rule had already seen the establishment of Greek cities throughout Judea and the process of Hellenization had begun. Antiochus III affirmed the right of the Jews to live according to their traditional laws, but Seleucid policy towards the Hellenization of their newly conquered territory changed under Antiochus IV. Some Jews had already embraced Hellenism, usually for economic advantage, by the time Antiochus IV came to power, but the new king was determined to Hellenize the Jewish community in its entirety. He manipulated the appointment of his choice for high priest, Jason of the Oniad family, and through him began a series of measures that ultimately led to revolt. His first major decision as part of his program to Hellenize the Jews was to order the construction of a gymnasium in close proximity to the Temple, bringing Greek culture into the very center of Jewish life. This action could not help but enrage traditional Jews since entrance to the gymnasium required nudity while Judaism strictly forbade being naked in public. For traditional Jews, those Jews who entered the gymnasium were violating the covenant.

---

[112] The Seleucid Empire was founded by Seleucis, who was another one of Alexander's generals.

[113] *From Text to Tradition: a History of 2nd Temple and Rabbinic Judaism* by L.H. Schiffman (1991). KTVA Publishing House.

[114] *From Text to Tradition: a History of 2nd Temple and Rabbinic Judaism* by L.H. Schiffman (1991). KTVA Publishing House.

Antiochus IV understood this only too well and enacted a law requiring males with sufficient means to visit the gymnasium at least once. Some Jews even went so far as taking steps to reverse their circumcision so that they could attend the gymnasium without fear of embarrassment. Many Jews obeyed the new law, but following a relatively minor rebellion occasioned by the edict, the Seleucids took the opportunity to vandalize the temple and erect a statue on the altar. Other repressive laws were introduced banning circumcision and Sabbath celebrations. Even more offensive to traditional Jews, altars to Greek gods were set up in every town and Jews were forced to worship them on pain of death.

Even many of those Jews who had voluntarily welcomed some aspects of Hellenism were appalled and resented what was a clear intention to destroy Judaism as a practising religion. Matters came to a head when Seleucid troops entered the town of Modiint to enforce the laws on worship. The local priest was Mattathias, who refused Seleucid instructions to sacrifice an animal on the altar of one of the Greek gods and murdered the army officer in charge. He tore down the statue and called upon the people to follow him in rebellion: "Let everyone who is zealous for the law and who stands by the covenant follow me."[115]

Together with his five sons, he roused the Jewish population to rebellion. At about the same time, the family became known as the Maccabees, meaning the hammers. They did not have the advantage of seasoned troops, so they resorted to guerrilla warfare. They were initially most successful in northern Judea, where they destroyed Greek temples and killed many non-Jews and Hellenized Jews.

Mattathias died in 166 B.C. leaving his son, Judah, to lead the insurrection. Judah proved to be a skilled general and succeeded in defeating a number of Seleucid forces sent against him. In response, the Seleucids, now totally enraged at their humiliations, sent their most famous general, Lysias, with an army of 60,000, with the intention of totally exterminating the Jewish population of Judea. In 161 B.C., Judah asked for Roman assistance against the Seleucids.[116] Even massive superiority in numbers and the leadership of Lysias proved to be of no avail, and Judah defeated the Seleucids. Jerusalem was taken back and the Temple was rededicated.[117]

In the coming years, Judah succeeded in throwing all the Seleucids out of Judea and hastened the ultimate demise of their empire. Simon was the last of the Maccabee brothers to rule in Judea until he died in 134 B.C. One of the major results of this successful revolt was the foundation of the Hasmonean dynasty, which provided more or less autonomous Jewish rule over the region for a generation.

Simon secured Roman recognition for Judea in 139 B.C., but while Roman support helped initially in expelling the Seleucids for a time, it also paved the way for direct Roman

---

[115] I Maccabees, 2:27.
[116] I Maccabees, 7.7.
[117] I Maccabees, 4:36.

involvement in the affairs of the country.

Simon was the first of the Hasmonean dynasty, a name derived from his ancestor Asamonaios. His successors were John Hyrcanus, Aristobulus I, Alexander Jannaeus and his widow Salome Alexandra, Aristobulus II, John Hyrcanus II and finally Antigonus, the last of the Hasmoneans before he was deposed by Mark Antony.

Simon ruled between 142 B.C. and his death, though his assumption of power was not confirmed until the following year, when an assembly "of the priests and people and the elders of the land" agreed that "Simon should be their leader and High Priest forever until there should arise a faithful prophet."[118] When he was assassinated in 135 B.C., he was succeeded by his son, John Hyrcanus.

The Seleucids at this point tried to reestablish control, and Antiochus VII attacked Judea. John, according to Josephus,[119] paid the invaders to leave and continued to pay tribute for the next 20 years. The Seleucid Empire, already weakened by the loss of the eastern part of their empire to the Parthians, was further weakened by civil war following the death of Antiochus.

The opportunity provided by a Seleucid Empire riven by internal disorder was too good to miss, and John led a successful revolt against the last vestiges of Seleucid control of Judea.[120] He then embarked on an expansionist program of his own, taking Madaba and Shechem before turning his attention to Transjordan, Samaria, Galilee and Edom. He was no less harsh on those he conquered than the Seleucids had been to the Jews: "John subdued all the Edomites and permitted them to stay in that country, if they would circumcise their genitals and make use of the laws on the Jews and they were so desirous of living in the country of their forefathers that they submitted to the use of circumcision and the rest of the Jewish ways of living at which time therefore this befell them that they were hereafter no other than Jews."[121]

John died in 104 B.C. and was succeeded by his son, who, after starving his mother to death, died himself in 103 B.C. He was succeeded by his brother, Alexander, who ruled from 103 B.C. until 76 B.C. During his reign he put down a Jewish insurrection in 87 B.C. and crucified over 800 of the insurgents, but he was unable to hold on to the gains made by his father in Transjordan and was soundly defeated at the Battle of Gadara in 93 B.C. by the Nabateans, who were not prepared to allow the Judean annexation of Transjordan. Alexander died while besieging the fortress of Ragaba in 76 B.C. and was succeeded by his wife, Salome Alexandra, who reigned until 67 B.C., becoming the only ruling Jewish Queen. During the period of Salome's rule the Pharisees expanded their influence into all aspects of Jewish life. Many rulings

---

[118] 1 Maccabees 14:41.
[119] Josephus, *The Jewish Wars*.
[120] *Heritage and Hellenism: The Reinvention of Jewish Tradition* by E.S. Gruen (1998). University of California Press. .
[121] Josephus, *Antiquities of the Jews*, xiii, 9.1.

on how the pious Jew should conduct his affairs were set down at this time and remain in force to this day.

Salome's death was significant in one particular regard, as it brought to a head the growing conflict between the Pharisees and the Sadducees, a conflict the led to direct Roman involvement in Judea. It is not entirely clear when the Pharisees emerged as a political force, though Josephus mentions them in connection with John.[122] As a group, they were distinguished by their fanatical belief in the necessity of all Jews observing the purity laws and total opposition to the adoption of any non-traditional, foreign practices. Their knowledge of, and adherence to, Jewish law were the cornerstones of their beliefs. They did not support the expansionist policies of the Hasmoneans and were vehemently opposed to the forced conversion of conquered people. They also demanded that the posts of king and high priest should be separated and tried to force Alexander to renounce one or other role. His response was to side with the rivals of the Pharisees, the Sadducees, and adopt their rites in the Temple. This caused riots in the city and a brief civil war, during which Alexander suppressed the Pharisees.

Salome's brother was Shimon ben Shetach, who was a leading Pharisee, and through this relationship the conflict between the two rival parties was kept in check. However, upon her death, her son, Hyrcanus, sought Pharisee support for his claim to the throne, while her younger son, Aristobulus, sought Sadducee support. Civil war broke out between the two and only ended in 63 B.C. when Romans led by Pompey the Great captured Jerusalem and ushered in a period of direct Roman involvement in Judea.

The Romans sent Marcus Aemilius Scaurus to Syria at the same time Judea was experiencing its civil war and took possession of the Seleucids' holdings. With Roman troops so close, both the warring brothers appealed directly for support from Scaurus, who initially supported Aristobulus, but when Pompey arrived in Syria in 63 B.C., Roman attitudes changed. Pompey had been awarded the title "Conqueror of Asia" following his victories over the Seleucids and Pontus, and he was now determined on bringing Judea under Roman rule. He favored Hyrcanus, deeming him to be a more suitable ward for Rome.

The brothers and a third party that wanted the dissolution of the Hasmonean dynasty altogether, the People's Party, presented their cases to him, but he prevaricated and refused to reach any definitive conclusion. Aristobulus raised an army with the intention of making the decision for him, but he proved no match for Pompey's troops. Jerusalem had to be surrendered to the Romans and Pompey entered the Holy of Holies in the Temple, only the second time anyone had done this. Judea was now forced to pay an annual tribute to Rome and was placed under the authority of the Roman Governor of Syria: "In 63 B.C. Judea became a protectorate of Rome. Coming under the administration of a governor, Judea was allowed a king, the Governor's business was to regulate trade and maximise tax revenues."[123]

---

[122] (Josephus Ant. Xiii, 5.9).

Jean Fouquet's painting depicting Pompey in the Temple of Jerusalem

In 57 B.C., Aulus Gabinius, the Governor of Syria, split Judea into Galilee, Samaria and Judea and set up five Sanhedrins, or councils, to administer them. He then divided the three areas into five, corresponding to the territory allocated to the five councils. The five sections were run from Jerusalem, Gadara, Amathus, Jericho and Sepphoris.

Judea quickly became a pawn in the increasingly tense rivalry between Julius Caesar and Pompey. Caesar contemplated using the defeated Aristobulus, who had been taken to Rome as a prisoner. Hyrcanus had been left as high priest and Caesar hoped to replace him with Aristobulus, who he believed would be more amenable to his cause.

Pompey reacted by having Aristobulus poisoned, but if Pompey assumed that he had secured the support of Hyrcanus, he was soon disappointed: "At the beginning of the civil war between Caesar and Pompey, Hyrcanus, at the insistence of Antipater, prepared to support the man to whom he owed his position; but when Pompey was murdered Antipater led the Jewish forces to

---

[123] Chapter 1, *Josephus* by N. Bentwich (1914). Philadelphia.

the help of Caesar, who was hard pressed in Alexandria. His timely help and his influence over the Egyptian Jews recommended him to Caesar's favour and secured for him an extension of his authority in Palestine and for Hyrcanus the confirmation of his ethnarchy. Joppa was restored to the Hasmonean domain, Judea was granted freedom from all tribute and taxes to Rome and the independence of the internal administration was guaranteed."[124]

---

[124] Chapter 1, *Josephus* by N. Bentwich (1914). Philadelphia.

Gautier Poupeau's picture of a bust of Caesar

Caesar's appointment of Hyrcanus as ethnarch in 47 B.C. took place at the same time he appointed Antipater as the first Roman Procurator. Josephus wrote of the favor Antipater had found with Caesar: "Caesar appointed Hyrcanus to be High Priest and gave Antipater what principality he himself should choose, leaving the determination to himself, so he made him Procurator of Judea." [125]

This elevation of a relatively obscure administrative assistant enabled Antipater to secure the position of his own family and ultimately led to the foundation of the Herodian Dynasty through his son, Herod the Great. Initially, he appointed his sons to as many positions of influence as he could: Phasael became Governor of Jerusalem, and Herod became Governor of Galilee.

Herod was appointed governor of Galilee at the age of 25 and immediately gained popularity by capturing and executing Ezekias, who was leading bandit raids throughout Galilee and Syria. Hyrcanus, in Jerusalem, was persuaded by his court that Herod was getting too powerful and had broken Jewish law by executing Ezekias and his followers. Herod was summoned to Jerusalem to stand trial before the Sanhedrin, the politically ruling body of the Jews.

Rather than arriving as a prisoner, Herod arrived in royal robes with a bodyguard. Hyrcanus was ordered by Sextus Caesar, governor of Syria, to declare Herod innocent in order to avoid consequences. Herod fled to Sextus in Damascus, where Herod was appointed governor of Coele-Syria, which included all of Syria, except Phoenicia. With this appointment, Herod became involved with the affairs of state between Rome and Syria. To avenge the humiliation at the hands of Hyrcanus, Herod began a march against Jerusalem. his father and brother persuaded him to refrain from violence and Herod returned to his own territory.

Sextus Caesar, Herod's political benefactor, was murdered by Caecilius Bassus, a faithful follower of Pompey, Julius Caesar's enemy. Antipater, Herod's father, a loyal friend of Julius Caesar, sent troops led by his two sons, Herod and Phasael, to fight against Bassus for about three years. After Cassius, Brutus and their followers murdered Julius Caesar, Cassius arrived in Syria, defeated Bassus and became ruler over Syria. Cassius exacted taxes on Judea, which had to be raised by Antipater. Antipater enlisted two of his sons, Herod and Phasael, and Malichus, a Nabatean king, to generate tax revenue for Cassius.

---

[125] Josephus, *Antiquities of the Jews*, xiv.

Cassius

Herod became so successful in collecting taxes that Cassius reappointed him as ruler over all of Syria and promised to make him king over Judea after the war that he and Brutus were fighting against Octavian and Antony. Because the Herodians were becoming very powerful under Roman domination, Malichus, the Nabatean king, bribed a butler to poison Antipater in 43 B.C. To avenge the death of his father, Herod stabbed Malichus to death.

Cassius left Syria to join in the campaign against Octavian and Antony, leaving a power vacuum in the region. Hyrcanus led a revolt, which Herod was able to calm with some difficulty. Shortly after this rebellion was squelched, another arose. Ptolemy had taken Antigonus, son of Aristobulus, Hyrcanus' brother, into his protection and attempted to use him to gain power. Herod defeated Ptolemy and was received by the people with praise and congratulated by Hyrcanus.

Herod's family life was closely related to his political life, and just as complicated. Herod married Doris, from Jerusalem, but most likely of Idumean descent. Doris was the mother of Herod's first son, Antipater, named after his grandfather.

During this time, Herod was betrothed to Mariamne, the granddaughter of both brothers, Hyrcanus and Aristobulus. She was also the niece of Antigonus, who was Herod's archrival. This betrothal secured many political advantages for Herod. By marrying Mariamne, he would marry into the Hasmonean royal family, securing him the position of regent upon Hyrcanus' death. Since Mariamne was Idumean, Herod gained acceptance into Judean circles.

In 42 B.C., Cassius was defeated by Antony at Philippi. As Antony proceeded into Asia Minor, he was met by Jewish leaders who brought accusations against the brothers, Herod and Phasael, claiming that they had overruled the powers of the government and placed Hyrcanus in a high position. Herod's defense against the accusations resulted in the charges being dropped.

In the next year, Antony was in Antioch and the Jewish leaders again brought accusations against Herod and Phasael. Antony asked Hyrcanus for advice concerning the most qualified rulers for the region. Herod and Phasael were recommended by Hyrcanus and appointed by Antony as tetrarchs (rulers of a fourth part) of Judea.

The newly appointed tetrarchs had only a brief period of peace before trouble from outside of the kingdom began. The Parthians, from northeastern Iran, appeared in Syria, and wanted to replace Hyrcanus in Jerusalem with Antigonus, supported by Pacorus, a Parthian prince. Several incidents arose which eventually led to the siege of Jerusalem by the Parthian invaders.

Hyrcanus and Phasael attempted to negotiate with the Parthians but were captured en route by Antigonus, who put the former to death and cut of the ears of the latter, thus rendering him ineligible for the high priest position. Antigonus took both the titles of high priest and king, assuming the name Mattathias, but his tenure lasted only three years. Herod had fled into exile once more when learning of Phasael's fate, and he sought help from the Romans. Antony took him under his wing, and in 40 B.C. The Roman Senate recognized him as King of the Jews. "Antony resolved to get Herod made king of the Jews and told the Senate that it was for their advantage in the Parthian War that Herod should be king; so they gave their votes for it. And when the Senate was separated Antony and Augustus went out with Herod between them while the consul and the rest of the magistrates went before them, in order to offer sacrifices to the gods and lay the decree in the Capitol."[126]

Once Rome had defeated Parthia, the Romans turned their attention to securing Herod's throne. Three years after being named King of Judea, Herod led troops to Jerusalem to begin a siege. After delegating responsibilities among his subordinates, Herod returned to Samaria to marry Mariamne, with whom he had been betrothed for almost five years. Not necessarily motivated by love, this move clearly strengthened Herod's claim to the Judean throne, as his new bride was a Hasmonean.

---

[126] Josephus, *Wars of the Jews*, xiv, 4.

Jerusalem fell to the Romans in the summer of 37 B.C. Herod's desire for power drove him to protect the wealth of Jerusalem and the purity of the Temple. He did not want to be a ruler over a wasteland and he wanted to have the favor of the Jews, so he had to keep the Roman soldiers from pillaging the city and desecrating the temple. Rather than letting the soldiers plunder and take what they wanted, Herod offered them a financial reward, a particularly high one for the commanders. The offer was accepted and the troops left Jerusalem with money in their pockets and Antigonus in chains. Herod bribed the Romans to have Antigonus eliminated, and he was apparently beheaded, thus ending the Hasmonean dynasty. Herod was now actually the king of Judea.

A depiction of the siege of Jerusalem in 37 B.C.

Herod the Great's reign over Judea lasted from 37-4 B.C. The first ten years witnessed a concerted effort to consolidate his powers, strengthening his control over this unsettling portion of the Roman Empire. Herod faced opposition from the remaining Hasmonean family members, the Jewish people and the Pharisees, the ruling class of Judea and Cleopatra of Egypt.

The people, who were under the persuasion of the Pharisees, were the most present threat to Herod. The Pharisees did not think that Herod was a rightful ruler, since he was Idumean and not a full-blooded Jew. The fact that Herod was a friend of the oppressing Romans did not help his standing before the people either. Herod's tactic in dealing with the people was to punish those who were against him, while rewarding those who were on his side.

The ruling class sided with Antigonus, also claiming that Herod was not a rightful ruler. Herod's solution to this threat was to execute forty-five of the most wealthy and prominent of the aristocracy. Their properties were confiscated and Herod's coffers were replenished as a result of their deaths.

The Hasmoneans, the previous dynasty in Judea, also maintained that Herod was not a rightful ruler. Although Herod had married into the family, it was his mother-in-law, Alexandra, who was most resistant to Herod. Since Hyrcanus had been mutilated and therefore no longer qualified to serve as high priest, Herod needed to appoint a replacement. Herod installed Ananel, an insignificant priest of the Zadokite family, considered to be descendants of Moses' brother, Aaron.

Alexandra took this as an insult to the Hasmonean dynasty and insisted that her son, Aristobulus, should have the position. Alexandra solicited help from Cleopatra of Egypt, who put pressure on Herod through Antony. Mariamne, Herod's wife, also put pressure on her husband to have her brother installed as high priest. Herod succumbed to the pressure and unlawfully removed Ananel and made Aristobulus high priest at 17 years of age.

Herod and Alexandra never trusted each other again. Alexandra attempted to escape from Jerusalem to Egypt with her son in two coffins. Herod uncovered the plot, causing him to keep a closer eye on his mother-in-law.

Aristobulus was gaining popularity, so Herod felt compelled to eliminate this Hasmonean threat to his throne. At Jericho, Herod was Alexandra's guest and invited Aristobulus to go swimming to cool off from the Judean heat. Some of his swimming companions had been bribed by Herod and they drowned Aristobulus. Herod mourned greatly and held a magnificent funeral, but Alexandra devoted her life to avenging the mysterious death. Again she called on Cleopatra to engage Antony in putting pressure on Herod. Herod was called to answer for his charges. Antony had the power to sentence Herod to death, so Herod put his wife under careful watch. his instructions were to assassinate her if he were killed, because he did not want her to become another man's lover. Mariamne's guard, Joseph, his uncle, was accused by his wife of infidelity with the king's wife. Herod believed his wife at first, but then had Joseph killed without an opportunity to defend himself. Alexandra was also put in chains and placed under guard for her role.

In addition to her role with Alexandra, Cleopatra was also a threat to Herod. Cleopatra was gaining more control of the region and Herod was eventually forced to turn over some of the most fertile areas of his territory to her. When Antony was defeated by Octavian in the Battle of Actium, Herod had to prove his right to the Judean throne to Octavian. Before leaving to meet Octavian, he had his wife and mother-in-law placed under the custody of his steward and a trusted friend. Again, the instructions were to kill these two women if anything were to happen to Herod. He did not want them to take over the kingdom, but wanted it to be left in the hands of his sons.

After securing his throne, Herod enjoyed several years of peace and prosperity (25-14 B.C.). This period is marked by massive building projects which Herod undertook, reshaping the Judean landscape and the Jerusalem skyline. Some of his buildings endeared him to the Jewish people, while others caused friction in the kingdom.

The first building project attributed to Herod was the introduction of the quinquennial (repeated every five years) games to honor Caesar. The Caesars were considered to be deities, so to the Jews this went against the Law of Moses. Other athletic and civic venues were built throughout the kingdom, providing entertainment and culture to the region, although not particularly appropriate to the Jewish laws and customs.

A royal palace was built, as well as fortified cities, including Caesarea. his greatest architectural achievement was the rebuilding of the Temple in Jerusalem. Contemporary commentary indicates that it was the greatest, most attractive building in the region. Others suggested that it was Herod's effort to atone for his killing many of the Jewish sages and leaders.

With so many disaffected groups antipathetic to his rule, it comes as no surprise that Herod had to resort to force to maintain his rule. His reign is particularly known for the introduction of what was in effect a secret police force. Exercising his power only re-enforced Jewish assessment of him as more Roman than Jewish and such beliefs were only confirmed by Herod's own references to himself as *philokaisar*, the emperor's friend. When a golden eagle, the symbol of Roman power, was erected on the new Temple gate, all pious Jews were scandalized, and when Herod, on the instructions of Augustus, ordered the Temple priests to sacrifice twice daily on behalf of the Roman Senate and people, the population was incensed. Rumors also circulated that Herod had violated Jewish tombs and stolen valuable objects from them.

Throughout all of this, Herod seemed either totally oblivious, or totally disinterested, in the hatred he was engendering, both of himself and his Roman masters. He married 10 women during his lifetime, all of them unhappy, though they did provide him with a total of 15 children.

Given all of the circumstances, it was no surprise that Herod's reign did not end well. When he fell ill, those who opposed him, led by two well-known religious teachers, Matthias and Judas, took the opportunity to remove the eagle from the Temple gatehouse. These two, and a number of their students, were burned alive. This action coincided with a number of scholars concluding that 76 generations had passed since the creation of the world. Some branches of Judaism foretold the coming of the Messiah who would deliver Israel from foreign domination in the 77th generation.

It is at this time in Herod's life that he becomes a character in the biblical account. Shortly before his death, the Magi from the East came to Jerusalem to worship the newborn king of the Jews (Mt 2). Herod, who had been murdering, plotting and conniving to hold onto his kingdom over thirty years, was duly distraught.

Matthew records that the entire city of Jerusalem was troubled along with the king about this news (Mt 2:3). At first, this appears to be odd. The Jews were being oppressed by the Romans, in particular their regional king, Herod the Great, a tyrant with little regard for his own people. Wouldn't the local populace be rejoicing in the birth of a true king of the Jews? Perhaps someone who would liberate them from the crushing reign of Herod was finally on his way. Perhaps the promised Messiah from Isaiah and the prophets would set them free from the strong arm of the far away Roman emperor.

But they were troubled. Considering the well-known history of Herod and his strong-arm rule over Judea and the squashing of any possible threat to his throne, the reason for their troubled spirits becomes clear. If there truly was a Jew who claimed to be the rightful king of Israel, what would this hot-headed Herod do? Would there be a manhunt? Would homes and villages be destroyed in his search of this pretender for the throne? Would there be even more bloodshed? What would happen to those who sympathized with this claimant to the throne? The citizens of Jerusalem were troubled. It was not for fear of a new king, but out of concern for what the current king would do to keep his throne.

The priests and scribes were summoned to tell Herod where this king was to be born. Matthew's record seems to indicate that Herod's encounter with the Magi was not known to the religious leaders. Herod knew enough of the Old Testament prophecies that he was able to cunningly cloak his question as a mere question about the prophetic writings. He said nothing of a king, but asked where the Christ, the Messiah, was to be born. Whether or not they had to research to find the answer, they reported that the prophet Micah had prophesied that the ruler would come from Bethlehem of Judah (Mic 5:2).

Herod summoned the Magi to determine when the star had appeared (Mt 2:7). He wanted more details without revealing his own plans. Herod wanted to be able to calculate the earliest possible time that this pretender to the throne could have been born. In his mind a plot was developing to eradicate anyone born in Bethlehem from the time of the appearance of the star until the arrival of the Magi in Jerusalem. Apparently, based on Herod's later actions, the Magi stated that it had been two years since the appearance of the celestial phenomenon (Mt 2:16).

He sent them to Bethlehem, deceiving them to tell him where the child was, under that pretense that he would also worship him (Mt 2:8). Upon leaving, the star reappeared, causing the Magi to rejoice. This second appearance of the celestial phenomenon verified to the Magi that they were headed in the right direction. The Magi visited and worshipped the child in a house in Bethlehem, not at the manger (Mt 2:11). Having presented costly gifts of gold, frankincense and myrrh, they were warned in a dream not to return to Herod, but to travel to their home via an alternate route.

Joseph, the earthly father of Jesus, was warned in a dream to flee to Egypt to escape Herod's wrath. Herod discovered that the Magi had deceived him and became furious. He ordered the execution of all male children in Bethlehem two years and younger, based on the timing that he had learned from the Magi (Mt 2:16-18).

Herod, now nearly 70 years old, was failing rapidly and his power was waning. During the last decade of his reign, he was haunted by the thoughts of a rival to the throne. his climb to power had occurred over the corpses of thousands of people, including those closest to him. The paranoia and his age were wearing on the king in his last days. Tormented by fears, history records that Herod often called out to his beloved wife, Mariamne, and her sons, whom he had murdered. Bouncing between suicidal thoughts and blood-thirsty delirium, Herod the Great was on the verge of insanity during his last years.

This may have been the basis for the Biblical story of the slaughter of the innocents though Herod's nature was such that such an act of brutality would not have been out of character. His illness was such that his family realised that his end was inevitable though it proved more protracted than they had assumed. Factional strife within the family resulted and possibly in exasperation Herod executed two of his sons who were plotting to take his place, Aristobulus and Antipater, in 7 and 4 B.C. respectively. Herod died in 4 B.C., dividing his kingdom between Herod Antipas who was given Galilee, Philip who was given the north eastern area around the Golan Heights, and Archelaus who became the ethnarch of Samaria and Judea. Herod was buried in Herodion, one of the fortresses he had built.

Herod reigned for over 30 years, most of which was filled with violence and bloodshed. The complicated family tree and the intrigue which developed around it may seem irrelevant, but it helps the Bible student understand the culture in which the Gospels were set. As terrible as the story reads, it is particularly important to note that Herod's murder of the children in Bethlehem was not out of character for this king. He was constantly aware of threats to his reign and would stop at nothing to secure the throne for himself or his son. The massacre of innocent children in a small village outside of Jerusalem was nothing peculiar for this king.

Caesar's Invasions of Britannia

At the time of Julius Caesar's first visit to Britain in 55 B.C., Romans knew very little of this mysterious land, and myths and legends about the fearsome Druids and blue-painted savages abounded in the Roman world. By the late 1st century A.D., Britain was securely established within the Roman Empire and becoming an increasingly important and wealthy province that ultimately produced Roman Emperors of its own. The transition from a wild misty backwater into this wealthy addition to the Empire was not without difficulty. Rebellions, particularly those staged by the Iceni, were frequent occurrences. The savagery of these rebellions was such that it is difficult to understand how Roman rule was not only preserved, but how the process of Romanization, proven more successful in Britain than in most non-Latin provinces of the Empire, was achieved.

The reasons behind this success lie in the nature of the island's political situation, which facilitated a Roman policy of divide and rule. This was used in successful combination with their normal carrot and stick approach to pacifying what, for all intents and purposes, should have been an impossible challenge, seeing as how the Romans were operating so far from their center of power. The Britain invaded by Caesar in 55 B.C. was populated by a large number of Iron Age tribes, all of which belonged to a broadly Celtic culture. In the context of Britain, however, the term "Celtic" must be seen as a linguistic one, because despite suggestions of deep-seated cultural links with the Celts of Northern Gaul, there is, in fact, very little evidence of permanent, strong ties between the Celts in Britain and those in Gaul.

The Brythonic language spoken in Britain at this time was similar to that spoken both in Ireland and Gaul, all of which are considered Celtic. Nevertheless, while on-going links between the various centers of Celtic culture may not have been quite as widespread as earlier scholars had presumed, it is inevitable that people sharing a relatively common language would also share at least some cultural features. Fitzpatrick wrote: "It is clear then, that there is no intrinsic 'Celtic' European unity and that the idea of a Celtic Iron Age Europe has developed in an almost ad hoc fashion. When examined critically, the central idea of being 'Celtic' may also be seen to be weakly formulated."[127] Tacitus believed the Britons to be descendants of migrants from throughout Europe. He concluded the Caledonians were descendants of German settlers, while those in Wales, he argued, came from Iberia, and those in the south from Gaul: "Their physical characteristics are various and this is suggestive, overall however, it seems reasonable to believe that the Gauls occupied this island lying so near to them."[128]

Scholars have long debated the nature of these movements, but whether they were migrations,

---

[127] P. 242, 'Celtic Iron Age Europe: The theoretical basis' by A.P. Fitzpatrick in P. Graves-Brown *Cultural Identity and Archaeology: The Construction of European Communities* (1996). Routledge: London.
[128] Tacitus, *The Life of Cnæus Julius Agricola*, 11.

invasions, or simply a process of "diffusion" is largely unimportant. What matters is that tribes from various parts of the continent did settle in Britain, including the Belgae, who appeared on the island in the 2nd century B.C. Julius Caesar describes this migration in his *Commentaries on the Gallic War,* using the assumed unity of the Belgae and their descendants across the Channel in the war against Rome as the excuse for his invasion in 55 B.C.[129]

There were trading links between the groups in Britain. Archaeological evidence suggests that from the 8th century B.C. onward, Celts in Britain traded with their counterparts across the Channel, bringing new ideas on, for example, the manufacture of swords. Trade was not restricted to near neighbours, and evidence confirms that Phoenician traders began visiting the island at about the same time, too, bringing various Mediterranean products with them. Similarly, it is evident that traders from Scandinavia brought their produce to Britain. All of these visitors seemed particularly interested in the country's mineral resources and salt. Goods were imported from the Hallstatt culture and these, in particular, influenced art in Britain. From the 2nd century B.C. onward, Britons made use of trading routes developed by the Romans through Brittany and southwest France to access Italian produce and Hengistbury Head in Dorset became the center for the importation of Italian wine.[130]

Some estimates put the population of Britain in the Iron Age as high as four million by the end of the 1st century B.C., with the greatest density in the southeast. The average life expectancy was around 25-30 years old, although the rates were lower for women due to the many deaths in childbirth. Between 400 B.C. and 100 B.C., evidence suggests the development of regional identities, and populations rose steadily, as "growth of population was one of the factors which led to the crystallising out of well-defined social hierarchies accompanied, especially in the south, by a degree of territoriality."[131]

Far from being the painted savages depicted by the Romans, the tribes engaged in extensive trade and commerce. While coinage from around Europe was used for trading purposes by Britons, they also developed and minted their own. Tribal kings put their names on these coins in the continental manner, and there are examples naming, for instance, Tasciovanus from Verulamium and Cunobelinos from Camulodunum. A number of buried hoards have been found throughout England, all confirming both the use of native coinage and the very disparate number of tribes based on specific regional areas.[132]

The Britain that Julius Caesar began taking an interest in from 58 B.C. onward was, then, a relatively prosperous land with a large population and numerous, successful—if comparatively

---

[129] Julius Caesar, *Commentaries on the Gallic Wars*
[130] *Greeks Romans and Barbarians: Spheres of Interaction* by B.W. Cunliffe (1988). London.
[131] P. 598, *Iron Age Communities in Britain: An account of England, Scotland and Wales from the Seventh Century B.C. until the Roman Conquest, 4th Edition* by B. Cunliffe (2010). Routledge: London.
[132] Coins in Context: coinage and votive deposition in Iron Age South East Leicestershire' by I. Leins (2007). *The British Numismatic Journal* Vol. 77, pp. 2-45.

small—regionally-based tribes. Caesar's determination to conquer Gaul totally and completely brought his initial attention to those tribes in Britain, based on his assumption they were helping the Gauls in the war against Rome. His underlying focus, however, was always his long-term plan to take total control of Rome. To do that, he had to retain control of his army. To retain that control, he had to have an enemy the Senate perceived to be a real threat to Rome. Therein lies the basis of Caesar's attempts to paint the British, and especially the Druids, as barbarians able to threaten Roman civilisation. The tactics of demonization were not particularly new to the Romans—they had employed the same tactics in the wars against the Carthaginians (who were also accused of being practitioners of human sacrifice). For Caesar, Britain was never an end in itself, but simply a means to with which to attain his greatest objectives, which accounts for his relative lack of success in his invasions compared to his other military exploits. Nevertheless, he brought Britain into the Roman consciousness, and it was inevitable that at some point Rome would turn its full attention to the island.

Caesar's expeditions to Britain in both 55 B.C. and 54 B.C. have to be viewed against the backdrop of the political situation in Rome at that time. Caesar had control of a large army in Gaul, and his campaign was, to a very large extent, undertaken on the pretext of combating an external threat to the empire. This justified the maintenance of his control over these forces at a time when there was a move in Rome for him to be relieved of his command even before the end of his commission, which was scheduled for 54 B.C.

Thus, Caesar was determined to retain command of his troops at all costs, which was pivotal to his political plans. As outlined in his *Gallic Wars*, he claimed the Britons had been aiding the Gauls and posing a very real threat to the Roman attempt to pacify the newly-conquered country.[133] The English Channel was generally regarded by the Romans as defining the very edge of the world, and the symbolic significance of crossing the "Ocean" was not lost on Caesar, intent as he was on projecting himself as Rome's greatest general and politician.

The first invasion began in the late summer of 55 B.C., despite the fact that it was already very late in the campaigning season. Gaius Volusenis was sent in a single ship to scout the south coast area as Gaulish merchants had refused to provide any information about Britain to the Romans. He did not land, as "he did not dare leave his ship and entrust himself to the barbarians."[134] The scouting expedition lasted five days and furnished with what little information his tribune had been able to gather, Caesar planned his invasion. Various tribes in the south of Britain grew alarmed as soon as they realized the Romans were intent on invading, and a number of tribes sent envoys to Caesar, offering their submission. He sent these back to the island along with his ally, King Commius of the Atrebates, to win as many tribes over as possible before he landed.

---

[133] Julius Caesar, *Commentaries on the Gallic Wars*, 4.20. (Trans. by W. A. McDevitte and W. S. Bohn) [Online]. Available at: http://www.forumromanum.org/literature/caesar/gallic_e1.html

[134] Julius Caesar, *Commentaries on the Gallic Wars*, 4.22. (Trans. by W. A. McDevitte and W. S. Bohn) [Online]. Available at: http://www.forumromanum.org/literature/caesar/gallic_e1.html

The invasion fleet numbered 80 transport vessels with the capacity to transport the Legio VII, the Legio X, and other fighting ships, and the fleet was assembled at what is now Boulogne, then known as Portus Itius. In addition, Caesar arranged for a further 18 transport ships to take the cavalry from Ambleteuse after he had landed.[135] The fact that Caesar was in something of a hurry is exemplified by the fact he set sail well after midnight on August 23, 55 B.C., without the cavalry, any siege weapons, or any of the baggage assumed necessary for a serious attempt at conquest.[136] This lack of detailed planning has led many historians to conclude that Caesar did not intend the expedition to be one of total subjugation.

Whatever the original aim, it is clear the Romans had initially intended to land at Dover, but upon arrival offshore, the numbers of assembled tribesmen on the cliffs persuaded Caesar that discretion was the better part of valour, and he sailed a further seven miles up the coast to what he thought was an unguarded beach—now thought to be Pegwell Bay on the Island of Thanet—and landed there.[137] The establishment of a beachhead proved extremely difficult, as the British fiercely opposed the landings and were only driven back by ballistae fired from ships anchored off the coast.

A camp was established. Caesar received hostages from the surrounding tribes, but he was unable to consolidate his bridgehead as his cavalry did not arrive. He quickly realized he had not come equipped to deal with a typical (harsh) British winter. Aware of his precarious position, Caesar decided to return to Gaul rather than risk being stranded in Britain over the winter with the very real possibility of complete defeat. He successfully crossed back to Gaul and continued to receive hostages from two tribes on the southeast of the island. The other tribes, however, believed the threat from Rome to be over and decided not to honor their pledges.

No matter how this particular campaign is assessed—either as an intended invasion or a reconnaissance mission—it failed to achieve any real goals. Despite this, the Senate, awed by the fact that Caesar had gone beyond what they regarded as the "known world", declared a supplication—or thanksgiving—of 20 days in honor of his achievements.

On his return to Gaul, Caesar immediately began to plan for a second invasion, scheduled for 54 B.C. Cicero referred to these plans in letters to a friend, asking him to make sure he acquired a British war chariot for him.[138] The Romans had learned from their mistakes in 55 B.C., and instead of invading with only two Legions, on this occasion, the force was comprised of five plus 2,000 cavalry, and all personnel were carried on ships specially designed for beach landings. He also planned his supply route more carefully and leaving Labienus at Portus Itius to oversee the

---

[135] P. 19, *Britannia: History of Roman Britain* by S. Frere (1987). Routledge: London.
[136] Julius Caesar, *Commentaries on the Gallic Wars*, 4.30. (Trans. by W. A. McDevitte and W. S. Bohn) [Online]. Available at: http://www.forumromanum.org/literature/caesar/gallic_e1.html
[137] Julius Caesar, *Commentaries on the Gallic Wars*, 4.25. (Trans. by W. A. McDevitte and W. S. Bohn) [Online]. Available at: http://www.forumromanum.org/literature/caesar/gallic_e1.html
[138] Cicero, *Letters to Friends*, 7.6 and 7.7.

regular transport of all food and other equipment necessary to maintain an invading force.

The Romans landed at the spot Caesar had identified the previous year, but this time their landing was unopposed. As soon as the bridgehead was established, Caesar ordered Quintus Atrius to advance inland. By the end of the day, this force had covered nearly 12 miles and defeated a British force at Bigbury Wood.[139] The next day, the Romans prepared to march further inland, but a severe storm that wrecked numerous invasion fleet vessels caused Caesar to order his troops back to the coast for repairs.

In early September, Caesar marched inland once again, confronting the forces of Cassivellaunus, the king of a tribe living north of the Thames. Cassivellaunus had recently successfully defeated the Trinovantes and was now their war leader, as well. With a combined force, the Britons harried the Romans but realized they were not strong enough to inflict a decisive defeat on the invaders. Caesar continued his progress northwards, but the constant attacks meant that by the time he had reached the Thames, that one, fordable crossing had been heavily fortified by the Romans who had used an elephant to terrify the Britons and the defenders into abandoning the crossing due to fright.[140] The Trinovantes sent ambassadors promising aid and provisions against Cassivellaunus and the Romans restored Mandubraccius to the Trinovantine throne. Other tribes followed the Trinovantine lead—including the Cenimagni, the Segontiaci, the Ancalites, the Bibroci, and the Cassi—and surrendered. Caesar, now in a more secure position, laid siege to Cassivellaunus' last stronghold at Wheathampstead.[141]

As in the previous year, Caesar was eager for a resolution to the conflict and was fearful that he would be stranded in Britain over the winter. Consequently, he did not press the siege, and when Cassivellaunus offered to provide tribute and hostages and agree not to attack the Romans' new allies, the Romans agreed to the terms and promptly left the island. No garrison of any sort was left in Britain to enforce the settlement, and it is not known if any tribute was ever paid.[142]

While both of Caesar's two invasions failed to produce military or economic advantages, the second foray provided the Romans with a significant amount of knowledge about the island that they did not have prior to the campaigns. Geographical knowledge was collected, not by Roman advances, but in dealings with local populations. Caesar's discoveries were limited to Kent and the Thames Valley. In his *Commentaries on the Gallic War,* however, Caesar made note that "[t]he climate is more temperate than in Gaul the colds being less severe." He also wrote, "The island is triangular in form and one of its sides is opposite to Gaul. One angle of this side, which is in Kent, whither almost all ships from Gaul are directed, looks to the east. The lower looks to the south. This side extends about 500 miles. Another side lies toward Spain and the west, on which part is Ireland is less, as is reckoned, than Britain, by one half, but the passage from it into

---

[139] P. 22, *Britannia: History of Roman Britain* by S. Frere (1987). Routledge: London.
[140] Polyaenus, *Strategems*, 8.23.5.
[141] P. 25, *Britannia: History of Roman Britain* by S. Frere (1987). Routledge: London.
[142] Caesar, *Letters to Atticus*, 5.

Britain is of equal distance with that from Gaul. In the middle of this voyage is an island which is called Mona many smaller islands besides are supposed to lie there, of which islands some have written that at the time of the winter solstice it might be night for thirty consecutive days. We, in our inquiries about the matter ascertained nothing except that, by accurate measurements with water, we perceived the nights to be shorter there than on the continent. The length of this side, as this account states, is 700 miles. The third side is toward north to which portion of the island no land is opposite but an angle of that side looks principally toward Germany. This side is considered to be 800 miles in length. Thus the whole island is about 2,000 miles in circumference."[143]

The actual total circumference of the island, taking account of inlets and so on, is actually about 11,000 miles, but Caesar's figures denoting the approximate shape of the island are extraordinarily accurate. The ability to assess potential landing sites and harbors proved invaluable in the next century.

Caesar was also able to assess the Britons, informing Roman attitudes from that point onward. He explained, "The interior of Britain is inhabited by those of whom they say that it is handed down by tradition that they were born in the island itself. The maritime portion by those who had passed over from the country of the Belgae for the purpose of plunder and war, almost all of whom are called by the names of those states from which being sprung they went thither and having waged war continued there and began to cultivate the lands. The number of people is countless and their buildings exceedingly numerous for the most part very like those of Gaul. They do not regard it lawful to eat the hare, and the cock and the goose, they do, however, breed them for amusement and pleasure."[144]

Caesar concluded that the most civilized of the British tribes were those living in Kent, though he noted the Britons did not sow corn but tended to live on milk and flesh instead. He confirmed all of the tribes used blue woad to decorate themselves for war, wore their hair long, and used animal skins for clothing. He was intrigued by the custom of their shaving every part of their bodies except for the hair and upper lip, and even more fascinated by the practice of sharing up to a dozen wives between warriors. The father of any child born from such unions was, he recorded, always assumed to be that of the first husband.[145]

Caesar was also able to study British military tactics, and he provided details about chariot warfare, which was a specialty of the British: "Firstly they drive about in all directions and throw their weapons and generally break the ranks of the enemy with the very dread of their horses and the noise of their wheels and when they have worked themselves in between the troops of horse, leap from their chariots to engage on foot. The charioteers in the meantime withdraw some little

---

[143] Caesar, *Letters to Atticus*, 5.13.
[144] Caesar, *Letters to Atticus*, 5.12.
[145] Caesar, *Letters to Atticus*, 5.14.

distance from the battle and so place themselves with the chariots that if their masters are overpowered by the number of the enemy they may have a ready retreat to their own troops. Thus they display in battle the speed of horse, together with the firmness of infantry and by daily practice and exercise, attain to such expertness that they are accustomed, even on a declining and steep place to check their horses at full speed and manage and turn them in an instant and run along the pole and stand on the yoke, and thence betake themselves with the greatest celerity to their chariots again."[146]

Caesar undoubtedly respected the Britons' military attributes and even copied a style of boat he had seen on the island during the subsequent civil war he fought against Pompey years later.[147] He was less enthusiastic about the Druidic religion—which he believed originated in Britain—going so far as to claim the Druids in Gaul had all been trained there.[148] He also appreciated the economic potential of the island and was convinced it would be a valuable addition to the Roman Empire: "The number of cattle is great. They use either brass or iron rings, determined at a certain weight, as their money. Tin is produced in the midland regions in the maritime, iron…there is timber of every description."[149]

Caesar did not conquer Britain, but what he did do—especially by restoring Mandubracius to the Trinovantine throne—was begin the system of client kingdoms. In so doing, he brought the island within the Roman orbit. One of his most significant successes, although perhaps only realized retrospectively in 43 A.D., was that he established alliances with key kings. Trading links also developed significantly over the coming years.

Caesar's contribution to the eventual conquest of Britain is best summed up by Tacitus: "It was, in fact, the divine Julius who first of all Romans entered Britain with an army, he overawed the natives by a successful battle and made himself master of the coast, but it may be said that he revealed, rather than bequeathed, Britain to Rome."[150]

---

[146] Caesar, *Letters to Atticus*, 4.33.
[147] Caesar, *Letters to Atticus*, 1.54.
[148] Caesar, *Letters to Atticus*, 6.13.
[149] Caesar, *Letters to Atticus*, 5.2.
[150] Tacitus, *The Life of Cnæus Julius Agricola*, 13.

The Gallic Wars

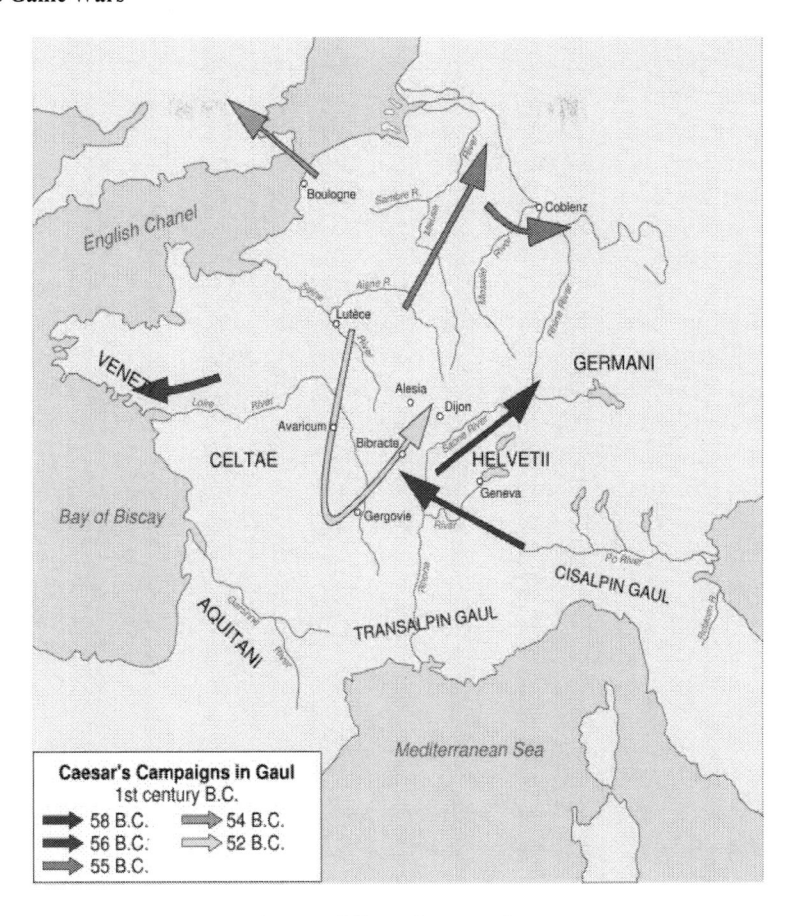

A map of Caesar's campaigns

In the early months of 58 B.C., the Helvetii, a Gaulish tribe inhabiting the lands abutting Gallia Transalpina, were pressured into seeking new lands by the fractious Germans now assailing their borders and conducting raids on their territory. As a result, they began a mass migration, destroying their homesteads as they began to march southwards. Although their destination lay outside of Roman territory and thus might not have affected the Romans to any great extent, their chosen route took them via modern Geneva into the lands of the Allobroges, a tribe under direct Roman control. This was a concern, because it meant there were tens of thousands of potentially bellicose Gauls crossing through what was in effect Roman territory. At best, the Allobroges could expect to have anything valuable which lay upon the Helvetii's line of march to go missing, while worst-case scenarios included raids by high-spirited young warriors or even a full-scale war.

Caesar, who at the time was pursuing his political ambitions in Rome, was notified of the crisis and headed north towards Gallia Transalpina as fast as possible. With only one legion to oppose the Helvetii (the personal retinue of the chief of the Helvetii alone outnumbered the Roman troops in the region two to one), Caesar was forced to quickly raise a levy of local auxiliaries. He then marched his troops to the strategic lynchpin of the region: the bridge over the Rhone. Caesar knew that the Helvetii must cross the Rhone at some point to continue their march westwards, and the easiest place for them to do so, slowed down by women and children as they were, was the bridge that had been built where the Rhone emptied into Lake Geneva. To thwart them, Caesar ordered it destroyed.

The advancing horde of the Helvetii arrived in sight of Geneva to find the bridge destroyed and a sizeable part of Caesar's forces encamped upon the far bank. High-ranking emissaries were immediately dispatched to Caesar by the Helvetii, ostensibly in an attempt to try and negotiate a peaceful passage. However, rather than entertain these dignitaries, Caesar stalled them for two weeks, using that time to recruit a large contingent of mercenary cavalry from the neighboring tribe of the Remi. He also bolstered his levies with slingers and javelineers, and more importantly, he had his legionaries complete a massive series of siege works. Without the bridge across the Rhone, the only place the Helvetii could proceed along their journey was through the Pas de l'Ecluse, a dangerous route which they had initially decided to avoid but was now their only hope. Caesar's fortifications aimed to deny this to them as well; his men constructed a rampart nearly 20 feet high and almost 20 miles long, reinforced by fortifications and fronted by a deep ditch, heavily garrisoned all along its length. For the Helvetii, there was no way forward without a fight.

Caesar, secure in his position, was able to refuse the Helvetii's overtures, and once the Helvetii became desperate enough, they attempted to launch a series of attacks across the river, only to have Caesar's troops repulse them with ease. The Helvetii would have to turn away, but whatever path they chose would still take them through lands belonging to Roman allies, and they were unlikely to be inclined to be peaceful. Caesar, sensing an opportunity for a campaign that would win him laurels and plunder and extend Rome's influence further to the north and west, resolved to come to their aid. Leaving his legion near Geneva, he hurried to Aquileia (in modern northwest Italy near the border with France) and took command of the three legions stationed there, raising Legio XI and Legio XII Fulminata as reinforcements. With about 25,000 men under his command, Caesar then marched north and elected to take the most direct route, confident that even though he had to cross hostile territory, his strength was enough to see any enemy attack off.

Despite being harassed by local tribes, Caesar was able to catch the Helvetii on the march as they attempted to ford the Avar River. The bulk of the Helvetii had already made it onto the far bank via improvised rafts and ferries, but a large portion of them remained on the near bank of the Avar. With three legions under his command, Caesar fell upon this rearguard and destroyed it. Caesar described this fight, and the personal connection he had with the enemy: "When Caesar was informed by spies that the Helvetii had already conveyed three parts of their forces across that river, but that the fourth part was left behind on this side of the Saone, he set out from the camp with three legions during the third watch, and came up with that division which had not yet crossed the river. Attacking them encumbered with baggage, and not expecting him, he cut to pieces a great part of them; the rest betook themselves to flight, and concealed themselves in the nearest woods. That canton [which was cut down] was called the Tigurine; for the whole Helvetian state is divided into four cantons. This single canton having left their country, within the recollection of our fathers, had slain Lucius Cassius the consul, and had made his army pass under the yoke. Thus, whether by chance, or by the design of the immortal gods, that part of the Helvetian state which had brought a signal calamity upon the Roman people, was the first to pay the penalty. In this Caesar avenged not only the public but also his own personal wrongs, because the Tigurini had slain Lucius Piso the lieutenant [of Cassius], the grandfather of Lucius Calpurnius Piso, his [Caesar's] father-in-law, in the same battle as Cassius himself."

In the wake of this victory, Caesar constructed a bridge across the Agar and set off in pursuit of the Helvetii. The Helvetii once again attempted to negotiate, but Caesar refused their overtures. His pursuit had now brought him deep into Aedui territory, so he was forced to negotiate with their chieftain Dumnorix for supplies for his men. Dumnorix, however, proved ambivalent at best in his support, and although a number of his cavalrymen served with Caesar's army, his promised supplies were not forthcoming. Rather than march his army into the ground, Caesar gave up his pursuit and headed for Bribacte, an Aedui stronghold, to demand the promised supplies at swordpoint.

However, the Helvetii had been emboldened by this apparent retreat and by an earlier reversal suffered by Caesar's Roman and Aedui cavalry at the hands of a smaller Helvetii mounted unit. Caesar explained, "These [cavalry], having too eagerly pursued the enemy's rear, come to a battle with the cavalry of the Helvetii in a disadvantageous place, and a few of our men fall. The Helvetii, elated with this battle, because they had with five hundred horse repulsed so large a body of horse, began to face us more boldly, sometimes too from their rear to provoke our men by an attack. Caesar restrained his men from battle, deeming it sufficient for the present to prevent the enemy from rapine, forage, and depredation."

With supplies running dangerously low and the Helvetii snapping at his rearguard's heels, Caesar chose to make his stand near the town of Bibracte in mid-June 58 B.C. By this point, Caesar had six full legions under his command, plus auxiliaries: Legio VII, Legio VIII, Legio IX, Legio X, Legio XI and Legio XII. Caesar placed the Seventh, Eight, Ninth and Tenth Legions at the foot of a steep hill in triple battle order, with the Eleventh and Twelfth under his direct command at the top of the hill. He then sent out his cavalry to engage their Helvetii counterparts, but they were repulsed. When the Helvetii advanced upon the Roman formation, however, the legionaries hit them with a double shower of javelins from about 10 yards away, throwing their ranks into utter chaos and causing them to break. Caesar described the carnage, "Caesar, having removed out of sight first his own horse, then those of all, that he might make the danger of all equal, and do away with the hope of flight, after encouraging his men, joined battle. His soldiers hurling their javelins from the higher ground, easily broke the enemy's phalanx. That being dispersed, they made a charge on them with drawn swords. It was a great hindrance to the Gauls in fighting, that, when several of their bucklers had been by one stroke of the javelins pierced through and pinned fast together, as the point of the iron had bent itself, they could neither pluck it out, nor, with their left hand entangled, fight with sufficient ease; so that many, after having long tossed their arm about, chose rather to cast away the buckler from their hand, and to fight with their person unprotected. At length, worn out with wounds, they began to give way, and, as there was in the neighborhood a mountain about a mile off, to betake themselves thither."

Caesar's men drove the Helvetii back nearly to their own baggage train, until they were in turn attacked in the flanks by a relief force of the Boii and Tulingi tribes arriving late to the battle. At this point, Caesar ordered his foremost elements to press on their attack, committing his reserve to fending off the Boii and Tulingi. The battle lasted for the better part of a day, but by evening Caesar was master of the field, and he had captured quite a few important prisoners: "The fight was carried on also at the baggage till late in the night, for they had set wagons in the way as a rampart, and from the higher ground kept throwing weapons upon our men, as they came on, and some from between the wagons and the wheels kept darting their lances and javelins from beneath, and wounding our men. After the fight had lasted some time, our men gained possession of their baggage and camp. There the daughter and one of the sons of Orgetorix was taken. After the battle about 130,000 men [of the enemy] remained alive, who marched incessantly during the whole of that night."

Karl Jauslin's painting of Caesar and Divico meeting after the Battle of Bibracte

According to Caesar's estimates, his 30,000 men had faced the better part of 90,000 enemy combatants, many of whom lay dead or dying on the battlefield. The remnants of the Helvetii, including tens of thousands of women and children, took refuge with a neighboring tribe, as Caesar and his men were not initially in a position to pursue them. However, once he had tended to his wounded, Caesar pushed on and was able to persuade the Helvetii to surrender. Caesar described the surrender terms in his commentaries: "The Helvetii, compelled by the want of every thing, sent embassadors to him about a surrender. When these had met him on the way and had thrown themselves at his feet, and speaking in suppliant tone had with tears sued for peace, and [when] he had ordered them to await his arrival, in the place, where they then were, they obeyed his commands. When Caesar arrived at that place, he demanded hostages, their arms, and the slaves who had deserted to them."

In the wake of his victory against the Helvetii, Caesar quickly became aware that he had forged a reputation throughout all of Gaul as a great general. He was approached by a congress of tribes, both allied and notionally neutral, who entreated him to deal with the problem of the fractious Ariovistus and his trespassing Suebi. The Suebi's encroachment was possibly part of the reason the Helvetii had decided to decamp from their ancestral lands in the first place. Caesar had plenty of incentive to undertake such a campaign; not only would it strengthen his standing with the Aedui and potentially bring other Gaulish tribes into the fold, it would also allow him the opportunity to expand Rome's borders into the lands held by the Suebi, cement his status among his legionaries as a successful general, increase his haul of plunder, and overtake Pompey the Great in the eyes of the Roman people and the Senate as Rome's foremost commander. On top of all that, the Gauls who approached Caesar also warned during negotiations that should Caesar refuse to aid them, they might well be forced to migrate, possibly even into Roman-controlled territory. Accordingly, Caesar marched.

Ignoring the fact that Ariovistus had been declared a "friend of the Roman people" by the Senate in 59 B.C., Caesar took advantage of the Suebi's breaching of an ultimatum he had posed (no more incursions across the Rhine) as his casus belli. Having received intelligence that Ariovistus planned to seize Vesontio, the Sequani's capital, Caesar ordered his legions to force-march towards the city, knowing it was imperative that he reach it before Ariovistus and his army. When several of his newly raised legions proved slow on the march, as the men were not hardened to such marching, Caesar proved himself a master at understanding the psychology of military morale by making a public speech to his men, claiming that only his personally raised Legio X was up to scratch. Desperate to prove him wrong, the men of the other legions outdid themselves on the march, with the result that Caesar reached the town of Vesontio before Ariovistus could.

Of course, Caesar wasn't terribly worried by such boasts. With the armies of the Suebi facing Caesar's legions across the plain of Vesontio, Ariovistus asked Caesar for a meeting, but this fell through when some soldiers from Ariovistus's army began hurling stones at Caesar's escort. Ariovistus attempted to negotiate a new meeting, but Caesar chose to send two fairly junior officers instead. Enraged by this perceived slight, Ariovistus had the pair imprisoned, then marched his army around Caesar's and parked it so that it straddled Caesar's lines of communication and supply with his Gaulish allies. When Caesar attempted to offer battle, Ariovistus refused to commit his armies to the fray, so to entice him into fighting, Caesar deliberately divided his force, placing a smaller part of it inside a fortified camp close to the Suebi's lines. The Suebi attacked this unit but were repulsed, and Caesar described the aftermath of that small skirmish: "Then at last Ariovistus sent part of his forces to attack the lesser camp. The battle was vigorously maintained on both sides till the evening. At sunset, after many wounds had been inflicted and received, Ariovistus led back his forces into camp. When Caesar inquired of his prisoners, wherefore Ariovistus did not come to an engagement, he discovered this to be the reason-that among the Germans it was the custom for their matrons to pronounce from lots and divination, whether it were expedient that the battle should be engaged in or not; that they had said, "that it was not the will of heaven that the Germans should conquer, if they engaged in battle before the new moon."

The following morning, Caesar advanced the bulk of his army in the customary triple rank against Ariovistus, who deployed his warriors in seven echelons. Caesar himself took command of the right flank. The battle was joined, and quickly turned into a slugging match, with neither side being able to win a clear advantage. Caesar again described the fighting in graphic detail: "There were found very many of our soldiers who leaped upon the phalanx, and with their hands tore away the shields, and wounded the enemy from above. Although the army of the enemy was routed on the left wing and put to flight, they pressed heavily on our men from the right wing, by the great number of their troops."

After several hours of confused fighting, the Suebi had succeeded in bending back the Roman left flank almost to the breaking point. At this point, one of Caesar's officers, Publius Crassus (son of the triumvirate Marcus Crassus), led a perfectly timed cavalry charge to smash into the flank of the Suebi advance on the Roman left, then ordered forward the reserve to reverse the attack of Ariovistus's men into a rout. The Romans then rolled up the Germanic line from their left, at which point the Suebi broke and fled. Tens of thousands were cut down in the ensuing slaughter as the broken lines of Ariovistus's men attempted to flee the battlefield (Caesar estimates 120,000, but this is likely high). Ariovistus and the shattered remnants of his army retreated across the Rhine and would never threaten Gaul again. As Caesar proudly put it in *De Bello Gallico*, "Caesar having concluded two very important wars in one campaign, conducted his army into winter quarters among the Sequani, a little earlier than the season of the year required."

Despite his most recent victory, which won him widespread acclamation in Rome and provided him and his legionaries with a vast amount of plunder, Caesar could not rest on his laurels. After winter interrupted the campaigning season, in 57 B.C. he took the field against the Gauls once more, this time marching against the Belgae, a group of tribes inhabiting modern Belgium. The Belgae had grown anxious about Caesar's apparent intent to eventually take over all of Gaul, since he and his army had made Rome the most powerful force in the region the year before. Accordingly, they formed a federation of over a dozen tribes and prepared for war, but Caesar countered this by raising a further two legions (XIII and XIV). His legions undertook a lightning action against the federation forces, which shattered their morale and caused the alliance to dissolve. Despite making great protestations of coming to each others' aid if attacked by the Romans, the Belgic tribes were subdued by Caesar one by one, but a hard core of four tribes refused to bow to Roman rule. These were the Nervii, the Atrebates, the Viromandui and the Aduatuci, a group of tribes that was both formidable, extremely hostile, and fiercely opposed to Roman ways.

Caesar decided to advance against this federation, among which the Nervii, as the most warlike tribe, claimed pre-eminence. By this point, his army had swelled to a total of eight legions, about 40,000 fighting men, plus soldiers from the Remi, an allied Belgic tribe. According to the reports passed on by his scouts, Caesar claimed that the Belgic federation could field in excess of 300,000 fighting men. While this is likely an exaggeration, they undoubtedly outnumbered Caesar's legionaries, likely by as many as two to one. Caesar, however, refused to be daunted by this and continued his march north into the Belgic heartland.

The Nervii, Atrebates and Viromandui (with the Aduatuci still en route) fortified a position on the banks of the Sabis River, placed their women, children and elderly behind the protection of a marsh, and waited for Caesar. Caesar obliged them, and in fact, for one of the first and only times in his career, he blundered. With the Belgic army drawn up in concealment behind a tree line on the far bank of the Sabis, Caesar decided to make camp on his side of the river. His column of march consisted of six legions in marching order, followed by the entire army's baggage train, behind which came the newly raised Thirteenth and Fourteenth legions. As his six legions began to construct the fortified camp behind which they would shelter for the night, the Nervii decided to spring their trap and poured out of the trees en masse, sprinting down the clear slope to the river, pouring across to the Roman side of the river's banks and, quickly overrunning the entire Roman position. Caesar vividly described the ambush and his role in rallying the Romans:

> "When the first part of the baggage train of our army was seen by those who lay hid in the woods, which had been agreed on among them as the time for commencing action, as soon as they had arranged their line of battle and formed their ranks within the woods, and had encouraged one another, they rushed out suddenly with all their forces and made an attack upon our horse. The latter being easily routed and thrown into confusion, the Nervii ran down to the river with such incredible speed that they seemed to be in the woods, the river, and close upon us almost at the same time. And with the same speed they hastened up the hill to our camp, and to those who were employed in the works.

> "Caesar had every thing to do at one time: the standard to be displayed, which was the sign when it was necessary to run to arms; the signal to be given by the trumpet; the soldiers to be called off from the works; those who had proceeded some distance for the purpose of seeking materials for the rampart, to be summoned; the order of battle to be formed; the soldiers to be encouraged; the watchword to be given. A great part of these arrangements was prevented by the shortness of time and the sudden approach and charge of the enemy. Under these difficulties two things proved of advantage; [first] the skill and experience of the soldiers, because, having been trained by former engagements, they could suggest to themselves what ought to be done, as conveniently as receive information from others; and [secondly] that Caesar had forbidden his several lieutenants to depart from the works and their respective legions, before the camp was fortified. These, on account of the near approach and the speed of the enemy, did not then wait for any command from Caesar, but of themselves executed whatever appeared proper.

> "Caesar, having given the necessary orders, hastened to and fro into whatever quarter fortune carried him, to animate the troops, and came to the tenth legion. Having encouraged the soldiers with no further speech than that "they should keep

up the remembrance of their wonted valor, and not be confused in mind, but valiantly sustain the assault of the enemy ;" as the latter were not further from them than the distance to which a dart could be cast, he gave the signal for commencing battle. And having gone to another quarter for the purpose of encouraging [the soldiers], he finds them fighting. Such was the shortness of the time, and so determined was the mind of the enemy on fighting, that time was wanting not only for affixing the military insignia, but even for putting on the helmets and drawing off the covers from the shields."

Caesar was suddenly faced with hostile Gauls assaulting him all across his line, smashing into the legionaries before they had time to hurl their javelins or form into a proper fighting line. To make matters worse, the Nervii had planted abatis of thorns and brambles across the battlefield, which prevented the Romans from forming ranks. Most of the legionaries were not even in armor, having been recalled from work details to the fighting line in a matter of moments, and most Romans just rallied around the closest centurion, trumpeter or standard they could find. Caesar was everywhere, directing what resistance he could, but there was no master-stroke to be delivered here, just a chaotic brawl in the mud.

Somehow, the four legions managed to rally and push the Belgae back, but this precipitated a crisis. With the Romans counter-attacking in two two-legion blocks, the Nervii under Buodognatus smashed down between the two of them and penetrated all the way to the Roman baggage train. While the Roman left flank fought its way uphill towards the Belgic rearguard, eventually taking the enemy encampment, the Roman right was being assailed front, flank and rear and was in danger of crumbling, with most centurions and senior officers dead or dying. According to Caesar, he personally snatched up a sword and shield to fight in the front rank like a common legionary, and he turned the tide. The Thirteenth and Fourteenth legions, force-marching to the battlefield, managed to complete the rout.

The Atrebates and Viromandui were put to flight, but the Nervii refused to budge. Although encircled, they fought on with the utmost ferocity, despite being subjected to an unrelenting hail of javelins, arrows and slingstones by Caesar's legionaries and auxiliaries. They were eventually cut down virtually to the last man, and Caesar noted the numbers when the Nervii's noncombatants sent emissaries to him to surrender: "This battle being ended, and the nation and name of the Nervii being almost reduced to annihilation, their old men, whom together with the boys and women we have stated to have been collected together in the fenny places and marshes, on this battle having been reported to them, since they were convinced that nothing was an obstacle to the conquerors, and nothing safe to the conquered, sent embassadors to Caesar by the consent of all who remained, and surrendered themselves to him; and in recounting the calamity of their state, said that their senators were reduced from 600 to three; that from 60,000 men they [were reduced] to scarcely 500 who could bear arms; whom Caesar, that he might appear to use compassion toward the wretched and the suppliant, most carefully spared; and ordered them to enjoy their own territories and towns, and commanded their neighbors that they should restrain themselves and their dependents from offering injury or outrage [to them]."

The Belgic wave had dashed itself to pieces against the rock of Caesar's legions, and though the battle had been a close-run affair, by its end there was no Belgic army left to take the field. Caesar moved northwards, subduing what little pockets of resistance remained, including the Aduatuci, who had failed to arrive in time to fight at the Sabis River. Caesar prepared to lay siege to the Aduatuci, and he reported in his commentaries how the movement of his siege engines compelled them to surrender:

> "But when they saw that it was being moved, and was approaching their walls, startled by the new and unaccustomed sight, they sent embassadors to Caesar [to treat] about peace; who spoke in the following manner: 'That they did not believe the Romans waged war without divine aid, since they were able to move forward machines of such a height with so great speed, and thus fight from close quarters; that they resigned themselves and all their possessions to [Caesar's] disposal: that they begged and earnestly entreated one thing, viz., that if perchance, agreeable to his clemency and humanity, which they had heard of from others, he should resolve that the Aduatuci were to be spared, he would not deprive them of their arms; that all their neighbors were enemies to them and envied their courage, from whom they could not defend themselves if their arms were delivered up: that it was better for them, if they should be reduced to that state, to suffer any fate from the Roman people, than to be tortured to death by those among whom they had been accustomed to rule.'

> "To these things Caesar replied, 'That he, in accordance with his custom, rather than owing to their desert, should spare the state, if they should surrender themselves before the battering-ram should touch the wall; but that there was no condition of surrender, except upon their arms being delivered up; that he should do to them that which he had done in the case of the Nervii, and would command their neighbors not to offer any injury to those who had surrendered to the Roman people.' The matter being reported to their countrymen, they said that they would execute his commands."

By the end of 57 B.C., Caesar was master of virtually all of modern Belgium, and his campaigning for the year was done.

The campaign against the Belgae was over, but after spending the winter refitting his depleted legions where he could, Caesar marched again in the spring of 56 B.C. This time his target were the Venetii, who headed a confederation of Armorican (Breton) tribes. Because the Venetii were seafaring folk, Caesar recruited sailors and shipwrights and constructed war-galleys to face them on the open sea. Caesar fought the Venetii for the better part of a year, frequently conducting complex amphibious operations which saw his fleet engage the Venetii on the waves while his legions struck against them on land. However, Caesar was ultimately victorious against the Venetii and their Armorican allies, thus adding Brittany to the haul of territories he had subdued on behalf of the Republic. By this point, Caesar had conquered or forced into alliance as Roman subjects the greater part of modern France and Belgium.

Not satisfied, the following year, in 55 B.C., Caesar took his legions across the Rhine into the dangerous territory of Germania, ostensibly to mount a punitive expedition against the Suebi, although they wisely made themselves scarce and did not engage Caesar's men during the course of his campaign. Later that year, in response to aid sent by the Britons across the English Channel to their fellow Celts in Gaul during his campaign in Armorica, Caesar put two legions aboard ships and sailed to Britain.

The expedition turned out to be a virtual disaster, as storms in the notoriously treacherous channel wrecked much of Caesar's war fleet, and when he assembled his remaining men in Britain he was met by wild enemies who painted their skins with war-paint and fought from the top of serried ranks of war-chariots. Caesar was able to leverage his legions' reputation into securing hostages from the British tribes, but the expedition was ultimately something of a humiliation for him. This rankled him enough that the following year, he returned with a more carefully executed plan and a larger army. This time, the Britons were forced to fight him, and their leading tribe, the Catuvellani, were defeated and forced to submit. Caesar left Britain without leaving a lasting impression (the conquest would only be completed much later) but the idea of Roman legions battling across the whole of Gaul, then taking ship beyond the Pillars of Hercules to take the fight to stranger and wilder enemies still, captivated the imagination of the Roman people. Caesar flooded the streets with plunder and exotic slaves and prisoners of war, elevating his popularity sky-high. Perhaps more importantly, the Romans eventually established enough of a presence to set up the outpost of Londinium, which ultimately morphed into one of the world's most famous cities: London.

While Caesar was dealing with the Britons, the European continent was up in arms, literally. Naturally, Caesar wasn't terribly popular among the Gauls he had so recently subdued, and during the winter of 54-53 B.C., when the close of the campaigning season kept most of the legions confined to their encampments, the Eburones, a tribe inhabiting northeastern Gaul, rose up against Roman rule. The Eburones and their allies, under their chieftain Ambiorix, fell upon a Roman garrison wintering at Atuatuca Tungrorum in Belgic territory and took it out completely, slaughtering the entire Fourteenth Legion. Caesar, notified of the revolt, marched his army against the Eburones just in time to rescue another beleaguered Roman garrison from annihilation, before then leading his legions in a punitive expedition which resulted in the virtual genocide of the Eburones. Most of the population was slaughtered, and the survivors were either displaced or sold into slavery. Despite that, Ambiorix managed to slip away and was never found by the Romans.

A statue commemorating Ambiorix in Tongeren, Belgium

Caesar returned to Italy after dealing with the Eburones, but he was not able to stay away from Gaul for long. In 52 B.C., there was an all-out insurrection of almost all of the previously subdued Gaulish tribes (including Rome's previously erstwhile allies, like the Aedui), which united under Vercingetorix, chieftain of the Arverni. The first blow of the insurrection was the murder of most of the Roman citizens, diplomats and merchants who had settled throughout Gaul, mostly in the major cities and trading hubs.

A statue of Vercingetorix in France

    Caesar, who was wintering in Cisalpine Gaul, heard of this from survivors of the massacre and force-marched across the snowbound Alps with ten legions. They quickly surprised the rebels, who were expecting no enemy movement until spring. Caesar dispatched four legions under Titus Labienus to quell unrest in the North, while he himself took command of the remaining six legions and his auxiliary cavalry and marched against Vercingetorix and the bulk of the rebel army.

    Vercingetorix initially refused to meet Caesar in open battle, preferring to withdraw or engage Caesar's cavalry and skirmishers in inconclusive actions that nonetheless sapped morale and caused casualties which were not easily replaced. Caesar's lines of supply were also stretched dangerously thin by this point, with little hope of local resupply in a country made barren by Vercingetorix's scorched earth policies. Eventually Vercingetorix made a stand at the hilltop town of Gergovia, and Caesar, possibly overconfident in himself and his men, attacked head-on. His legions were forced to slog uphill while the Gauls rained missiles on them and were completely exhausted by the time they were committed to the battle-line. The Gauls slaughtered thousands of Caesar's men, forcing him to pull them back before his army was annihilated, and the retreat left Vercingetorix master of the field.

    Over the course of the next year, the two armies fought a series of skirmishes as they attempted to outmaneuver each other, but Caesar's superior generalship meant that the various Gaulish contingents were scattered. Eventually, Vercingetorix and a large portion of the rebel army took up a defensive position atop the formidable earthworks of the hillfort at Alesia, hoping for the kind of result he had at Gergovia.

Of course, Caesar was too great a general to indulge him twice. His confidence now tempered by his defeat at Gergovia, Caesar reckoned that Alesia's defensive works, which were even mightier than Gergovia's, would cause him to lose his army entirely if he attempted a head-on assault. Instead, Caesar decided to bottle Vercingetorix in and starve him out. In September 52 B.C., with his allied cavalry acting as a screen, Caesar's legions spent two weeks constructing a massive set of fortifications, known as the circumvallation (the encircling wall): a rampart over 10 miles long and 12 feet tall, fronted by two ditches over 10 feet wide and 10 feet deep, the closest of which was flooded by diverting a neighboring river. Watch-towers topped with ballistae (heavy roman siege crossbows which launched a bolt several feet long), spiked ditches and other obstacles completed the defensive works. Vercingetorix was now trapped inside Alesia with 40,000-80,000 of his warriors, as well as the local population. Supplies could not be expected to last more than a few weeks.

However, before the circumvallation was completed a detachment of Vercingetorix's cavalry had succeeded in forcing a gap. Caesar explained Vercingetorix's strategy: "Vercingetorix adopts the design of sending away all his cavalry by night, before the fortifications should be completed by the Romans. He charges them when departing 'that each of them should go to his respective state, and press for the war all who were old enough to bear arms; he states his own merits, and conjures them to consider his safety, and not surrender him who had deserved so well of the general freedom, to the enemy for torture; he points out to them that, if they should be remiss, eighty thousand chosen men would perish with him; that upon making a calculation, he had barely corn for thirty days, but could hold out a little longer by economy.' After giving these instructions he silently dismisses the cavalry in the second watch, [on that side] where our works were not completed; he orders all the corn to be brought to himself; he ordains capital punishment to such as should not obey; he distributes among them, man by man, the cattle, great quantities of which had been driven there by the Mandubii; he began to measure out the corn sparingly, and by little and little; he receives into the town all the forces which he had posted in front of it. In this manner he prepares to await the succors from Gaul, and carry on the war."

Caesar assumed, rightly, that the Gauls' cavalry would return with reinforcements, so to ensure that his besieging army was not assaulted from the rear, he ordered the construction of an outer ring of fortifications pointing outward. Caesar's army was now protected from within and without, all while bottling in Vercingetorix's troops in the process. With time on his side, Caesar waited, and soon the supplies in Alesia were so exhausted that the Gauls turned their women and children out of the city, hoping that the sight of their plight would move Caesar to care for them. Caesar let them starve, and the defenders were forced to watch their families waste away in no-man's land.

However, just as the Gauls in Alesia were about to surrender, a relief force arrived to attempt their rescue. An army of around 50,000-60,000 Gauls (later sources claim as many as 300,000) fell upon the contravallation, and upon seeing this, Vercingetorix ordered his own men to sally out and attack the Romans simultaneously. All told, the Gauls may have outnumbered the Romans 4:1, and several hours of fierce fighting along virtually the entire double line of fortifications ensued, but the Gauls were unable to make or exploit a breach. They lacked siege engines and the knowledge to build them, and ultimately, they were forced to break off their attacks.

Despite repulsing the initial attack, there was no respite for Caesar and his men, because another double assault was launched the following day under cover of darkness, this time with greater success. While Vercingetorix's men struggled to make any impact against the circumvallation, the warriors of the relief force were able to capture large sections of the contravallation and were only prevented from gaining a stable foothold there by the tireless efforts of the Roman and allied cavalry under the command of Labienus and Mark Antony.

Bust of Antony

Caesar, himself now besieged, was also fast running out of supplies with no respite in sight. The following day, October 2, the entire relief force under the command of Vercingetorix's cousin Vercassivelaunus launched an all-out assault against a section of the contravallation where the Romans had been unable to erect a wall due to the nature of the terrain. Meanwhile, to prevent them from concentrating reinforcements there, Vercingetorix assaulted the entire length of the circumvallation from within. Caesar described the hectic nature of the fighting and how both sides understood the importance of the fighting: "Caesar, having selected a commanding situation, sees distinctly whatever is going on in every quarter, and sends assistance to his troops when hard pressed. The idea uppermost in the minds of both parties is, that the present is the time in which they would have the fairest opportunity of making a struggle; the Gauls despairing of all safety, unless they should succeed in forcing the lines: the Romans expecting an end to all their labors if they should gain the day. The principal struggle is at the upper lines, to which as we have said Vergasillaunus was sent. The least elevation of ground, added to a declivity, exercises a momentous influence. Some are casting missiles, others, forming a testudo, advance to the attack; fresh men by turns relieve the wearied. The earth, heaped up by all against the fortifications, gives the means of ascent to the Gauls, and covers those works which the Romans had concealed in the ground. Our men have no longer arms or strength."

For hours, the Romans battled on two fronts until, with the contravallation in serious danger of collapse, Caesar personally took command of a detachment of cavalry and led them in a lightning assault on Vercassivelaunus's rear. This turned the tide, and with the main body of the cavalry now in support, Caesar was able to start a panic in the relief force's rear. Within minutes, the entire assault had dissolved into a mass of desperately fleeing Gauls, and Caesar's cavalry and skirmishers attacked them at will, slaughtering as they went. According to Caesar, only sheer physical exhaustion prevented the Romans from completely wiping out the relief force, but they had nonetheless succeeded in destroying the Gallic army in the field: "Vergasillaunus the Arvernian, is taken alive in the flight, seventy-four military standards are brought to Caesar, and few out of so great a number return safe to their camp. The besieged, beholding from the town the slaughter and flight of their countrymen, despairing of safety, lead back their troops from the fortifications. A flight of the Gauls from their camp immediately ensues on hearing of this disaster, and had not the soldiers been wearied by sending frequent reinforcements, and the labor of the entire day, all the enemy's forces could have been destroyed. Immediately after midnight, the cavalry are sent out and overtake the rear, a great number are taken or cut to pieces, the rest by flight escape in different directions to their respective states."

Seeing his reinforcements cut to pieces from the walls of Alesia, Vercingetorix was left with no choice but to surrender, which he did the following day. The entire garrison of Alesia was sold into slavery, except for the Aedui and Arverni, who were forgiven for their crimes and allowed to return home as reinstated Roman allies. Caesar described the scene of the surrender: "Vercingetorix, having convened a council the following day, declares, 'That he had undertaken that war, not on account of his own exigences, but on account of the general freedom; and since he must yield to fortune, he offered himself to them for either purpose, whether they should wish to atone to the Romans by his death, or surrender him alive.' Embassadors are sent to Caesar on this subject. He orders their arms to be surrendered, and their chieftains delivered up. He seated himself at the head of the lines in front of the camp, the Gallic chieftains are brought before him.

They surrender Vercingetorix, and lay down their arms. Reserving the Aedui and Arverni, [to try] if he could gain over, through their influence, their respective states, he distributes one of the remaining captives to each soldier, throughout the entire army, as plunder."

Vercingetorix himself would eventually be paraded through the streets of Rome as part of Caesar's triumph in 46 B.C., after which he was executed. After Alesia, Gaulish resistance to Roman rule was effectively ended throughout the entire region for several centuries, and Gaul became one of the most prosperous, stable and loyal provinces of the Roman Empire.

In the end, Caesar had seemingly won Rome an incredible victory. Not only did he do so dazzlingly, far surpassing the most rosy expectations and extending the borders of the Republic from the Alps to the English Channel, but he did so against one of Rome's most ancient and hated enemies.

What makes the Gallic Wars even more significant, however, is that the campaigns established a legend that Caesar would use to wage a civil war against Pompey the Great and virtually destroy the Roman Republic, establishing a proto-empire in its place with Octavian as his heir. By the end of the Gallic Wars, the alliance between Caesar and Pompey had devolved from alliance to rivalry, and when his governorship ended in 50 B.C., Pompey was ready to gain an upper hand in Rome. In 50 B.C., with his term as governor having ended, Caesar received a formal order by the Senate, largely the product of Pompey's machinations, to disband his army and return to Rome, but Caesar was certain that he was going to be held to account for his debts and other irregularities. Assuming that any trial he participated would likely be a witch-hunt specifically designed to permanently tarnish him, he would have none of it.

In 50 B.C., Caesar would have to greatly rely upon Antony's loyalty. The great general's political troubles were coming to a head, and there seemed to be every likelihood he would be recalled to Rome and submitted to a trial by his political rivals, who were headed by Caesar's former friend and ally Pompey. Recognizing that he would need a powerful voice in the Senate, Caesar dispatched Antony to Italy, to speak for him and drum up popular support for his cause. Since Caesar's political mandate was expiring, he would soon lose his immunity from prosecution, so he prepared to march into Italy to pursue what he claimed where his rights.

Caesar's claims were not exactly legitimate, but Antony seems not to have cared. Indeed, he set about defending his friend with remarkable zeal. Once in Rome, Antony's dashing reputation as a model soldier and his skill at oratory secured him a position as tribune of the people, and also the rank of augur, which like many senior religious positions in Rome also carried significant political clout. Antony made sure that Caesar's voice was heard in the Senate. Caesar had abandoned the larger part of his armies north of the Alps and, with a single legion, he was marching southwards to put his case personally, or so he claimed, to the people. Caesar's optimate opponents wanted he and his party, the populares, to be heard as little as possible, lest their arguments sway those among the Senators who were still undecided. To that end, they made sure that the proclamations that Caesar routinely dispatched southwards were never heard, either by the Senate or by the common people. However, vested with the authority of tribune of the people, Antony was able to read Caesar's speeches himself, and the optimates were powerless to resist him.

Clearly the situation in Rome quickly became untenable. Having crossed into Northern Italy, Caesar was encamped close to the northern bank of the Rubicon River. This was a hugely momentous event, as the Rubicon marked the southernmost boundary a general could advance on Rome from the north with his army, and the last people to infringe upon this border had been the military dictators Marius and Sulla, the memory of whose purges was still fresh in the minds of many Romans. If Caesar crossed the river in arms, it meant civil war.

Since Caesar refused to obey the Senate, Pompey worked to have him accused of treason. Caesar, meanwhile, had taken his own initiative. After much deliberation, he figured that his opponents would never surrender peaceably. Leaving the majority of his forces in Gaul, Caesar headed south for Italy in January 49 B.C. at the head of the 13th Legion, despite repeated remonstrations by the Senate and threats by Pompey. That month, Caesar and his men crossed the Rubicon River into Italy, thus entering Italy as invaders, and it's likely that similar exploits by his uncle Marius and Sulla were playing in his mind. According to Suetonius and Plutarch, as his troops filed by, he famously quoted the Greek playwright Menander: "The die is cast". Within a few years, a costly civil war would end with Caesar victorious and the Roman Republic all but finished, paving the way for the establishment of an empire that would exist for more than 500 years.

While the Romans began to build and consolidate the ancient world's most famous empire, the years of war took a terrible toll on Gaul. The loss of life was huge and the damage to the rural economy was devastating. The damage was mainly due to the ravages of the Romans, but the scorched earth policy adopted by Vercingetorix also played its part. Caesar suggested that the casualties from battles and punitive actions ran into hundreds of thousands, and while the majority of the casualties were men, there were significant numbers of women and children killed as well.

Of course, from Caesar's point of view, however, the wars were enormously successful. He had been bankrupted in 63 B.C., but his success in Gaul delivered him from penury and provided him the wealth and control of troops that would enable him to embark on the next stage of his plan to become the sole ruler of Rome. The Senate declared 20 days of thanksgiving for Caesar's victory but refused him a triumphal parade. The refusal of a triumph was a rather ineffective attempt to put Caesar in his place, but the political reality was that the victory had given Caesar all he needed to take the next steps on his path to ruling over Rome.

Much of the profit that financed his political aspirations came from the sale of slaves captured during the various campaigns. Caesar claimed to have sold 53,000 members of the Aduataci tribe alone. These Gallic slaves were considered to be barbarians by the Romans, and consequently the vast majority ended up working on farms, mines or quarries.[151]

For Rome itself, the acquisition of Gaul was a great boon. It was a populous, relatively fertile area, and in the coming years successive emperors were able to develop its potential for wealth generation even further. Gaul went on to become a key component of the empire, delivering taxes and goods in significant quantities. More importantly, in many ways for the Romans, the age-old threat of Gallic incursions into Italy and the fear of the city of Rome being sacked again was eliminated.

Rome's advance into Cisalpine Gaul was undoubtedly motivated by the city's determination to secure itself from the ravages wrought by marauding Gauls in the 4th century B.C. The sack of Rome shaped Roman attitudes regarding the northern part of the Italian peninsula and the Gauls for centuries, so the acquisition of the region that eventually became fully integrated into the Roman Empire cannot be seen as a direct result of any planned program of expansion and conquest but rather as a result of intense feelings of insecurity. Similarly, the acquisition of the area of southern Gaul, Narbonensis, was due to the perception that Rome had to secure a land route to its new provinces in Hispania, which had fallen into Roman hands as a consequence of victory over the Carthaginians in the Second Punic War. Similarly, there is no evidence that expansion into the Iberian Peninsula was anything other than a way of weakening their Carthaginian enemies, and there was no conscious imperial ambition in play.

However, having acquired those areas, and indeed southern Italy, the Roman mindset became somewhat more aligned to the concept of further expansion as a policy, and by the mid-1st century B.C., the remaining unconquered parts of Gaul became inextricably bound up with the personal ambitions of Caesar. For him, Gaul provided an opportunity to match his great rival Pompey, who had won fame and great wealth fighting in the east. Caesar's military genius in dealing with overwhelming odds has to be admired, but his ruthlessness in his dealings with those he defeated taints the accomplishments, at least from a modern perspective.

The wars illustrated the differences between two very different styles of warfare and ultimately proved the superiority of the Roman military machine over what was arguably the next most potent force in the ancient world at the time. The victories against the Gallic tribes were stunning, and while the lack of unity between the tribes until the latter stages of the conflict was a major factor in Rome's victory, the impact of Roman military efficiency and tactics cannot be overestimated. The fact that Gaul was a relatively populated, cultured and wealthy area has often been overlooked primarily because of intense Roman propaganda that painted the Gauls as uncivilized barbarians who practiced human sacrifice. The fact that they were not actually adds to Caesar's success rather than diminishes it.

---

[151] Julius Caesar, *Gallic Wars*, 8.

Gaul under the empire became an even more prosperous region, but arguably the most important aspect of the acquisition of Gaul lay in the power it gave to Caesar. Without his success in Gaul, there would have been no crossing of the Rubicon, no dictatorship for Caesar, and no emperors to take on his mantle. Needless to say, the history of Rome, and the rest of the world, may have been very different.

The Collapse of the Egyptian Empire

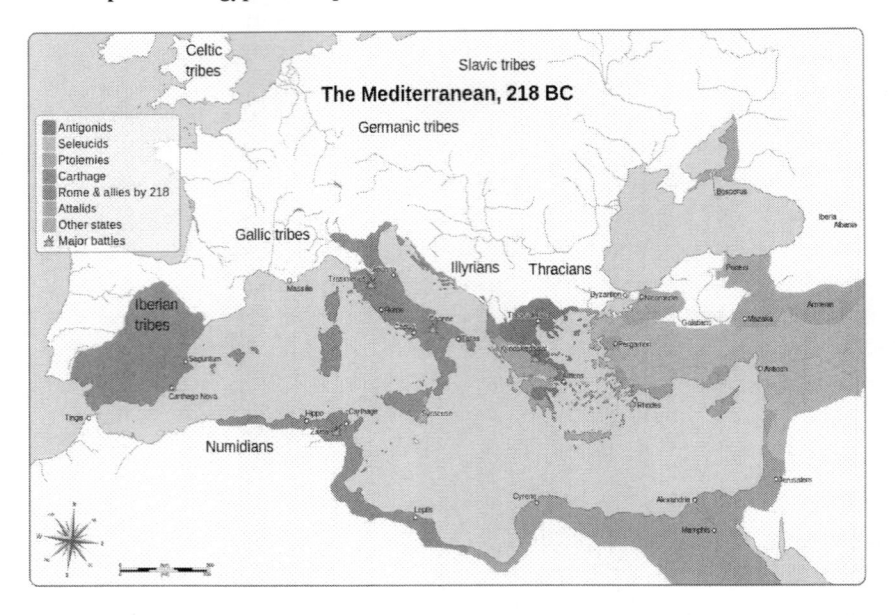

Goran Tek-en's map of the ancient empires in the Mediterranean in the late 3rd century B.C.

By the end of the 1st century B.C., the Ptolemies had transformed Alexandria into the greatest city on the planet, and in many ways, the city proved to be immortal. But while Alexandria is still an important center in the eastern Mediterranean, the dynasty that built it saw its prospects quickly decline.

The decline of the dynasty and the constant troubles that plagued it can be traced to the rule of Ptolemy IV Philopator (221-204 B.C.). The Ptolemies became too concerned with taking small tracts of land from the Seleucids in Coele-Syria while Rome became the preeminent power in the Mediterranean, and the most impressive achievement of Ptolemy IV was his victory over the Seleucid King Antiochus III (241-187 B.C.) in the Fourth Syrian War, during which the Seleucids pursued a campaign to wrest back Coele-Syria from the Ptolemies that culminated in a battle near the city of Raphia. Strabo explained, "After Gaza one comes to Rhaphia, where a battle was fought between Ptolemaeus the Fourth and Antiochus the Great" (Strabo, *Geography*,

XVI, 2, 31). The result was a victory for Ptolemy IV, but it proved to be ephemeral since a rebellion of native Egyptians had begun in Upper Egypt.

After Ptolemy IV's death, the instability inherent in his reign turned into a succession crisis, during which native Egyptian priests temporarily ruled in the south and a minor noble ruled in Alexandria (Chauveau 2000, 11). Stability was finally reestablished by the young Ptolemy V Epiphanes (204-181 B.C.) in 186 B.C. Ptolemy V is best known for marrying one of Antiochus III's daughters, Cleopatra I—the first royal Ptolemy woman of seven to take the now famous name—which brought temporary peace to the warring Ptolemies and Seleucids.

Although Ptolemy V reestablished order within Egypt's borders, others were waiting outside the gates for a chance to attack. The situation between the Ptolemies and Seleucids took another turn after Ptolemy V died and was succeeded by Ptolemy VI Philometer (180-145 B.C.), who spent most of his reign dealing with rebellious elements in the Alexandrian court. Sensing weakness in Egypt, the Seleucid King Antiochus IV (175-164 B.C.) attacked Egypt's possessions in Coele-Syria in 169 B.C. (Chauveau 2000, 13). The campaign was a stunning success for the Seleucids, who drove their forces deep into Egypt, where Antiochus IV had himself proclaimed pharaoh in the traditional capital of Memphis (Chauveau 2000, 13).

Throughout this, Ptolemy VI was more concerned with fighting his brother Ptolemy VIII Euregetes II (170-163 and again in 145-116). Antiochus supported Ptolemy VIII but was ultimately rebuffed by the Romans, who knew that a civil war in Egypt would be bad for their economy because that was where they got much of their grain. They also were not keen to see either the Seleucids or Ptolemies acquire too much power in the eastern Mediterranean.

For those reasons, the Roman Senate decided to take Ptolemy VI's side and gave Antiochus IV an ultimatum. The 3rd century A.D. Roman historian Cassius Dio explained, "Ptolemy, the ruler of Egypt, passed away leaving two sons and one daughter. When the brothers began to quarrel with each other about the sovereignty, Antiochus, the son of Antiochus the Great, sheltered the younger, who had been driven out, in order that under the pretext of defending him he might get his hands on Egyptian affairs. In a campaign directed against Egypt he conquered the greater part of the country and spent some time in besieging Alexandria. When the rest sought refuge with the Romans, Popilius was sent to Antiochus and bade him keep his hands off Egypt; for the brothers, comprehending the designs of Antiochus, had become reconciled. When the latter was for putting off his reply, Popilius drew a circle about him with his staff and demanded that he deliberate and answer standing where he was. Antiochus then in fear raised the siege." (Cassius Dio, *Roman History*, XX, 9, 25)

Roman intervention in the sixth and final Syrian War was a sign of things to come. Although the Greek kingdoms had long been the preeminent powers in the region, the upstart Romans now used a combination of their military might and diplomacy to shape the Mediterranean. After the Romans had wielded their might, the Seleucids focused their attention on reacquiring possessions they had lost in Coele-Syria, while Ptolemaic Egypt continued to decline.

While the young Ptolemy VI was on the throne, he had to contend with his older brother, Ptolemy VIII Euergetes II, who continued trying to replace him. Ptolemy VIII was temporarily successful and briefly ruled during the Sixth Syrian War, but he was deposed and exiled to the colony of Cyrene. Fate stepped in once more to give Ptolemy VIII a reprieve when his brother died and he was recalled to Alexandria.

Among the Ptolemaic kings, Ptolemy VIII would probably be the closest to one what thinks of as a stereotypical ancient despot. Unlike most of his predecessors, who had colorful nicknames—some of which are translated into English as "savior" (soter) or "flutist" (auletes)—Ptolemy VIII was given the moniker of "physkon," or "fat." Unlike the first three Ptolemies, Physkon was no patron of the arts, and despite being known for his weight, he was also notoriously thin-skinned. Instead of building on the accomplishments of his illustrious predecessors, Physkon spent most of his time going after his political enemies and those who had offended him. One of his most notable targets was the famed Library of Alexandria, home to many prominent free thinkers of the time. Once he learned that a fair amount of opposition had originated in the halls of the Library, he closed the institution's doors for the remainder of his rule (Chauveau 2000, 15). An example of the tactics Physkon used to suppress opposition was recorded by Strabo. "But after this mass of people had also been blotted out, chiefly by Euergetes Physcon, in whose time Polybius went to Alexandria (for, being opposed by factions, Physcon more often sent the masses against the soldiers and thus caused their destruction)." (Strabo, *Geography*, XVII, I, 12).

Ptolemy XII came to power after Ptolemy XI Alexander II (who only ruled for a few days in 80 B.C.) killed his wife and incurred the wrath of an Alexandrian mob, losing his life in the process (Chauveau 2000, 18). Besides being the father of Cleopatra VII, Ptolemy XII was known for his pursuit of the arts and humanities, earning the nickname the "flutist" in the process, but in terms of imperial policy, Ptolemy XII was weak and ineffective, and he nearly destroyed the Egyptian economy when he devalued the currency (Chauveau 2000, 22).

Ptolemy XII's accession to the throne was marked by plotting and bribery on a grand scale, and once he was in place he grew so paranoid that, suspicious of his provincial governors, he insisted on concentrating almost all executive powers in Alexandria, where he had his seat. Such a system of government could not hope to cope with, or indeed understand, the problems faced by the Egyptian kingdom's most far-spread provinces, and inevitably there were violent uprisings by those subjects at the borders of the kingdom who felt themselves abandoned to their fate. Cyprus and Cyrenaica were both lost, and other rebellions were crushed only with great difficulty and expense. At this time, Egypt had effectively become a client state of Rome – and a valued trading asset, as they provided the majority of grain imports to the capital – and, in 58 B.C., despite unrest at home, Ptolemy was obliged to travel to Rome on an official visit. He chose to take Cleopatra, then just a child, with him as well, but what was meant to be a short trip ended up becoming a three-year exile. Taking advantage of his absence, another Cleopatra seized the throne.

It is unclear which Cleopatra this was, as records from the period are sparse and not helped by the fact that the Ptolemies favored re-using the same names over and over again. She may either have been Cleopatra V, making her Cleopatra VII's mother, or Cleopatra VI, which would mean she was a sister. Either way, this Cleopatra's reign was to be short-lived, because within a few months of her accession to the throne, she died suddenly under mysterious circumstances. It is highly likely that she was murdered, most probably at the hand of Berenice IV, Cleopatra VII's older sister, who took the throne as soon as she died. Berenice reigned for just under three years in Alexandria, until Ptolemy XII finally returned at the head of a Roman army led by General Aulus Gabinius. Ptolemy had been forced to go hat in hand to Rome, having virtually no support outside of Alexandria and no chance of regaining his throne by raising armies of his own. Though this move allowed Ptolemy to recapture the throne of Egypt, he had effectively made his kingdom a vassal state of Rome, garrisoned by Roman armies, propped up by Roman spears, and dependent on Roman goodwill.

Betrayed by at least one of his eldest daughters, if not two (or his wife), Ptolemy XII seems to have turned to Cleopatra VII, his companion during his three-year exile, as his sole repository of trust. At age 14, he proclaimed her regent, a largely ceremonial position which nonetheless placed her in direct line to the throne in the event of his death. Ptolemy's reign limped on for another four years, amid further losses of crucial territory and an ever-growing dependence on Gabinius's troops, whose officers had established themselves – apparently permanently – in Egypt and promptly formed their own political faction, the *Gabiniani*, in order to try and carve themselves their own piece of the rich Egyptian pie.

Finally, in 51 B.C., Ptolemy XII died, leaving an 18-year-old Cleopatra at a crossroads. She could not assume sole rulership, for such an act would require her to get rid of her younger brother, Ptolemy XIII, with whom she was expected to share power. Cleopatra was also, in keeping with dynastic tradition, required to marry Ptolemy XIII, who was 10 years old at the time. With the weight of tradition upon her, Cleopatra complied, but it would certainly not be a happy union. The two seem not to have gotten along as brother and sister, never mind as husband and wife, and their joint rule was marked by more uprisings. To add insult to injury, the Nile stubbornly refused to deliver adequate floods. Egypt's fertile grain fields were dependent on the periodic flooding of the Nile basin, which would coat the fields with a natural fertilizer, and a sparse flood meant even sparser harvests, which meant not only that the people would go hungry but that Egypt would be unable to deliver sufficient grain to Rome, with all the perilous consequences that entailed.

Just a few months after ascending to the throne, Cleopatra effectively divorced her younger brother, whose influence was limited by his age. She no longer appeared with him at official ceremonies, and started being the sole signatory on official documents, a gross breach of tradition. In Ptolemaic tradition, female co-rulers were technically subordinate to their male counterparts, regardless of whether this was actually the case, so doing away with Ptolemy was a slap in the face to the many traditionalists at court. Having made enemies of the traditionalists, she promptly followed this political mistake in 50 B.C. by upsetting one of the most powerful political factions in Egypt, the *Gabiniani*. Having been in Egypt for approximately five years, the *Gabiniani* had essentially severed their ties to Rome.

When some exponents of the *Gabiniani* murdered the sons of Marcus Bibulus, the governor of Syria, who had been sent in friendship to request their aid in a military campaign against the neighbouring Parthians, Cleopatra saw a chance to intervene and cut the *Gabiniani* down to size. She had the assassins seized, put in chains, and delivered to Bibulus, but while this may have curried favour with the Roman governor, it did nothing to endear her to the *Gabiniani*, who promptly went from uneasy allies to sworn enemies. Cleopatra could hardly hope to rule long in the face of such massed political hostility, and in 48 BC, a plot spearheaded by Pothinus, a eunuch in the palace service, with the collusion of Cleopatra's many enemies, forced her from the throne and placed the more biddable, pliant Ptolemy XIII on it as sole ruler of Egypt. Cleopatra now found herself a fugitive.

Cleopatra VII was exiled to Upper Egypt and then fled to Palestine in order to escape a potential assassination, and at some point during this time, she made contact with Julius Caesar in order to elicit his support for her claim to the Egyptian throne. At the time, Rome was tearing itself apart, and the repercussions of this conflict were being felt across the Mediterranean. Caesar, former consul and governor of Gaul, had marched across the Rubicon, illegally bringing his armies onto Italian soil and threatening Rome itself, with the purpose of making himself dictator. Caesar was opposed by his former ally, the once-great general Pompey Magnus. By this time, Pompey was an old, spent man, while Caesar was still vigorous, and Caesar had chased Pompey's army from Rome, hounded it all the way to southern Italy, and then, when Pompey escaped across the Mediterranean to Greece, he had loaded his army onto a fleet and shipped it across the sea, where he had annihilated Pompey's armies at Pharsalus in 48 B.C.

Pompey barely escaped with his life, and virtually alone and penniless, he had taken ship for Egypt, where he arrived as a supplicant, possibly hoping for military assistance from the *Gabiniani*, or from Ptolemy XIII himself. Having heard a rumor that Pompey was attempting to raise men against him in Egypt, Caesar took ship for Alexandria, only to find upon his arrival that Pompey had been murdered on the orders of Egypt's young pharaoh, the boy-king Ptolemy XIII. Possibly encouraged by Pothinus, Ptolemy had Pompey Magnus put to death almost immediately after his arrival in Egypt, the end result apparently being that he hoped to ingratiate himself with Caesar, whose victory at Pharsalus had, by default, made him the uncontested ruler of Rome and thus the most powerful man in the known world.

An ancient bust of Pompey

Ptolemy XIII, however, had completely misunderstood Caesar. When the Roman general arrived in Egypt a bare two days later, hot on Pompey's heels, Ptolemy XIII received Caesar with great pomp and presented him with Pompey's head. Pompey had been a close friend of Caesar's before their rivalry spiraled out of control, and had even married Caesar's daughter, who had died in childbirth before the war.

The year was 48 B.C., and Rome's strongest man was now in Egypt and positioned to decide who would rule. Dio noted, "Cleopatra, it seems, had at first urged with Caesar her claim against her brother by means of agents, but as soon as she discovered his disposition (which was very susceptible, to such an extent that he had his intrigues with ever so many other women—with all, doubtless, who chance to come in his way) she sent word to him that she was being betrayed by her friends and asked that she be allowed to plead her case in person…She asked therefore for admission to his presence, and on obtaining permission adorned and beautified herself so as to appear before him in the most majestic and at the same time pity-inspiring guise…Afterward he entered an assembly of theirs, and producing Ptolemy and Cleopatra, read their father's will, in which it was directed that they should live together according to the custom of the Egyptians and rule in common, and that the Roman people should exercise a guardianship over them." (Cassius Dio, *Roman History*, XLII, 34-35)

The peace did not last very long, and Caesar had to demonstrate his martial abilities to the supporters of Ptolemy XIII in no time. According to Caesar's own account, taking the Pharos Island—where the Lighthouse had been located—was crucial for taking and holding Alexandria. He wrote, "On the island there is a tower called Pharos, of great height, a work of wonderful construction, which took its name from the island. This island, lying over against Alexandria, makes a harbor [sic], but it is connected with the town by a narrow roadway like a bridge, piers nine hundred feet in length having been thrown out seawards by former kings. On this island there are dwelling-houses of Egyptians and a settlement the size of a town, and any ships that went a little out of their course there through carelessness or rough weather they were in the habit of plundering like pirates. Moreover, on account of the narrowness of the passage there can be no entry for ships into the harbour [sic] without the consent of those who are in occupation of Pharos. Caesar, now fearing such difficulty, landed his troops when the enemy was occupied in fighting, and seized Pharos and placed a garrison on it. The result of these measures was that corn and reinforcements could be safely conveyed to him on shipboard." (Julius Caesar, *The Civil Wars*, III, 112).

Gautier Poupeau's picture of a bust of Caesar

After Caesar had won the Egyptian civil war for Cleopatra, he demonstrated his diplomatic abilities by bringing the two factions back together. Since Ptolemy XIII had died in his attempted escape from Caesar's clutches, the Roman general ordered that Cleopatra "marry" her other brother in a very Ptolemaic-style wedding. Dio explained, "In this way Caesar overcame Egypt. He did not, however, make it subject to the Romans, but bestowed it upon Cleopatra, for whose sake he had waged the conflict. Yet, being afraid that the Egyptians might rebel again, because they were delivered over to a woman to rule, and that the Romans might be angry, both on this account and because he was living with the woman, he commanded her to "marty" her other brother, and gave the kingdom to both to them, at least nominally. For in reality Cleopatra was to hold all the power alone, since her husband was still a boy, and in view of Caesar's favour [sic] there was nothing that she could not do. Hence her living with her brother and sharing the rule with him was a mere pretence [sic] which she accepted, whereas in truth she ruled alone and spent her time in Caesar's company." (Cassius Dio, *Roman History*, XLII, 44)

After assuring the situation in Alexandria was stable once more, Caesar returned to Rome, where he was proclaimed "dictator for life." He did, however, leave Cleopatra with more than one gift. From 47-30 B.C., Cleopatra VII would rule Egypt as sole monarch, but unfortunately few documents, either Greek or Egyptian, exist that can shed more details on her rule (Chauveau 2000, 24). Cleopatra gave birth to Caesar's son—whom she named Ptolemy Caesar—on July 23, 47 B.C. She then traveled to Rome with her son three years later and was in the Eternal City when Caesar was assassinated by the Senate on March 15, 44 B.C., the Ides of March (Chauveau 2000, 25).

The assassination sparked a new round in the civil wars, pitting the Senate against the Second Triumvirate of Octavian, Mark Antony, and Lepidus. Once the triumvirate won the war, Cleopatra sided with them and developed a close personal relationship with Mark Antony.

Antony

As per the agreement between Antony, Octavian, and Lepidus, Antony was given control of

Rome's eastern provinces, which included Egypt, although it was still nominally independent. In 37 B.C., Antony and Cleopatra began their infamous affair, which saw the Roman general adopt more and more Hellenistic and Egyptian styles and nomenclature, much to his reputation's detriment back in Rome (Chauveau 2000, 27).

As Antony and Cleopatra struggled with unrest in the east, back in Rome Octavian had dismissed Lepidus, the third member of the Second Triumvirate, and assumed sole power over his domains, while also continuing a vigorous smear campaign against Antony. Octavian denounced him for abandoning his wife Octavia and his children, and he accused Antony of going native with his wanton Egyptian queen. Octavian's public relations offensive blamed Antony's recent failure and the consequent loss of Roman life on the wrath of the gods for Antony's sins.

An ancient bust of Octavian

Antony and Cleopatra, however, seem to have been unconcerned with Octavian's threats, or the growing popular resentment with Antony that Octavian was fomenting in Rome. It seems quite likely that Antony simply did not care anymore and just wanted to be left alone in his Alexandrian idyll with the woman he loved. Like Caesar, Antony was fully charmed by the quixotic and exotic Egyptian lifestyle, and he immersed himself in it even more than his famous mentor. Despite repeated demands from Octavian that he return to Rome immediately to answer for his conduct, Antony remained happily in Alexandria, and instead waged a new campaign against the Armenians in 34 B.C., this time achieving success and annexing the territory to his and Cleopatra's domains.

It was in the aftermath of this war that Cleopatra and Antony finally overstepped their mark. Cleopatra organised a lavish, Roman-style Triumph in Alexandria to mark Antony's successful conquest, during which Antony's children (now numbering three) by Cleopatra were all granted royal titles in the East, Cleopatra herself was named Queen of Queens and ruler of the East, and crucially, Cleopatra's son Caesarion was named King of Kings, ruler of Egypt and the East, living God, and above all – Caesar's formal sole son and heir, thereby by default disowning Octavian in the eyes of the East. Additionally, Antony officially declared his alliance with Octavian over, proclaiming that from then on the East was free and independent of Rome. It was the biggest blunder of their lives.

In 32 B.C., Octavian declared war against Cleopatra, not Antony, a calculated move intended to ensure the Romans did not feel he was continuing the legacy of the fratricidal civil war. Perhaps Octavian overestimated his support, for Cleopatra and Antony were delighted to discover that both consuls and a full third of the Senate had decamped from Rome and defected to their side wholesale. The royal couple met the defectors in Greece, and for a while felt so secure in their position they even considered an invasion of Italy itself.

Their victory was to prove short-lived, however. In 31 B.C., Octavian's forces set sail for Greece, and the legions there immediately went over to his side, spurred by the veterans in their ranks who had once fought for his adoptive father Caesar. Both Cyrenaica and Greece fell to Octavian, essentially without a blow struck, and Cleopatra and Antony were forced to retreat back to Egypt, where they rallied the Eastern navies and prepared to contest Octavian's passage across the Mediterranean.

On September 2, 31 B.C., Antony and Cleopatra found themselves in a tactically disadvantageous position, facing Octavian's navies off the coast of Actium, in Greece. With the risk of being bottled up and surrounded at Actium by Octavian's naval forces a very real possibility, Cleopatra advised Antony to give battle, although it appears the Roman general thought victory was an unlikely possibility. Antony and Cleopatra appeared, to the untrained eye, to have the advantage: their fleet numbered over 500 vessels, almost half of which were giant five-decked quinquiremes, ramming warships that carried full-blown siege engines on board, while Octavian had only 250 far lighter craft.

However, the sea was rough that morning, favoring Octavian's more maneuverable ships, which were less affected by the rolling swells, and to make matters worse, Antony's fleet had been wracked by disease, meaning that many of his mighty quinquiremes were undermanned. The giant craft were ponderous to begin with, but without the requisite number of rowers and fighting men, they could never hope to achieve proper ramming speed. Octavian's lighter, more agile craft, filled with veteran sailors, were able to dance around the ponderous quinquiremes, showering them with hails of fire arrows, ramming and boarding where they could, and sprinting away before the heavier craft had a chance to bring their rams to bear. As the day wore on, it became more and more apparent to Antony and Cleopatra, on their twin flagships, that the battle would be lost. More and more of their craft were being sunk, scattered or overwhelmed, and still more were burning down to the waterline, their skeleton crews being insufficient to man their battle stations and extinguish fires at the same time. As night approached, Antony and Cleopatra spotted a gap in the now thoroughly jumbled enemy line, and ordered their ships to speed through it without delay, making for Alexandria with all speed and abandoning their entire navy to its fate. It was a crushing blow, for Octavian and his generals had virtually annihilated Egypt's seaborne power.

As one of Rome's most famous battles, and one of the most famous events in Cleopatra's life, the Battle of Actium has taken on a life of its own in popular memory. One of the longest-held myths about the battle is that Cleopatra, sensing defeat, began to sail away from the fight in the middle of the day, and the lovestruck Antony followed her with his own ship, abandoning his men in the middle of the fight. While that popular myth would be in keeping with explaining Cleopatra's irresistible charm and magnetism, contemporary accounts of the battle do not suggest it was actually the case.

Once the Battle of Actium was over, Mark Antony and Cleopatra were forced to flee back to Egypt. Dio wrote, "At the time he sent a part of the fleet in pursuit of Antony and Cleopatra; these ships, accordingly, followed after the fugitives, but when it became clear that they were not going to overtake them, they returned. With his remaining vessels he capture the enemy's entrenchments, meeting with no opposition because of their small numbers, and then overtook and without a battle won over the rest of the army, which was retreating to Macedonia." (Cassius Dio, *Roman History*, LI, 1, 4).

After the loss at Actium, it was just a matter of time before Octavian caught up with Antony and Cleopatra. According to Dio, Antony attempted to enlist the help of some of his former allies in North Africa who had rebuffed his advances, before concentrating his energies on the defense of Alexandria. Dio explained, "Now among the other preparations they made for speedy warfare, they enrolled among the youths of military age, Cleopatra her son Caesarion and Antony [and] his son Antyllus, who had been born to him by Fulvia and was then with him. Their purpose was to arouse the enthusiasm of the Egyptians, who would feel that they had at last a man for their king, and to cause the rest to continue the struggle with these boys as their leaders, in case anything untoward should happen to the parents." (Cassius Dio, *Roman History*, LI, 6, 1-2)

While preparations for the defense of Alexandria were being made by Antony, Cleopatra once more demonstrated how she had reached the pinnacle of Ptolemaic power by sending overtures to Octavian behind Antony's back: "Meanwhile Cleopatra, on her part, unknown to Antony, sent to him a golden scepter and a golden crown together with the royal throne, signifying that through them she offered him the kingdom as well; for she hoped that even if he did hate Antony, he would yet take pity on her at least. Caesar accepted her gifts as a good omen, but made no answer to Antony; to Cleopatra, however, although he publicly sent threatening messages, including the announcement that, if she would give up her armed forces and renounce her sovereignty, he would consider what ought to be done in her case, he secretly sent word that, if she would kill Antony, he would grant her pardon and leave her realm inviolate." (Cassius Dio, *Roman History*, LI, 6, 5-6)

The end was near for the lovers, but the classical sources disputed the details of their legendary deaths. Of all the fictionalized portrayals of Cleopatra VII's rise and fall, perhaps the most memorable scenes involve her and Antony's deaths. Once again, Dio provided the most detailed account of the events. According to him, after Antony had lost a pivotal battle to Octavian near the Egyptian Delta city of Pelusium, Antony attempted to flee, but he was tricked by Cleopatra into believing that she was dead, the purpose being that she would subsequently conclude a peace deal with Octavian. Dio wrote, "After his unexpected setback, Antony took refuge in his fleet, and was preparing to give battle on the sea or at any rate to sail to Spain. But Cleopatra, upon perceiving this, caused the ships to desert, and she herself rushed suddenly into the mausoleum, pretending that she feared Caesar and desired by some means or other to forestall him by taking her own life, but really as an invitation to Antony to enter there also. He had a suspicion, to be sure, that he was being betrayed, yet in his infatuation he could not believe it, but actually pitied her more, one might say, than himself. Cleopatra, doubtless, was fully aware of this and hoped that if he should be informed that she was dead, he would not wish to survive her, but would die at once…He first asked one of the bystanders to slay him; but when the man drew his sword and slew himself, Antony wished to imitate his courage and so gave himself a wound and fell upon his face, causing the bystanders to believe that he was dead…Now when some of them saw her peering out at this point, they raised a shout so that even Antony heard. So he, learning that she survived, stood up, as if he had still the power to live; but, as he had lost much blood, he despaired of his life and besought the bystanders to carry him to the monument and to hoist him up by the ropes that were hanging there to life the stone blocks." (Cassius Dio, *Roman History*, LI, 10, 5-9)

Cleopatra then tried to save her own life - and possibly her position as regent of Egypt - by negotiating with Octavian, but the future emperor wanted to bring her back alive to Rome, where he would presumably parade her through the streets during his triumph and then ritually strangle her. Once Cleopatra realized the ramifications of Octavian's plans for her, she made the decision to commit suicide.

The manner of Cleopatra's death has been debated for millennia, shaped in popular memory by everyone from Shakespeare to Hollywood. Ancient historians wrote that she had a venomous snake, most likely a cobra, concealed in her private apartments, and that when she realised that escape was impossible, she provoked it into administering a fatal bite on her arm. Today most people unfamiliar with those accounts believe that Cleopatra had an asp bite her on the breast, which was how Shakespeare depicted it in his famous play. Stories differ as to what snake was used (the term "asp" is most likely a generic name for any venomous snake, but Egypt is renowned for its deadly King Cobra) and if it was kept deliberately or came to be there by accident. Some historians even argue that there was no snake at all, and that Cleopatra poisoned herself with hemlock, as Socrates had done. Still others claim Octavian had her killed, which seems contrary to the widely-assumed belief that Octavian intended to parade her as a captive through the streets of Rome in a triumph.

Although people are now familiar with the venomous snake bite version, Dio was adamant the method of death she had chosen for herself is unknown. "But when she could accomplish nothing, she feigned a change of heart, pretending to set great hopes in him and also in Livia. She said she would sail of her own free will, and she made ready some treasured articles of adornment to use as gifts, in the hope that by these means she might inspire belief that it was not her purpose to die, and so might be less closely guarded and thus be able to destroy herself…She put on her most beautiful apparel, arranged her body in most seemingly fashion, took in her hands all the emblems of royalty, and so died. No one knows clearly in what way she perished, for the only marks on her body were slight pricks on the arm." (Cassius Dio, *Roman History*, LI, 13-14, 1).

Although Dio's account of Cleopatra's death is probably the most detailed, Strabo, who was a contemporary of Cleopatra's, declared it had been an asp that had killed the queen. "Having passed through the Hippodrome, one comes to Nicopolis, which has a settlement on the sea no smaller than a city. It is thirty stadia distant from Alexandria. Augustus Caesar honoured [sic] this place because it was here that the conquered in battle those who came out against him with Antony; and when he had taken the city at the first onset, he forced Antony to put himself to death and Cleopatra came into his power alive; but a little later she too put herself to death secretly, while in prison, by the bite of an asp or (for two accounts are given) by applying a poisonous ointment; and the result was that the empire of the sons of Lagus, which had endured for many years, was dissolved." (Strabo, *Geography*, XVII, I, 10)

Regardless of how it happened, Cleopatra's death marked the end of Egyptian independence. Egypt became a province of Rome, but that did not necessarily mean the Ptolemaic Dynasty was finished. Although Octavian was never known as a military genius, he was adept in many other respects, especially when it concerned the art of politics and the ability to see things in the long-term. Octavian knew that even with Cleopatra VII dead, her children, especially Caesarion, might claim the throne of Egypt, and Octavian could not let that happen. Dio explained, "Such were these two and such was their end. Of their children, Antyllus was slain immediately, though he was betrothed to the daughter of Caesar and had taken refuge in his father's shrine, which Cleopatra had built; and Caesarian while fleeing to Ethiopia was overtaken on the road and murdered." (Cassius Dio, *Roman History*, LI, 15, 5).

Incorporating Egypt as a Province

Once his conquest was complete and all potential rivals were exterminated, Octavian immediately set to work incorporating Egypt into the Roman Empire. The nuances of the transition of power from the Ptolemies to the Roman empire were described by Dio as follows: "In the case of the Egyptians and Alexandrians, he spared them all, so that none perished. The truth was that he did not see fit to inflict any irreparable injury upon a people so numerous, who might prove very useful to the Romans in many ways; nevertheless, he offered as a pretext for his kindness their god Serapis, their founder Alexander, and, in the third place, their fellow-citizen Areius, of whose learning and companionship he availed himself. The speech in which he proclaimed to them his pardon he delivered in Greek, so that they might understand him. After this he viewed the body of Alexander and actually touched it, whereupon, it is said, a piece of the nose was broken off. But he declined to view the remains of the Ptolemies, though the Alexandrians were extremely eager to show them, remarking, "I wished to see a king, not corpses." For this same reason he would not enter the presence of Apis, either declaring that he was accustomed to worship gods, not cattle...For in view of the populousness of both the cities and country, the facile, fickle character of the inhabitants, and the extent of the grain-supply and of the wealth, so far from daring to entrust the land to any senator, he would not even grant a senator permission to live in it, except as he personally made the concession to him by name. On the other hand he did not allow the Egyptians to be senators in Rome...Thus was Egypt enslaved. All the inhabitants who resisted for a time were finally subdued, as, indeed, Heaven very clearly indicated to them beforehand." (Cassius Dio, *Roman History*, LI, 16, 3-17, 4).

Augustus' domination of Rome was largely achieved through patronage dependent upon his control of Egypt, which he exercised through the equestrian class rather than the traditional senatorial families. Senators had to apply for special permission to visit the province. The prefects he personally appointed had unrestricted independent jurisdiction. In the system introduced by Augustus and maintained with minor changes by his successors, the prefect was at the top of the governmental tree followed by the *juridicus*, also someone appointed from the equestrian class and directly appointed by the princeps himself. This office holder had judicial power over all of Egypt. The *archdicasres*, chief judge, came next in the hierarchy, though he was not actually a judge but rather, an official linked to Alexandria, usually from one of Rome's leading families. He had control of debt collecting and the Public Record Office, as well as anything connected to Alexandria. The next in seniority was the *idiologus*, who was the financial officer in charge of the *idios logos*, or special account, for Egypt. This account included the more irregular or uncertain sources of income, such as fines and confiscations.

Strabo praised the system initiated by Augustus for the governance of the Egypt: "Egypt is now a Province and it not only pays considerable tribute but also is governed by prudent men, the prefects who are sent there from time to time. Now he who is sent has the rank of the king and subordinate to him is the administrator of justice who has supreme authority over most of the law suits and another is the official called Idiologus who enquires into all properties that are without owners and that ought to fall to Caesar and these are attended by freedmen of Caesar as also by stewards who are entrusted with affairs of more or less importance."[152]

Augustus was always aware of the importance of the army in maintaining control, and he paid particular attention to Egypt in this regard. Strabo describes the force garrisoned in the new province: "There are three legions of soldiers, one of which is stationed in the city and the others in the country. Apart from these there are nine Roman cohorts, three in the city, three on the borders of Ethiopia in Syene as a guard for that region, and three in the rest of the country. There are also three bodies of cavalry, which likewise are assigned to the critical points."[153]

A flotilla of ships was also stationed on the Nile, making Egypt the most militarized of all Roman provinces. While initiating a supervising administrative authority, Augustus utilized much of the administrative system set up by the Ptolemies, and Strabo confirms this policy: "Of the native officials in the city one is the Interpreter who is clad in purple, has hereditary prerogatives and has charge of the interests of the city and another, the Recorder, and another the Night Commander. Now these officers existed also in the time of the kings but since the kings were carrying on a bad government the prosperity of the city was also vanishing on account of the prevalent lawlessness."[154]

Officials called e*pistrategi, nomarchs,* and *ethnarchs* were appointed throughout Egypt to oversee a whole range of issues relating to daily life, as had been the case in the time of the Ptolemies. Polybius, who had visited Alexandria, described it as being inhabited by three distinct classes. The first was the Egyptians, whom he characterized as quick-tempered and disinclined to what he termed civic life. The next was the mercenary class, whom he believed was "severe, numerous and intractable."[155] The final class was the Alexandrians, whom he had a similarly poor opinion of their potential for civil life as he did of the Egyptians, but grudgingly conceded they were better than the others. From his perspective, being Greek—or at least, partly Greek— meant they had some veneer of Hellenistic civilization.

As an imperial province rather than a senatorial province, Egypt was always governed on the emperors' behalf by prefects, a total of 110 of them, until the empire split centuries later. The normal period of rule was a maximum of four years, but the time served often depended on factors such as changing emperors or assessments of success or failure. The prefects were all drawn from the equestrian class, a group that Augustus quite consciously promoted as a counter to the Senate. These knights, as they are sometimes called because of their association with horses, were the second rank in Roman society after the senatorial class. The rank was passed from father to son, but each *eques* had to meet the property threshold at the five year census. The

---

[152] Strabo, *Geography*, 17.1.12.
[153] Strabo, *Geography*, 17.1.12.
[154] Strabo, *Geography*, 17.1.12.
[155] Strabo, *Geography*, 17.1.12

property threshold was approximately 50,000 denarii in the Republican period, but this was doubled by Augustus.

During the reign of Augustus *equites* came to fill the senior administrative and military positions within the empire. The most senior were reserved for the senatorial class, but the two most powerful positions to which a member of the equestrian class could aspire were prefect of the Praetorians and prefect of Egypt. There was a degree of similarity between the normal careers of those in the top two tiers of Roman society. A young Roman in those classes would usually start his career in a number of junior administrative positions in Rome or Italy. This would be followed by about 10 years of military service as an officer, and then, assuming all had gone reasonably well, he would take on senior administrative or military position in the provinces.

The two classes combined never reached more than approximately 10,000 in number in an empire with a population of between 50 and 70 million, but this small group dominated political and military power and tended to monopolize economic power in different ways. The strictures on members of the senatorial class indulging in trade meant they tended to concentrate on the acquisition of land while the equestrians, although owning large estates, dominated trade, shipping, mining, and manufacturing.[156] In the Roman system, the tax-farming companies, which were so lucrative, were almost monopolized by *equites*.

The number of senators was restricted to 600 under Augustus and was maintained at this level until 312 A.D. The sons of senators held the equestrian rank until they were given a senatorial seat, but Augustus initiated a fundamental change in the system by altering a number of key elements regarding who could become a senator and who would be accorded equestrian status. These included raising the property qualification for membership of the Senate to 250,000 denarii, and as already noted, *equites* to 100,000 denarii. His aim was to create two distinct groups, but he avoided potential objections by allowing the sons of senators to wear the tunica – *laticlavia* - the exclusive tunic worn only by those of the senatorial class when they reached manhood, even though they were not yet actual members of the Senate.[157] Augustus created specific career paths for the sons of senators, known as the *cursus honorum,* usually involving being appointed to serve on the Committee of Twenty. This committee included those holding minor roles, such as *augurs*. This period was followed by service at a senior level in the legion, perhaps as a deputy commander.

Augustus also legislated for the marriage of sons of senators to the third generation as a distinct group. This had the effect of widening the numbers of those with senatorial rank and creating a distinction between serving senators and *senatorii,* those of senatorial rank.[158] If a senatorial

---

[156] Livy, *History of Rome*, XXI.63.
[157] Suetonius, *Augustus* 38.2.
[158] Roman Law Library (Lex Iulia de manitandis ordinibus).

family lost its senator, the whole family reverted to normal equestrian status. The numbers of those who were accorded equestrian status but who were not considered as full members of that class, rose under Augustus as he sought to use more and more equestrians in government positions that reported to and were responsible to him directly. This, in effect, created tiers within the equestrian class, ranging from those who were full members of the order to those whose status depended on their lineage.

Augustus' other major innovation with regard to the equestrian class was its organization along quasi-military lines. All equestrians were enrolled into one of six national cavalry squadrons called *turmae*. Each of these had a commander, and the six commanders formed a governing committee. To encourage the *equites* to identify themselves more closely with their peers, Augustus resurrected a defunct Republican practice called the inspection of the equites, *recognito equtum*, a ceremony involving all equites parading with their horses in front of the consuls every year.[159] Augustus cemented the separation of the senatorial class and the equites, including the sons of senators, by naming them *clarissimus*—most distinguished—and *egregious*—distinguished gentleman.[160] He also reserved a significant number of administrative posts exclusively for those of equestrian rank,[161] the most prestigious of which was the *praefectus Augusti* of Egypt. Similarly, the procurators Augusti, the chief financial officers of the imperial provinces, were also drawn exclusively from the ranks of the equestrians, and this post in Egypt was the aspiration of many.

After Augustus, equestrians took on even more of the administrative posts, including the Treasury and the directorship of grain supply.[162] As well as filling the key military post of Commander of the Praetorian Guard, equestrians also provided the *praefecti classis*, admirals of the Roman fleets at Misenum and Ravenna, and the Vigiles.[163] As the importance of the equestrians developed, they came to dominate Rome's law courts, providing judges and state secretaries. Hadrian exempted these post-holders from military service.[164] All of Augustus' innovations provided members of the equestrian order with ample opportunities to enrich themselves. The salaries of imperial prefects ranged from 15,000 denarii for smaller provinces to 75,000 per annum for Egypt. An equestrian *praefectus* of an auxiliary cohort was paid approximately 10,000 denarii per year, 50 times as much as a foot soldier and as much as two could earn in their entire enlistment.

Inevitably, Augustus trusted and relied on this class far more than the senators. Augustus

---

[159] 'Equites', *Encyclopaedia Britannica* (2009).
[160] P. 8, *The Later Roman Empire* by A.H.M. Jones (1964). Oxford.
[161] P. 64, *The Complete Roman Army (The Complete Series)* by A. Goldsworthy (2003). Thames and Hudson: London.
[162] P. 65, *The Complete Roman Army (The Complete Series)* by A. Goldsworthy (2003). Thames and Hudson: London.
[163] P. 340, 'The Senate and Senatorial and Equestrian Posts' by R. Talbert. *Cambridge Ancient History Vol. X* (1996). Cambridge University Press.
[164] P. 8, *The Later Roman Empire* by A.H.M. Jones (1964). Oxford.

always saw senators as potential rivals, whereas equestrians were very much dependent on his good offices to maintain and advance themselves in the Roman world.[165] In due course, powerful equites came to be seen as threats in the same way as senators, explaining why Augustus, late in his reign, extended his ruling that senators could only visit Egypt with his express permission to equestrians, a policy retained by his successors.[166] Augustus' system proved to be extremely stable, and senators and equites cooperated in the smooth running of the empire until well into the 3rd century A.D. The use of equestrians in the imperial service was crucial to Augustus and his vision of the Principate, and the fact that equestrians came to control such huge swathes of government, the economy and the military were the key to his success. Central to his ability to promote the equestrian class and retain its loyalty was his control of Egypt and its wealth.

The first Prefect appointed to Egypt was Cornelius Gallus, a close friend of Augustus who found one of his first tasks to be the suppression of an uprising in the Thebaid, the area surrounding the old capital of Thebes. He was successful and set up an inscription at Philae to record his achievements: "Gaius Cornelius Gallus son of Gnaeus, Roma eques, first prefect of Alexandria and Egypt after the overthrow of the kings by Caesar, son of a god, having been victorious in two pitched battles in the fifteen days within which he suppressed the revolt of the Thebans, capturing five cities, Boresis, Coptus, Ceramice, Diospolis Magna, and Ophieum and seizing the leaders of these revolts having led his army beyond the Nile cataract…dedicated this thank offering to his ancestral gods and to the Nile as his helpmate."[167]

---

[165] Tacitus, *Annals*, II 59.
[166] Tacitus, *Annals* II 59.
[167] CIL 3.14147, *Roman Civilization: Selected Readings, Vol. 2: The Empire* by N. Lewis and M. Reinhold (1990). Cambridge University Press.

An ancient bust of Cornelius Gallus

What is interesting is that the prefect made a dedication to his own family gods and the Nile, a sign of Augustus' policy of paying due honor and respect to local deities. He was, however, apparently prone to making exaggerated claims, and Augustus was not enamored of either his boasting or his forays into Sudan. He mysteriously committed suicide after being recalled to Rome.

Cornelius Gallus is best remembered today not for his limited political or military achievements, but his reputation as a poet, though very little of what he wrote has survived. In

1978, nine lines of his verse were discovered in Nubia, and this is now thought to be one of the oldest surviving examples of Latin poetry. Ovid rated him as the first of Rome's elegiac poets,[168] and he was held in the highest esteem by some of his contemporaries. One of his most famous contemporaries, Ovid, put him on a par with Virgil.[169]

The second prefect was Aelius Gallus who served two years, from 26-24 B.C. His rather unfortunate claim to fame rests with another disastrous expedition, on this occasion to Arabia. Augustus ordered the attempt to take Arabia under Roman control in the belief it was a repository of great hidden wealth.

Like his predecessor, this Gallus is also remembered for matters other than his military success. He is credited by Galen with discovering numerous medical remedies which, unfortunately, he had to utilize to the fullest during the campaign.[170] Aelius Gallus was a close friend of Strabo, and he provided detailed information about the attack on Arabia. Cassius Dio and Pliny the Elder also wrote about the expedition, and all concurred it had been an unmitigated disaster.[171] According to Strabo, Gallus' big mistake was relying too heavily on one Nabatean guide. Whether that was true or not, the net result was that the Roman force was almost entirely wiped out by a combination of thirst, disease, and military defeats. The Romans inherited small parts of Arabia when they had taken power in Egypt but even these were lost, and a disgruntled Augustus recalled his prefect to send another close friend, Gaius Petronius, to take over. Petronius does not seem to have learned much from the experiences of his predecessors, and he embarked on a foreign expedition himself. He invaded the kingdom of Kush but was not able to secure permanent gains. Instead, he razed the city of Napata to the ground and retreated to Egypt. The destruction of their capital and the enslavement of many of its citizens did not deter the Kushites from their raids into Roman territory. It was not until 22 B.C., when Petronius repulsed another Kushite raid, which they accepted client kingdom status. From then on, they became a lucrative trading partner.[172]

The prefects who followed were a relatively undistinguished group, none of whom experienced any major adventures or undertook revisions of the administrative system, ordered to secure maximum outcomes in terms of wealth and the maintenance of the grain supply that had become so vital to any emperor's hopes of a long reign. Romans never settled in Egypt in any great numbers, and as a result, civic life and culture remained largely Greek in the Roman period. Alexandria had become a major center for Jews who had fled from Judea for various reasons, and their abhorrence of what they had seen as the idolatry and paganism of both Greek and native religions led to direct conflict between the groups. The first major confrontation came during the reign of Caligula (34-41 A.D.). On this occasion, the Romans placed the blame

---

[168] Ovid, *Tristia*, IV.
[169] Suetonius, *Augustus*, 66.
[170] Galen, II.
[171] Strabo, Geography, XVI; Cassius Dio, LIII, Pliny, *Natural History*, VI.32.
[172] P. 350 *The Nubian Past* by D.N. Edwards (2004). Routledge: London.

squarely at the feet of the Jews and savagely put the riots down.

This pattern of the Romans supporting the Greeks against the Jews was repeated in all subsequent confrontations. After the destruction of Jerusalem in 70 A.D., Alexandria, already home to a large Jewish population, became the main centre for Judaism in the Mediterranean world, and the religious conflicts between Greeks and Jews became commonplace, intense, and extremely violent. A major Jewish revolt erupted during Trajan's reign in 115 A.D., bringing severe reprisals by the Romans against the Jewish community, including the loss of a number of privileges. The two-year insurrection came to be known as the Kitos War, but there is very little contemporary evidence or commentary about the episode. The uprising had come about due to increasing tensions between Jews and Greeks within Alexandria, and during the conflict, the Great Synagogue in the city was destroyed and thousands of Jews were massacred by the Romans.[173]

The result was that the vibrant Jewish community, which once numbered in excess of a quarter of a million people, was drastically reduced and never achieved anything like the status it had before the insurrection. However, while the traditional Jewish community's fortunes plummeted, a new sect born out of Judaism would begin to take hold in Egypt.

Christianity in Egypt dates to the very earliest years of the religion. Tradition assigns its introduction to Saint Mark 33 A.D., though the Bishop of Caesarea, in his *History of the Early Church*, makes the claim that the introduction of Christianity to Egypt occurred a bit later, somewhere between 41 and 44 A.D. There is debate as to whether Mark the Evangelist, who had founded the Coptic Church in Egypt, is the same as John Mark, cousin of Barnabas, but Hippolytus writes of them as distinct individuals who were both among the Seventy Disciples sent out by Christ to spread the gospel.

Mark is said to have composed his gospel based on accounts of Christ's life provided by the Apostle Peter, whom he had accompanied on his early travels. He left Peter to travel to Alexandria in the eighth year of Nero's reign, where he became the first Bishop of that city.[174]

The issue as to whether Mark, this first Bishop, actually wrote Saint Mark's Gospel is still a matter of scholarly debate, but his place as the founder of the Coptic Church in Egypt cannot be denied. The word "coptic" derives from the Greek word for Egypt, and the Coptic Church in Egypt is still very active, with followers numbering over 22 million with 18 million of them living in Egypt.

Today, Saint Mark's place as a central figure in Christianity is evident, and he is credited with, among other things, hosting the Last Supper and being present at the Marriage Feast at Caana. He is thought to have been born somewhere in North Africa, possibly Libya, and his African

---

[173] *The Ancient Jews from Alexander to Muhammad* by S. Schwartz (2014). Cambridge University Press.
[174] Eusebius, *Ecclesiastical History*, 2.14.6.

birth may have helped him in his missionary work in Egypt.

When he began his evangelical crusade, the Egyptians were still mostly loyal to the old gods, even after they came under Roman rule. While they made allowances for the state-sponsored worship of the emperor, they were as reluctant as their Hellenistic counterparts to countenance any acceptance of what they saw as another Jewish sect. According to Eusebius, the first convert to Christianity was a shoemaker named Anianus around 62 A.D., and he went on to become the Patriarch of Alexandria after Saint Mark's martyrdom in 68 A.D.

Initially, Christian converts came mainly from the Jewish community, but by the end of the 3rd century A.D., almost all of the native Egyptian population had converted. The reasons for this very rapid rate of conversion have been the subject of speculation amongst historians for many years. The Egyptians, throughout their history, had been a very religiously-oriented people, as evidenced by their religious buildings and the symbiosis between everyday life and preparation for the afterlife. The Roman conquest subtly undermined Egyptian confidence in their religion, but the Roman concepts of religion were alien to their traditions and culture, whereas Christianity, on the other hand, contained many familiar and similar concepts, such as death and resurrection of a god, the judging of souls, and an afterlife that would be better than the present one for the true believers. Even the symbols had some similarities, with the shape of the Coptic cross and ankh, and the story of Mary and Joseph's flight to Egypt to escape Herod proved particularly powerful, as it proclaimed God had chosen Egypt as the safe haven for his infant son.

The transition to Christianity was not without its difficulties though, and the conflicts between Jews and followers of the polytheistic religions of Greece and Rome re-emerged in disputes between the latter and the new Christian groups. It was primarily to counter Hellenistic philosophy that the Alexandrian Church founded the Didascalia in the 2nd century A.D., which codified Christian philosophy and belief. It was this school that provided the core of Christian dogma and was the centre of intellectual debate regarding Church doctrines. Most of the early teachers and orators of the Church, such as Clement and Origen, were in the intellectual vanguard of the battle against polytheism and in the forefront of the missionary movement. Pantaenus, the founder of the Didascalia, was particularly successful in converting Egyptians and wrote extensively using the Greek alphabet to explain the new religion. The Didascalia was taught in Greek, and the teaching became accessible to virtually all elements of Egyptian society.

The greatest persecutions faced by Christians came, in the end, not from the local Hellenized population or native Egyptians but the Romans, and it was in Egypt that Christians were subjected to the greatest of this persecution. Unlike their Christian counterparts in Rome who had worshipped in catacombs and kept their religious beliefs secret whenever possible, the Egyptian Christians were totally open from the start, building their churches in the most public spaces they could acquire. Diocletian was particularly savage in his persecution of Egyptian

Christians. His brutality was so great that the Coptic Church dates itself from 264 A.D., the year in which the greatest numbers of Christians were martyred in Egypt.[175]

G. Dallorto's picture of a bust of Diocletian

Roman attitudes to Christianity are known from a number of writers who expressed their views around the time of Trajan. From these works, it is clear the Roman view of Christianity was that it was depraved and "*superstitio*", a word applied to all cults or movements not officially sanctioned. Tacitus recorded that Domitian classified Christianity as a *superstitio Iudaica*,[176] which indicates much of the criticism against Christianity was based on earlier charges against Judaism, including the claim that both hated the human race. The refusal to swear allegiance to Roman gods and the emperor as a god marginalized Christians from the rest of society and was something the Roman authorities would not accept. In the specific case of Christianity, the Roman perception was that it encouraged sexual immorality and what they termed abominations, such as the eating and drinking of the blood of their god.[177]

The most damning comments came from Pliny the Younger, who accused Christians of being obstinate despite the generous pardons offered to recant. Meanwhile, Suetonius, as with most

---

[175] Eusebius, *Martyrs of Palestine; p.* 10, *Athanasius and Constantius: Theology and Politics in the Constantinian Empire* by T. Barnes (1993). Harvard University Press.
[176] Tacitus, *Annals*, XV.
[177] Tacitus, *Annals*, XV.

Roman writers, didn't distinguish between the Christians and the Jews. He wrote that "since the Jews were continually involved in disturbances at the instigation of Christ, Emperor Claudius expelled them from Rome."[178] In his *Life of Nero,* he commented that Christians "were a set of men who adhered to a new and mischievous superstition."[179]

On the night of July 18th, 64 A.D., the most significant event of Nero's time in power – and the one which, for better or for worse, would seal his name in infamy throughout the ages – took place. What became known as the Great Fire of Rome erupted sometime between the night of the 18th and the earliest hours of the 19th, and it consumed almost a quarter of the city while it burned out of control for five days. Interestingly, though there is archaeological evidence for the fact that the fire actually took place, and its extent was as significant as the sources seem to indicate, Tacitus is the only one who gives a comprehensive account of the fire, with other biographers not even mentioning it (aside from Pliny, who mentions it in connection to another incident). Yet the fire was definitely a momentous event, and one which would live on in history as Nero's worst hour.

The aftermath of the fire must have been a sight to behold. Much of Rome was a scorched and smoking ruin, and Nero was now faced with the unenviable task of trying to finance a rebuilding effort with state coffers that were already dangerously close to being empty. Part of his economic policy included the transportation of rubble from the blaze to nearby Ostia, where it was poured into the marshes both to get rid of it and to drain them of water, creating what eventually would become fertile farmland. Nero also ordered the reconstruction of the areas affected by the fire, having modern, evenly spaced and comfortable residences erected under his own supervision, and presumably employing many of those whose livelihoods were destroyed by the flames.

Nero capitalized on that unpopularity by accusing Christians of being responsible for the blaze, though it does not appear as though any motive was ever ascribed to them. Several were seized and, after being tortured, confessed (it is unclear whether they confessed to being Christians, or to the arson itself, but most sources are in accord in saying that they confessed *because* they were tortured). Scores of Christians were martyred, some draped in the skins of wild animals and then torn apart by dogs in the arena, others crucified in a mockery of Jesus's martyrdom, and still more were burned alive, nightly, to serve as illumination for Nero's garden banquets. The first institutionalized persecution of the Christians in the history of the Roman Empire (but not the last) had begun.

Tacitus described Nero's scapegoating of the Christians, writing, "Consequently, to get rid of the report, Nero fastened the guilt and inflicted the most exquisite tortures on a class hated for their abominations, called Christians by the populace. Christus, from whom the name had its origin, suffered the extreme penalty during the reign of Tiberius at the hands of one of our

---

[178] Suetonius, *Life of Claudius,* XXV.4.
[179] Suetonius, *Life of Nero,* XVI.

procurators, Pontius Pilatus, and a most mischievous superstition, thus checked for the moment, again broke out not only in Judaea, the first source of the evil, but even in Rome, where all things hideous and shameful from every part of the world find their centre and become popular. Accordingly, an arrest was first made of all who pleaded guilty; then, upon their information, an immense multitude was convicted, not so much of the crime of firing the city, as of hatred against mankind. Mockery of all sorts was added to their deaths. Covered with the skins of beasts, they were torn by dogs and perished, or were nailed to crosses, or were doomed to the flames and burnt, to serve as a nightly illumination, when daylight had expired."

Tacitus himself went on to describe Christianity as a "pernicious superstition," and he wrote that the Christians arrested for starting the fire had not been punished for that crime as much as for "their hatred [of] the human race. Besides being put to death they were made objects of amusement: they were clothed in the hides of beasts and torn to death by dogs. Others were crucified, others set on fire to illuminate the night after sunset."[180]

The persecution suffered by Egyptian Christians was possibly even more brutal than that suffered in other parts of the empire. Although the persecution reached its height under Diocletian, there were similarly savage repressions of Christians under Septimus Severus and Maximinus I. In Egypt, special equipment was developed to enhance the pain of those being tortured, and there are numerous examples of Christians being lashed, stoned, blinded, and castrated. From the Roman perspective, the torture was not a punishment so much as a device to make recalcitrant Christians recant and acknowledge Roman gods and the emperor. If they did so, they would be released, but if they did not, then the torture invariably resulted in death.

As is often the case, the deaths of so many martyrs had the opposite effect of the one the Romans intended, and each new martyr seemed to lead to more converts. In Egypt, Christianity came to be adopted as the people's religion, and the Church flourished and spread its influence throughout the Roman world.

One particular aspect of Christianity developed in Egypt with a great impact on later European history was monasticism. Saint Antony is generally credited with the foundation of the ascetic monastic life, and he is often referred to as Antony the Great or Antony the Abbot to distinguish him from a number of other Saints named Antony. He is also known as Father of All Monks. He was born in Egypt, and his life and work are relatively well-known thanks to *Life of St Anthony*, a biography written by Athanasius of Alexandria. He was brought up in Coma in Lower Egypt by wealthy parents, but after their death, when he was about 18, he renounced his worldly goods to follow Christ's injunction, selling all he had and giving to the poor so he could have "treasures in heaven."[181] He became an ascetic, living in and around his hometown for the next 15 years.

---

[180] Tacitus, *Annals*, XV.
[181] Eusebius, 1878.

Antony went even further in the next period of his life by retreating to the desert to live an essentially hermetic life. Although he was not the first of the ascetic hermits since there had been Pagan hermits before him, he took the concept to the extreme and located himself in the barren Nitrian Desert about 60 miles from Alexandria, where he remained for 13 years.[182]

Athanasius describes Antony's sufferings in the desert and the temptations he had to overcome through prayer. Having moved to live in a tomb, he was, it is claimed by his biographer, beaten mercilessly by the devil who resented his piety. His experiences in the tomb presumably prompted him to move on, and he spent the next 20 years even deeper in the desert, at a place named Pispir. There, he blocked himself into a cell and communicated only rarely with visitors through a small hole through which food was also passed.[183]

After his years of self-imposed incarceration, he emerged to help spread the gospel and bolster the Christian community which was, by that time, undergoing the worst of the Diocletian persecutions. He arrived in Alexandria in 311 A.D., ignored warnings from the Romans, and began preaching. For whatever reason, he was not arrested, unlike so many of his followers, and when the persecutions ended, he returned to the desert. By then, however, his fame was so great that he was constantly beset by visitors seeking his counsel. Many of these visitors became his disciples, and he organized them into communities that spread throughout Egypt and the Roman world.[184] One disciple, Macarius the Great, carried on his work, providing the key elements of monasticism Saint Benedict had used in the development of his Rule 200 years later.

Antony's sayings and those of his major disciples were incorporated into the *Sayings of the Desert Fathers,* which profoundly influenced Christian thinking. It is said that Emperor Constantine wrote to Antony personally asking for his advice. Toward the end of his life, he returned to Alexandria to lead the opposition to the Arian heresy.[185]

Antony's influence on the early Church cannot be overestimated. He played a major role not only in promoting the concept of monasticism but in consolidating Christianity in Egypt, and through his disciples and personal influence, the whole Roman Empire.

Another Egyptian who played a significant part in the development of coenobitic or communal monasticism was Saint Pachomius. Born in Upper Egypt, he was conscripted into the Roman auxiliaries where he met Coptic Christians and converted. He became a follower of Antony and withdrew into the desert near Thebes around 314 A.D. Pachomius had a talent for administration and was soon involved in building monastic enclosures where the scattered monks could live in communities. He drew up routines for the monks that balanced work and prayer and his monasteries, with their hierarchical structures, became models for those that came later.

---

[182] *Butler's Lives of the Saints edited by* M. Walsh (1991). Harper Collins.
[183] Athanasius, *Life of St. Anthony.*
[184] Eusebius, 1878.
[185] *The Story of Christianity: Volume 1* by J. Gonzalez (1984). Harper Collins.

Pachomius' life was recorded by Palladius in his *Lausiac History*. One specific legacy among many was that he was known by the title Abba, meaning father, which became the title Abbot and was used by leaders of subsequent monasteries. He founded 11 monasteries, but many more were founded throughout Egypt, the Middle East, and later Western Europe.[186]

Given Egypt's pivotal position within the empire, it is no surprise it was embroiled in complex political battles for the ultimate control of Rome. No one unable to control Egypt could aspire to rule the empire for long. In 139 A.D., native Egyptians, led by Isidorus, rose in rebellion in what became known as the Bucolic War. The insurrection was put down by Avidius Cassius after several years of fighting, after which he declared himself emperor in 175 A.D. Marcus Aurelius was despatched to deal with the usurper, and Cassius was defeated. A similar train of events occurred in 193 A.D. when Pescennius Niger was proclaimed emperor in Egypt; he, too, was defeated.

Caracalla was responsible for the next major changes in Egyptian social structure when he gave Roman citizenship to all Egyptians, though it is more likely he did so to extort additional taxes rather than as a notion of fairness.[187] The economic resources Egypt provided did not change to any great extent in the Roman era as compared to the Ptolemaic period, but what did change was the efficiency with which the wealth was extracted through ever more sophisticated taxation systems. Assessments were made of the value of land, and taxes were paid in kind. In addition, smaller taxes were levied through custom duties on a variety of goods.

The grain exported to Rome, however, always remained the key issue, and securing an uninterrupted supply was the primary objective of every prefect. They also took the opportunity to increase their wealth, and in doing so, helped benefit the general economic well-being of the province.

Successive prefects encouraged the purchase of land and promoted private enterprises in commerce, manufacturing, and trade through reduced taxation rates. The poor, on the other hand, had to scratch a living from the land they'd rented from the state or private landlords and bore the brunt of the taxation system. Egyptian economy was complex, and even at the local level, the use of coinage was commonplace. The net result was that Egypt economically thrived from the reign of Nero, and was at the height of its economic power by the end of the 2nd century A.D.

By the end of the 3rd century A.D., the debasement of the currency began to have a negative impact on Egypt's economic situation.[188] The economy degenerated to such an extent that Diocletian and Constantine enacted drastic reforms that played a part in the empire's split, and Egypt became a part of the eastern half.

---

[186] Pp. 73-76, *Pachomius: The Making of a Community in Fourth Century Egypt* by P. Rousseau (1985). University of California Press.
[187] Provided for under the statutes of the *Constitution of Antoninus*.
[188] *Coinage in Roman Egypt* by E. Christiansen (2004). Aarhus University Press.

It is probably true to say there is no one overarching reason for the emergence of two separate, imperial entities following the split of the empire into east and west. Some writers highlight the problems created by the vast size of the empire, which encompassed over two million square miles at its height and spanned over three continents, resulting in significant problems in communication and making governance difficult. It is certainly true that the empire was enormous and communication between Rome and its furthest reaches could involve months of travel. In such circumstances, it was relatively easy for local figures to ignore or modify Roman dictates or to operate semi-autonomously.

Other academics point to underlying economic issues confronting the empire. It has been suggested that the western part was essentially consumer and debtor, and the eastern part the provider of wealth and food. In this context, Egypt was vital, particularly in relation to the provision of grain. The western part of the empire was much poorer and more rural than the east, but despite this rural nature, the real wealth of the empire lay in agriculture from the African continent, particularly Egypt. This is what kept Italy from starvation. The underlying economic weakness of the western empire was masked by the wealth of the eastern. These economic imbalances contributed to the instability in the empire in the 3rd century A.D., leading to Diocletian's attempt to impose far-reaching, centralized control on the economy as a means of protecting the empire's integrity.

He instituted price controls by forcing workers into hereditary professions, but punitive taxation fomented dissatisfaction so he had to create more reasons to find ways around the system. In rural areas, the net result was less tax revenue, not more, as local aristocrats conspired with the rural population to avoid taxation. In the urbanized and populous east, it was much harder to evade taxation, resulting in the growth of a highly bureaucratic, hierarchical administrative structure. Unlike rural areas in the west, the aristocrats of the east became the bureaucracy. This only added to the growing cultural gulf between the two parts of the empire already manifesting itself through things like the west speaking Latin while the east spoke Greek. Diocletian then took a step preparing the way for the split by dividing the empire into four administrative regions in an attempt to make it more manageable. These reforms could not mask the simple truth that the west faced a situation in which food prices were high and rising, as well as a huge deficit with nothing to offer in exchange for the goods it imported from the east. To address the issue, the coinage was debased, but this led to further inflation, instability, and imbalance.

Apart from these economic problems and those associated with the difficulties of efficiently administering such a vast territory, some writers have concluded the real reason for the division lay in the fact the empire was fundamentally rotten at its core. By this, they mean that the system set up by Augustus and his successors had some superficial success in its early years in terms of securing the power of the emperor, but that maintenance of power was purely based on military might. By creating a more mobile class system, the way was opened for a wider selection of people to aspire to power, when what was actually needed was the ability to control military forces. Things eventually started coming to a head in the 3rd century.[189]

On a more positive note, Diocletian's administrative reforms also involved a restructuring of the systems in Egypt which proved helpful in securing Egypt's continued prosperity once the empire finally split. These systems were built upon by Constantine once he took complete control of the empire. The province was divided into four administrative areas, each of which had further subdivisions to create smaller units that were more easily managed. The reforms also involved the splitting of a number of official posts and the creation of separate military and civil officials, known as the *praeses* and the *dux*. For the first time, the whole province was also placed under the overall supervision of the most senior official in Antioch. Constantine consolidated these reforms in Egypt, and they proved vital in ensuring Egypt remained as the most important exporter of food in the ancient world.

Diocletian's answer to Rome's problems was the introduction of a system of devolution, known as the Tetrarchy, in 293. The word itself comes from the Greek, meaning leadership of the people by four. The Tetrarchy lasted until 313, when the four became two. Shortly after that, under Constantine, the system ended when he assumed sole rule. The Tetrarchs were made up of two co-emperors and two Caesars, or junior emperors, each ruling from their own capital. None were based in Rome, as it was felt that each should be based on the borders of states with actual or potential enemies. Thus, the empire was ruled by Nicodemia in Asia Minor, Trier in Germany, Sirmium in modern-day Serbia, and Mediolanum in northern Italy. Rome remained the nominal capital of the empire under its own prefect.

Diocletian's reforms ultimately failed, and his pathological hatred of Christians contributed to the highly volatile situation, but it could still be argued that his policies served to keep the empire together in some sense. The consolidation of division was always likely to cause difficulties.

It was into this very unsettled scenario that Constantine, known historically as Constantine the Great, emerged. Rome was engulfed in another civil war in the early 4th century, and according to both Eusebius and Lactantius, two of Constantine's principal biographers, the day before the Battle of the Milvian Bridge, Constantine was stricken by a vision. Lactantius claims that Constantine was visited by an angel as he dreamt the night before battle, while Eusebius's version is even more theatrical. According to Eusebius, while Constantine's army was on the march, a fiery symbol, shaped like the crossed X and P of the Latin Alphabet (☧) and bearing beneath it the legend "Εν Τούτῳ Νίκα" ("by this sign, you will conquer"), appeared in the sky above. The X and P represented the Greek letters Xhi and Rho, the first two letters of Christ's name in the Greek spelling.

---

[189] *Rome and its Emperors A.D 193-284 A.D* by O. Hekstedt (2008). Edinburgh.

Jean-Christophe Benoist's picture of a bust of Constantine

Presumably, such a divine manifestation would have prompted an on-the-spot conversion, and Constantine certainly alluded to that in later propaganda, but there is significant evidence that the original manifestation was actually viewed as a pagan divine revelation. In that version, the revelation was interpreted as being the halo of *Sol Invictus,* the Sun God with whom Constantine claimed a long-standing association and whose iconography was depicted in coins issued by Constantine even years after the battle.

This gold coin, minted in 313, depicts Constantine with *Sol Invictus*.

One problem with the theory that Constantine merely observed what he thought was a divine revelation from *Sol Invictus* is that accounts agree he changed the appearance of his equipment before the battle. Some scholars have rather optimistically suggested that the fiery symbol was in fact a sun dog, but whatever the source of Constantine's divine inspiration, whether miraculous, scientific or simply clever propaganda, on the day of battle his armies apparently approached Maxentius's forces with the Xhi Rho painted on their shields. According to Eusebius: "Assuming therefore the Supreme God as his patron, and invoking His Christ to be his preserver and aid, and setting the victorious trophy, the salutary symbol, in front of his soldiers and body-guard, he marched with his whole forces, trying to obtain again for the Romans the freedom they had inherited from their ancestors."

Having consolidated his position within his own domains, Constantine then set about securing his borders from invasion. Matters outside the Western Roman Empire were still on a knife's edge with Maximin and Licinius at each other's throats, and so to smooth matters over Constantine suggested that he and Licinius meet in Mediolanum and talk peace. Accordingly, the two Emperors met in the city in 313, with Constantine asking that Licinius make good on his previous promise to marry his sister Constantia.

However, the most famous and significant result of the encounter was not the renewal of their alliance but their joint edict, later dubbed the Edict of Milan, on religious freedom. The Edict of Milan was not quite the landmark that Christian scholars declared it to be, given that Galerius had issued a similar edict shortly before his death. In Galerius's edict in 311, Christians who "followed such a caprice and had fallen into such a folly that they would not obey the institutes of antiquity" were excused from their "errors": "Wherefore, for this our indulgence, they ought to pray to their God for our safety, for that of the republic, and for their own, that the commonwealth may continue uninjured on every side, and that they may be able to live securely in their homes."

With that said, the Edict of Milan certainly went further than Galerius did, by declaring all religions exempt from persecution and proclaiming freedom of worship for all, with a special emphasis on Christianity. Not only were Christians freed from any persecution and allowed to worship in peace, but their property (including entire churches) and wealth that had previously been seized in various religious purges over the years were granted to them with full restitution.

Affairs within the Church did not immediately begin to run smoothly though. Even before the threat of persecution had been removed, the Christians were divided by a series of internal disputes, particularly virulent in Alexandria. The basis of the conflict was the disagreement among Christians regarding the doctrines of Arius, known as Arianism. Arius was an Alexandrian who had propounded a non-Trinitarian doctrine relating to the nature of Christ.[190] He asserted that Christ was the Son of God who had come into existence at a specific point in time created by God the Father and so was separate from the Father and subservient to him.[191] These views were very different from beliefs held by many Christians, known as Homoousian, who contended that Christ had always existed and was equal to the Father. The two sides argued long and hard in the School in Alexandria, even though, initially, the two doctrines had co-existed side-by-side. Both were considered orthodox, but conflicts developed as each side tried to win converts to its interpretation.

The disagreements continued until Constantine finally took control of the empire and Homoousianism was adopted as the official doctrine at the Council of Nicaea in 325 A.D. At that council, Arianism was declared heretical, and the Nicene Creed adopted as the summary of Christian beliefs. Of the 300 bishops at the council, only two did not endorse the Creed condemning Arianism.[192] Constantine imposed the death penalty on those who refused to hand over Arian texts: "If any writing by Arius should be found it should be handed over to the flames, so that not only will the wickedness of his teachings be obliterated but nothing will be left to remind anyone of him. I hereby make a public order that if someone should be discovered to have hidden a writing composed by Arian and not to have immediately brought it forward and destroyed it by fire his penalty shall be death."[193]

---

[190] 'Arianism', *Encyclopaedia Britannica* (2009).
[191] 'Arianism', *Encyclopaedia Britannica* (2009).
[192] 'Nicaea, Council of', *Encyclopaedia Britannica* (2009).

It is a fairly safe assumption that most Christians did not understand the issue in dispute.[194] The matter resolved at Nicaea was thrown into confusion again when the First Synod of Tyre declared Arius was not a heretic after all in 335 A.D.,[195] and Constantine was baptised by Arian Bishop Eusebius.[196] Later councils re-imposed the ban on Arianism, but in the period up to Constantine's death, the dispute proved extremely divisive and caused a very real disruption in the Egyptian cities that had given rise to these so-called heresies.

Nevertheless, despite this favoritism towards Christianity, there is still no definitive proof that Constantine was a Christian at this stage. Indeed, two years later, when he erected the famous Arch of Constantine, he made sacrifices to Victory and other deities. Though there are religious motifs on the Arch itself, and in the way it was constructed and sited, they are all pagan. There is no Christian iconography to be found anywhere on the arch.

In his time, Constantine affected nearly every conceivable cultural aspect of the Roman Empire, most notably in its religion but also even in attire and appearance. Constantine revived the clean shaven look, which Augustus himself had favored 300 years earlier. Given his conversion of the empire and relocation to Constantinople, Constantine directly shaped the histories of Europe, the Byzantine Empire, the Roman Empire, and the growth of the Catholic

---

[193] Athanasius, *Life of Constantine*, 18.
[194] p.267, *Church History Vol. I: From Christ to the Pre-Reformation* by E. Ferguson (2013). Zondervan.
[195] Socrates of Constantinople, *Church History*, I.33.
[196] *The Story of Christianity: Volume 1* by J. Gonzalez (1984). Harper Collins.

Church. While he was being venerated as a saint by the Eastern Orthodox Christians in the Byzantine Empire, Charlemagne was claiming his mantle in Western Europe about 400 years later, making sure that his own court was adorned with monuments to Constantine. Constantine's popularity even extended to Britain, where 12th century Britons were trying to claim him as a native son by claiming Helena actually originated from Colchester. To this day, Constantine's name has remained popular and in use.

At the same time, Constantine was shaped by his times just as much as he shaped them. His decision to regard Rome an unsalvageable Imperial capital was the consequence of a deeply rooted pragmatism; after all, Constantine himself had conquered Rome. It may also be argued that his conversion and successive edict of religious tolerance were also politically pragmatic. The traditional Roman religious worship, which had endured for hundreds of years, had begun to be supplanted by a new wave of "mystery cults", secretive sects with obscure rituals which had gained enormous popularity. The most popular of these, of course, was Christianity, whose adherents had forgone the traditional initiation mysteries which made each separate cult an elitist affair and opened it to all as a populist religion. Christianity was no longer an obscure sect whose members inspired fear and could thus be conveniently scapegoats for tragedies like the great fire of Rome. In the 1st century, they could be persecuted and even slaughtered with relative, but by Constantine's time, they had become a burgeoning and powerful religious force whose faithful could cause serious political problems if they were not appeased. By proclaiming himself a Christian and publishing his edict of religious tolerance, Constantine was pragmatically acknowledging that Christianity was, or was fast becoming, the dominant religious group in the Empire.

Constantinople, Constantine's "new" city, was founded in 324, dedicated in 330, and renamed Constantinople almost immediately after Constantine's victory over Licinius. The dedication ceremonies included both Pagan and Christian rites, but in this "new Rome," Pagan temples and cults were conspicuous by their absence.[197] The reunification of the empire, albeit not particularly long-lived, allowed Constantine to complete many of Diocletian's reforms, as well as allow him to introduce innovations of his own. His major reforms included the creation of a new field army and military positions that reported directly to the emperor. This extended the principle initiated by Diocletian of separating civil and military functions in the administration of provinces and was particularly relevant to the governance of Egypt.

Once he had decided to live more or less permanently in the Christianized east, Constantine promoted Christianity more aggressively. He openly rejected Paganism, though he never persecuted them. He promoted Christians into new posts and welcomed bishops to his court.[198] Constantine's patronage was a decisive turning point in the history of the Church as he supported it financially and had a large number of basilicas built, exempted Christians from some taxes,

---

[197] P. 508, *The Oxford Dictionary of Byzantium* edited by A. Kazhdan (1991). Oxford University Press.
[198] It was he that summoned the First Ecumenical Council at Nicaea in 325 A.D. mentioned above.

and returned property that had been seized by Diocletian as well as land granted to the Church.[199] The architecture of his new city was overtly Christian, and churches were built inside the city walls, a very visible illustration of the religion's status. No Pagan temples were built, and as there were no pre-existing ones, Paganism was not represented in the city.[200] Significantly, Constantine made non-Christians contribute to the building of Christian churches.

Constantine increasingly employed Christians in senior positions, but he never stopped utilizing the non-Christian aristocratic elites, and right up until his death, approximately two-thirds of senior positions were held by Pagans. He did change laws to bring them more in line with his Christian leanings, though. For example, in deference to Christian piety and sensibilities, he abolished crucifixion, replacing it with hanging. He was also responsible for making Sunday, a day sacred to both Christians and followers of Sol Invictus, an official day of rest. Markets were forbidden, and public buildings closed on that day, though agricultural work was allowed.[201] Other changes also reflected his Christian leanings; for example, a prisoner could be branded on his feet but not on his face, which was deemed to have been made in God's image. Gladiatorial games were also abolished.[202]

A particularly important order given directly by Constantine to Bishop Eusebius was that 50 Bibles be produced for the Church of Constantinople. Athanasius wrote that 340 Alexandrian scribes were employed to fulfill the commission.[203] These Bibles, along with the Codex Alexandrinus, are the earliest extant Christian Bibles, which testifies to the importance of the Egyptian Church in the spread of Christianity within the empire.[204] Though Constantine never made Christianity the official state religion of the empire, he did pave the way for that to happen in 380 A.D. His policies established the precedent for having a Christian emperor in the Church. What emerged was that the bishops took responsibility for doctrine, but the emperor had the responsibility for maintaining orthodoxy and rooting out heretics. In the later years of his reign, he ordered the destruction of Pagan temples, reversing his earlier, more tolerant approach to the older religions.[205]

Constantine believed he had a greater chance of salvation if he waited until he was dying before being baptized. He died in May 337, leaving his son, Constantius II, an Arian, to take over in the east. He received Egypt, while his half-brother, Constantine, was left the western half, restoring the position that had existed under the Tetrarchy.

As far as it is known, Constantine never visited Egypt himself, but his influence on its history

---

[199] *Christianizing the Roman Empire A.D. 100-400 A.D.* by R. MacMullen (1984). Yale University Press.
[200] P. 55, *Medieval Worlds* by R. Gerberding and J.H. Moran Cruz (2004). New York.
[201] *New Catholic Encyclopaedia* (1908); *Christianizing the Roman Empire A.D. 100-400 A.D.* by R. MacMullen (1984). Yale University Press.
[202] P. 700, *The Word Made Flesh: A History of Christian Thought* by M.R. Miles (2004). Blackwell.
[203] Ath. Apol. Const. 4.
[204] P. 414, *The Canon Debate* edited by L.M. McDonald & J.A. Sanders (2002). Hendrikson Publishers.
[205] P. 14, *The Popes and the Papacy in the Early Middle Ages* by J. Richards (1979). Routledge & Kegan.

was immense. If the early Christian writers are to be believed, Egyptian Christians, such as Saint Antony, were highly significant in persuading him to treat Christianity with much greater tolerance than his immediate predecessor, and in his final deathbed conversion.

Perhaps most importantly, while Constantine's reunification of the empire under his rule proved short-lived and the split after his death became permanent, historians still point to the fact he secured the Roman Empire, at least in the east, for another 1,000 years. In that sense, he also irrevocably linked Egypt to the Byzantine Empire, rather than with Western Europe, and Egypt's wealth and fertility guaranteed it would remain an important part of the Byzantine Empire throughout the Middle Ages.

The Final Subjugation of Britannica

From Caesar's second invasion in 54 B.C. to Emperor Claudius's invasion nearly 100 years later, the status quo between Rome and Britain—involving hostages and tribute—was maintained without direct military occupation of the island. Caesar's presumptive heir, Octavian, prepared to invade in 34 B.C., 27 B.C., and 25 B.C., but two of these dates were abandoned due to pressing problems elsewhere in the empire and the third was preempted because the British tribes came to terms with Rome.[206]

Strabo reflected on Augustus' policy toward Britain during this period, concluding it was founded on pure pragmatism: "And for the purposes of political power, there would be no advantage in knowing such distant countries and their inhabitants, particularly where the people live in islands which are such that they can neither injure or benefit us in any way, because of their isolation. For although the Romans could have possessed Britain, they scorned to do so, for they saw that there was nothing at all to fear from Britain, since they are not strong enough to cross over and attack us. No corresponding advantages would arise by taking over and holding the country. For at present more seems to accrue from the customs duties on their commerce than direct taxation could supply, if we deduct the cost of maintaining an army to garrison the island and collect the tribute. The unprofitableness of an occupation would be still more marked in the case of the other islands near Britain."[207]

The next potential invasion of Britain was led by Caligula in 40 A.D., initially reported on by Suetonius and then Dio Cassius, who recounted the story of Caligula collecting huge amounts of sea shells and declaring this the tribute he had won from Neptune. "Having secured these spoils for it was evident that he needed booty for his triumphal procession, he became greatly elated, as if he had subdued the Ocean itself. He gave many presents to his soldiers. He took back the shells to Rome in order to exhibit his booty there as well."[208]

---

[206] Dio Cassius, *Roman History*, 49.38.
[207] Strabo, *Geography*, 2.5.8.
[208] Dio Cassius, *Roman History*, 59, 25.1.3.

Louis le Grand's picture of a bust of Caligula

By 40 A.D., the political situation in Britain was in turmoil due to the emergence of the Catevellauni as the most powerful tribe. They displaced Rome's allies, the Trinovantes, which prompted Rome to consider invasion. It is not known what made Caligula decide to abandon his invasion plans, though he certainly took steps that aided Claudius three years later. Most notably, it was under Caligula that the Romans built a lighthouse at what is now Boulogne, a structure that stood until the 16th century.

Dio Cassius wrote extensively on the real invasion, which began in 43 A.D. From his work, it is known that the invasion force was led by Aulus Plautius, the distinguished senator, and comprised four legions, one of which was commanded by Vespasian, the future emperor. The army assembled at Boulogne, crossing over to Britain in three phases and apparently landing at Richborough on the east coast of Kent. Richborough had a large, natural harbor, and excavations do seem to confirm this was the landing place. That said, some historians argue the landing place was in the vicinity of Noviomagus, Chichester, in territory formerly ruled by Verica. Ostensibly, the invasion had taken place to restore Verica as ruler.[209]

---

[209] Strabo, *Geography*, 4.5.2.

British resistance to the Romans was more organized than in the time of Caesar and was led by two formidable commanders, Togodumnus and Caratacus, son of Cunobeline, King of the Catevellauni. The two armies met near Rochester on the River Medway, and after two days of intense fighting, the Romans emerged victorious. The Britons retreated to the Thames, where Togodumnus was killed. Caratacus evaded capture, however, and fled to the west to continue his resistance against the Romans.

Aulus Plautius was, he believed, assured of victory and sent for Claudius to join him for the final push. Dio Cassius claimed Aulus Plautius sent for Claudius because he needed the emperor to secure the victory: "On receiving his message Claudius committed affairs in Rome including the command of the troops to his fellow consul Lucius Vitellius, whom he had kept in office, like himself, for the full half year and set out for Britain...Taking over the command of the troops in Britain himself he crossed the Thames and engaged the barbarians who had assembled to oppose him. He defeated them and captured Camulodunum, the capital of Cunobelinus. After this he won over a number of tribes some by diplomacy some by force and was saluted as Imperator several times, contrary to precedent."[210]

Claudius was certainly no military man, and on his triumphal arch in Rome, it is claimed that Claudius received the surrender of 11 kings without any losses. In *Twelve Caesars*, Suetonius states that Claudius received the surrender of the Britons without battle or bloodshed.[211] It is more likely that by the time Claudius arrived, the Britons had, in effect, been beaten, so the elephants and heavy war engines brought by Claudius were superfluous. They would, however, have presented an imposing spectacle for Claudius's march to Camulodunum, where the Romans had established their new capital.

Despite having had very little to do with the actual defeat of the Britons, Claudius milked the victory for all it was worth. Dio Cassius noted, "The Senate on hearing of his achievements voted him the title Britannicus, and gave him permission to hold a triumph. They also voted an annual festival to commemorate the event and decreed that two triumphal arches should be erected, one in Rome and one in Gaul, since it was from Gaul that he had crossed over into Britain. They bestowed on his son the same title and indeed in a way Britannicus came to be the boy's usual name."[212]

---

[210] Dio Cassius, *Roman History*, 60.19.1-21.5.
[211] Suetonius, *Life of Claudius*, 17.
[212] Dio Cassius, *Roman History*, 60.22.1-23.6.

Marie-Lan Nguyen's picture of a bust of Claudius

Vespasian pursued Caratacus west and set up a legionary base at Exeter. While this was going on, the Legio IX was sent north and established a Roman center at Lincoln.

Josephus seemingly exaggerated Vespasian's role in the conquest of Britain, claiming it had been he who had added Britain to the Empire, "and thus provided Claudius, the father of Nero, with a triumph which cost him no personal exertion."[213] Regardless of whoever was most responsible, within only four years of the invasion, the area south of a line from the Humber to the Severn estuary was under Roman control.

Roman consolidation of their new province continued apace under the new Governor Publius Ostorius Scapula who, in 47 A.D., began a campaign against the Welsh tribes.

Key to the Roman success was their defeat of Caratacus whom they bested in the Battle of Caer Caradoc. He sought sanctuary with the Brigantes, whose queen, Cartimandua, promptly handed him over to her Roman allies. His wife and daughter were already in Roman hands,

---

[213] Josephus, *The Wars of the Jews*, 3.1.2(4).

having been captured after the battle. Tacitus described Caratacus in fairly glowing terms, writing, "The natural ferocity of the inhabitants was intensified by their belief in the prowess of Caratacus whose many undefeated battles and even many victories had made him pre-eminent among British chieftains. His deficiency in strength was compensated by superior cunning and topographical knowledge. Transferring the war to the country of the Ordovices he was joined by everyone who found the prospect of a Roman peace alarming."[214]

Tacitus recalls that Caratacus was held in some esteem in Rome despite nine years of warfare, and although he was paraded through Rome as a prisoner, Claudius pardoned his erstwhile foe after he had made a noble speech to the Senate. He may have lived the remainder of his life in the city.

The defeat of Caratacus was not, however, the end of the disturbances in Britain, and further trouble erupted with the Silures and the Brigantes. Ostorius died shortly after Caratacus's defeat and was succeeded by Aulus Didius Gallus, who, upon his arrival in Britain, found that a Roman brigade under Manlius Valens had suffered a reversal. The whole incident was magnified, for various reasons, by both sides in an internal struggle between Brigantine factions. Having resolved that issue, Gallus turned his attention to the consolidation of Roman gains in Wales. Nero became Emperor in 54 A.D., and he was keen to expand the invasion even further north. He appointed Quintus Veranius as governor, and he and his successor, Gaius Suetonius Paulinus, extended Roman control in Wales, destroying the seat of Druidical power on Mona, present-day Anglesey, in 60 A.D.

The Romans seem to have had an almost pathological hatred of the Druids since the days of Julius Caesar, and this sentiment was shared by Claudius. It was the determination to exterminate them that led to a significant part of the Roman forces in Britain being in the north when the Iceni revolt erupted.

The reason for the intensity of this antipathy towards the Druids is difficult to fathom, as all the evidence available suggests the individuals that were called Druids seem to have been high-ranking members of a professional class that served Celtic society. They were, of course, religious leaders, but they also served as legal authorities, lore keepers, doctors, and political advisers. They were thought to have been literate, but they were prevented by their doctrine from recording their knowledge in any written form. They left no written accounts of themselves or their beliefs. Consequently, the modern understanding of what they did and who they were comes only from the Greek and Roman sources.

Caesar provided the most detailed information on the Druids in his *Gallic Wars*, though later writers, such as Cicero and Tacitus, also offered etails. Caesar claimed the Druids were one of the two most important groups amongst the British tribes, the other being the nobles. He said

---

[214] Tacitus, *The Annals*, 12.31-3.

they were exempt from military service or the payment of taxes and could excommunicate individuals, thus making them outcasts from society.[215] Druidic lore was learned by rote in remote locations, deep in forests, or on isolated islands such as the major center on Mona. The instruction apparently took the form of making initiates learn large numbers of verses by heart and full training is said to have taken up to twenty years to complete. The exact content of the verses is lost—not one single verse has come down to modern times.

The most obvious cause of Roman antipathy towards the Druids was the belief that they practiced human sacrifice. Caesar claimed the preferred sacrifice was a criminal, but if none were available, anyone would do. Caesar went on to assert that the most common form of sacrifice was burning the victim alive in a large, wooden effigy, known today as a wicker man. Other writers claim that victims were also drowned or hanged, depending on whether the sacrifice was to Teutates, Esus, or Taranis. Significantly, Diodorus Siculus wrote that a sacrifice was invalid unless a Druid was present: "These then predict the future by observing the flight and calls of birds and by the sacrifice of holy animals, all orders of society are in their power and in very important matters they prepare a human victim plunging a dagger into his chest, by observing the way the limbs convulse as he falls and the gushing of his blood, they are able to read the future."[216]

There is some evidence from continental Europe that Celtic shamans practiced human sacrifice. Mass graves have been unearthed in Gaul dating from this period that seem to confirm that it was a Druidical practice, but there is debate as to whether the bodies are, in fact, those of honored warriors who fell in battle, rather than sacrificial victims. Modern scholars now tend to doubt whether the Druids ever practiced human sacrifice at any time or any period.[217]

The major philosophy of the Druids centered on the immortality of the soul: "The Pythagorean doctrine prevails among the Gauls' teaching that the souls of men are immortal and that after a fixed number of years they will enter into another body." [218] Caesar noted, "With regard to their actual course of studies the main object of all education is, in their opinion, to imbue their scholars with a firm belief in the indestructability of the human soul which according to their belief merely passes at death from one tenement to another, for by such doctrine alone, they say, which robs death of all its terrors, can the highest form of human courage be developed. Subsidiary to the teachings of this main principle, they hold various lectures and discussions on astronomy, on the extent and geographical distribution of the globe, on the different branches of natural philosophy and on many problems connected with religion."[219]

---

[215] Julius Caesar, *Gallic Wars*, VI 13-18.
[216] Diodorus Siculus, *Bibliotheca Historicae*, V 21.
[217] P. 85, 'Human Sacrifice among the Pagans and Christians' by J.Rives (1995). *Journal of Roman Studies*, 85, 65-85.
[218] Alexander Cornelius Polyhistor.
[219] Julius Caesar, *Gallic Wars*, VI.13.

There does not appear to be too much in the Druid philosophy as understood by the Romans at the time that should have caused them undue concern. Nevertheless, it did.

Whether the Romans believed the Celtic idea of immortality would imbue them with no fear of death, thus making them more effective weapons of war, is not known. Whether the influence the Druids had over the local kings was seen as a barrier to Roman attempts to manipulate local leaders or whether the Druidical aversion to bribery marked them for special treatment is a matter of conjecture. What is clear is that Roman leaders took every possible step to exterminate the Druids throughout the Celtic world. Their efforts were ultimately so successful that by the end of the 1st century A.D., there is little evidence of any Druids still practicing their religion.

John Opie's painting of Queen Boudicca

The final subjugation of Wales and the suppression of the Druids had to be deferred in 60 A.D. because the Romans had to turn their attention to the biggest threat to their invasion since 43 A.D.: the Revolt of the Iceni.

While the death of Prasutagus and the subsequent treatment of his wife and daughters was undoubtedly a major factor in the Iceni rebellion, the whole uprising had more deep-seated causes. Tacitus recorded, "Prasutagus, King of the Iceni, after a life of long and renowned prosperity, had made the emperor co-heir with his own two daughters. Prasutagus hoped by this submissiveness to reserve his kingdom and household from attack. But it turned out otherwise.

After his death, the kingdom and household alike were plundered like prizes of war, the one by Roman officers the other by Roman slaves. As a beginning his widow Boudicca was flogged and their daughters raped. The Icenian chiefs were deprived of their hereditary estates as if the Romans had been given the whole country. The king's own relatives were treated like slaves and the humiliated Iceni feared still worse now that they had been reduced to provincial status. So they rebelled."[220]

The Iceni had rebelled in 47 B.C., and it appears that Prasutagus had been put onto the throne by the Romans as a way of keeping control of the area. Prasutagus's will omitted Boudicca—contrary to normal Celtic practice—which has been assumed by some historians to be because of her open hostility to Rome. The terms of his will, it is suggested, were constructed in such a way as to help his daughters continue his policy of cooperation with Rome and thereby sideline Boudicca.[221]

Whether Boudicca was a long-standing opponent of Rome or not, she certainly seized the opportunity—presented by her own ill-treatment and that of her daughters—to begin another revolt against the Romans. The trouble quickly spread to the Trinovantes, who had their own grievances against Rome. Britons felt generally angry at the establishment of Rome's imperial cult, which was, of course, specifically intended to impress the natives with the might and majesty of both Rome and the emperor, as well as to act as the focal point for loyalty. The Romans used the cult in a number of ways, including enrolling the local aristocracy as priests, thus involving them in Roman public life. The intention was to Romanize the class of natives that would become the governing class, and who would then undertake the burden of running and administering the province in Rome's interests.

The attempt misfired badly, and the spark of rebellion created by Boudicca's treatment quickly lit fires elsewhere. Dio Cassius, however, put forward an alternative explanation for the outbreak of the revolt: "Claudius had given sums of money to the leading Britons and according to Catus Decianus, the procurator of the island, the money had to be returned together the rest. The confiscation of this money was the pretext for war. In addition, Seneca, with a view to a good rate of interest, had lent the reluctant islanders 40,000,000 sesterces and had then called it all in at once and not very gently. So rebellion broke out."[222]

As well as resentment about the collection of money, Cassius Dio blamed Boudicca for the rebellion, and his description of her atrocities against the Romans is both graphic and damning. She first struck at Camulodunum, where she massacred the entire population and razed the settlement to the ground. Suetonius was busily engaged in Mona and could not help. The Ninth Roman Division, led by Rufus, marched to aid the settlement but was routed by the Iceni.

---

[220] Tacitus, *The Annals*, 14.31.
[221] *Boudica Britannia; Rebel War Leader and Queen* by Aldhouse-Green (2006). Harlow, Pearson Longman.
[222] Dio Cassius, *Roman History*, 62.2.1-4.

Suetonius marched south to defend Londinium, but upon reaching the city, he decided his forces could not match the rebels, so he left it to its fate. "He decided to sacrifice the one town to save the general situation. Undeflected by the tears and prayers of those who begged for his help he gave the signal to move, taking into his company any who could join it. Those who were unfit for war because of their sex, or too aged to go or too fond of the place to leave were butchered by the enemy."[223]

Having taken Londinium, the rebels quickly moved on to Verulamium, where the massacres continued. "The same massacre continued at Verulamium, for the barbarian British, happiest when looting and unenthusiastic about real effort, bypassed the forts and garrisons and headed for where they knew lay the maximum of undefended booty. Something like 70,000 Roman citizens and other friends of Rome died in the places I have mentioned; the Britons took no prisoners sold no captives as slaves and went in for none of the usual trading of war. They wasted no time in getting down to the bloody business of hanging, burning and crucifying. It was as if they feared that retribution might catch up [to] them while their vengeance was only half complete."[224]

While the Britons were busy destroying Verulamium, Suetonius was scouting out the best possible site for a decisive battle. He chose a place where his troops would not be subjected to ambush and settled in to wait for the Britons, who duly arrived in huge numbers. Their confidence in victory was such that they brought their wives and children with them and left them in carts stationed at the edge of the battlefield.[225] Both leaders are said to have inspired their troops with rousing speeches before Suetonius gave the signal for the battle to commence.

His infantry moved forward, throwing their javelins, and Boudicca's superior numbers gave her no advantage in the narrow battlefield the Romans had chosen. Indeed, the vast throng impeded each other, providing easy targets for the Romans. The rebels were forced back, and the Romans advanced in their famous wedge formation, easily cutting through the enemies' lines. As Suetonius ordered in his cavalry and auxiliaries to press home his advantage, the Britons turned to flee. The carts they had arranged around the battlefield slowed their retreat, and the rout turned into an absolute massacre. Tacitus wrote that "the remaining Britons fled with difficulty since their ring of wagons blocked the outlets. The Romans did not spare even the women. Baggage animals too, transfixed with weapons added to the heaps of dead."[226] Boudicca and her daughters escaped, but it is thought they later committed suicide.

---

[223] Tacitus, *The Annals*, 14.33.
[224] Tacitus, *The Annals*, 14.33.
[225] Tacitus, *The Annals*, 14.33.
[226] Tacitus, *The Annals*, 14.33.

A. Brady's picture of a statue depicting Boudicca in her chariot before the battle

The location of the Battle of Watling Street is still unknown today. Theories range from King's Cross in London to Church Stowe in Northampton. Whatever the case, Boudicca's defeat was followed by a program of severe suppression of the indigenous population, initiated by Suetonius. Indeed, the measures he introduced to pacify Britain were so severe that he was eventually recalled to Rome and replaced by Publius Petronius Turpilianus, who tried a gentler approach to pacification. Neither approach proved entirely successful, and sporadic revolts continued to break out until Agricola put a definitive end to any hope the Britons had of expelling their conquerors.

A statue of Agricola

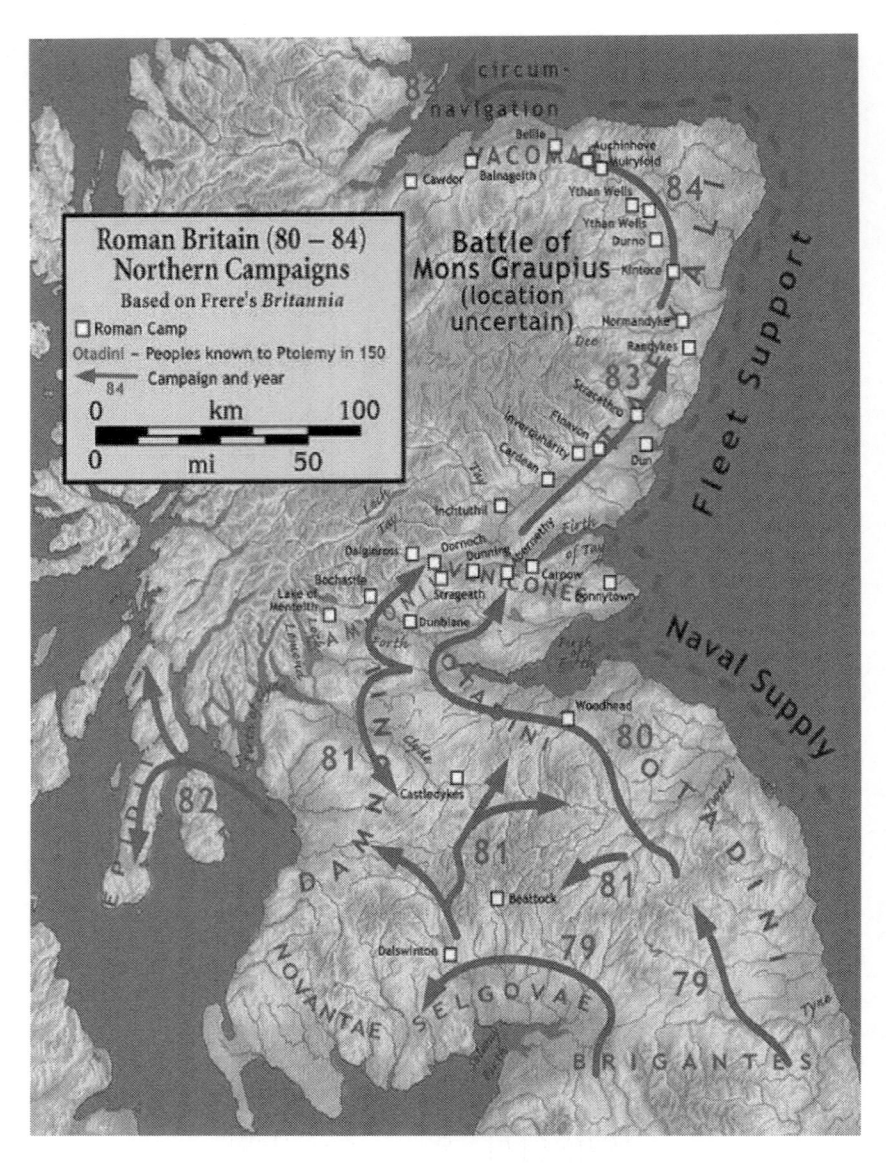

A map of Roman campaigns and conquests in Britain during the time of Agricola

Not all of the British tribes had taken part in the revolt, but according to Tacitus, whether they were hostile or neutral, they all suffered from the effects of the conflict. One of the major disasters stemming from the revolt was famine caused by the failure to sow crops. The situation created difficulties between the tribes who all jostled to secure food and security for their people. In due course, the basic problems of supply were resolved, but the underlying dissatisfaction remained, and internal wars became endemic. Tacitus records further revolts against the Romans by Cartimandua and Venutius in 69 A.D. He described Venutius as a "man of barbarous spirit who hated the Roman power."[227] He also had a grievance against his former wife, Cartimandua, who had thrown him out and taken his armor bearer, Vellocatus, as her husband. The Brigantes were shocked by their queen's actions and declared for her former husband. In desperation, she turned to the Romans—against whom she had so recently fought—to restore her to her throne.

While the Romans secured the queen's safety, as Tacitus had put it, "they were left with a war to fight."[228] In 70 A.D., Quintus Petillius Cerialis took a Roman force from Lincoln to York to defeat Venutius near Stanwick, resulting in the Brigantes and Parisii tribes being further assimilated into the empire and increasing the Romanization of the population. Frontinus succeeded Cerialis as governor in 74 A.D. and subdued the Silures and a number of smaller tribes in Wales, establishing a new base at Caerleon. To secure the area, he also built a series of smaller forts, approximately 10 miles apart, where auxiliary units were stationed. It is likely he built the fort at Pumsaint in the west of Wales to guard the gold mines at Dolaucothi. He retired in 78 A.D. and was replaced as governor by Gnaeus Julius Agricola, Tacitus's father-in-law, which ensured that his deeds were well known throughout the Roman world.

Agricola was born in what is now Frejus in the south of France, which was then a colony known as Forum Julii. His parents were members of the Gallo-Roman political class, of senatorial rank. Both of his grandfathers served as imperial governors and his father, Lucius Julius Graecinus, was a praetor and a member of the Roman Senate. Graecinus was unfortunate in that his time as a Senator in Rome coincided with Caligula's rule, and he fell afoul of the emperor when he refused to prosecute Caligula's cousin, Silanus. Caligula subsequently had him executed.[229] His mother was Julia Procilla, but little is known of her other than that Tacitus described her as a woman of singular virtue.

Agricola was brought up and educated in Massilia—present-day Marseille—and was interested in philosophy, even as a young boy. He began his career in Roman public life, as did so many of his classmates, as a military tribune, and he served in Britain under Gaius Suetonius Paulinus from 58-62 A.D. It is thought that he was attached to the Legio II Augusta but served on Suetonius's staff.[230] In this capacity, he would almost certainly have been involved in putting down the Iceni revolt in 61 A.D. Shortly after the revolt, he returned to Rome and married Domitia Decidiana, who quickly bore him a son.

In 64 A.D., Agricola was appointed quaestor in Asia under Proconsul Lucius Salvius Otho Titianus. During this period, his daughter, Julia Agricola, was born, but his son died in the same year. He became a tribune of the plebs in 66 A.D. and praetor in 68 A.D., working for Galba.

---

[227] Tacitus, *Histories*, 3.45.
[228] Tacitus, *Histories*, 3.45.
[229] *Coins and Power in Late Iron Age Britain* by J. Creighton (2000). Cambridge University Press: Cambridge.
[230] Suetonius, *Life of Caligula*, 44-46.

When Nero committed suicide, the Year of the Four Emperors found Agricola's family involved in the conflicts. Agricola's mother was murdered by Otho's troops in 69 A.D., and Agricola sided with Vespasian. When Vespasian succeeded in becoming emperor, Agricola was given command of the Legio XX Valeria Victrix, stationed in Britain.

At this point, Bolanus was the governor of Britain, and when Agricola arrived to take up his new post, he found that there was considerable unrest once again on the island. Agricola's first task was to re-impose discipline within his own legion, which had grown lax under his predecessor. He then set about helping to consolidate Roman rule. In 71 A.D., Bolanus was replaced as governor by Quintus Petillius Cerialis, and it was under him that Agricola was able to display his talents in the campaign against the Brigantes. In 73 A.D., Agricola's command came to an end, and he was appointed to govern Gallia Aquitania, where he remained until 77 A.D. before being recalled to Rome. Once there, he was appointed suffect consul, and he betrothed his daughter to Tacitus, with the wedding scheduled to take place the following year. It was quite the year for Agricola, for he was also appointed to the College of Pontiffs and became the new governor of Britain.

Once more, Agricola arrived to a Britain riven with unrest. He employed a two-pronged policy to pacify the island: short-term military action and longer-term programs of assimilation. Initially, he had to deal with the Ordovices in Northern Wales, as they had wiped out the Roman garrison there. He marched north and routed them in a short, bloody campaign. He then headed to Mona to complete the campaign that had been started by Suetonius and interrupted by Boudicca's revolt. There, he forced the local population to surrender.

In conjunction with this and other campaigns, Agricola sought to accelerate the process of Romanizing the native aristocracy, which had proven unsuccessful in the past. From the bungled attempt, he learned to involve the locals in the Imperial cult at Colchester, adopting a more systematic and extended policy. "The following winter was taken up with the soundest projects. In order to encourage rough men who lived in scattered settlements, and were thus only too ready to fall to fighting, to live in a peaceful and inactive manner by offering them the consequent pleasures of life, Agricola urged them privately and helped the officials to build temples, public squares with public buildings and houses. He praised those who responded quickly and severely criticized the laggards. In this way competition for public recognition took the place of compulsion."[231]

Agricola realized the long-term future of Roman rule depended on the younger generation of Britons being won over to the Roman way of life. To this end, he ensured that the children of all the leading figures in British society were given a Roman education that promoted the arts. The Latin language was taught, and the result, according to Tacitus, was that those who had once shunned the language now sought fluency and elegance in it.[232] Roman dress was encouraged,

---

[231] Tacitus, *The Life of Cnæus Julius Agricola*, 21.

and the wearing of the toga became commonplace. Romans introduced British aristocracy to the delights of assembly rooms, bathing, and smart dinner parties. In one of his more cynical moments, Tacitus noted, "In their inexperience the Britons called it civilization when it was really all part of their servitude."[233]

Agricola, however, found there was still work to be done on the military side. In 79 A.D., he moved against the Brigantes in the north and the Selgova in the south of Scotland, and by dint of overwhelming military superiority, he forced them into submission.

Cerialis's earlier campaigns against the Brigantes had brought Scotland to the attention of the Romans, and archaeological evidence suggests that following their success against the Brigantes, the Romans penetrated Scotland and built military camps as far north as the Gask Ridge, controlling the glens and providing access to and from the Scottish Highlands and Lowlands. In his account of Agricola's campaign in Scotland, Tacitus does not state that the Romans had returned to lands they had previously occupied, but it is almost certain this was the case. Whether these early attempts at settlement were overrun by the northern tribes or simply abandoned is unclear.

From Tacitus, it is known that Agricola advanced into Scotland. In 80 A.D., he reached the River Tay and remained in Scotland until 81 A.D. During this period, he quashed what was relatively ineffective opposition and established forts throughout the south of Scotland.[234] He returned to Scotland after a brief visit to the south in 82 A.D., and he sailed to Kintyre in Argyllshire, moving slowly northward along Scotland's eastern and northern coasts in the following two years. In this campaign, he used a coordinated strategy, employing both land and naval forces, and it was during this period that he also sent ships to investigate the island of Ireland.[235] He gave sanctuary to an exiled Irish king, and according to Tacitus, he considered invading Ireland by sending a small force to reconnoiter. No trace of it has ever been found, and no invasion materialized.

Agricola's attention then refocused on the campaign at hand, during which the only major confrontation with the indigenous population took place at the Battle of Mons Graupius, where the northern British tribes united briefly under Calgacus to try to defeat the invaders. The exact location of this battle and the date are unknown, but it was most likely fought in 84 A.D. The possible locations range from Perthshire to north of the River Dee, Grampian Mount, Kempstone Hill, Megray Hill, or a spot near the Roman camp at Raedykes. The sites in Aberdeenshire are most similar to the site described by Tacitus, but to date, no archaeological evidence for the battle has been found anywhere in Scotland.[236]

---

[232] Tacitus, *The Life of Cnæus Julius Agricola*, 21.
[233] Tacitus, *The Life of Cnæus Julius Agricola*, 21.
[234] Tacitus, *The Life of Cnæus Julius Agricola*, 19-23.
[235] Tacitus, *The Life of Cnæus Julius Agricola*, 24.
[236] Tacitus, *The Life of Cnæus Julius Agricola*, 21-22.

At the battle, the Romans were heavily outnumbered by the tribesmen. Normally, British tribes like the Caledonii avoided pitched battles, but on this occasion, for whatever reason, they decided to test themselves directly against the Romans, presumably in an attempt to stop the Roman pillaging of their lands. Tacitus says the Roman force was made up of approximately 17,000 men, 11,000 of whom were auxiliaries recruited from British tribes and other parts of the empire. The number of legionnaires is not known, but there were 3,000 cavalry, suggesting their numbers were not great.[237] Tacitus estimated the Caledonian forces at 30,000.

The tribesmen stationed themselves on higher ground, with some troops placed at the foot of the rise. The whole force was arranged in horseshoe-formation around the hill. On the plain between the opposing armies, the Caledonian chariots raced along both front lines. As was normal in battles at the time, the battle opened with both sides firing missiles at each other, followed by a frontal attack by the Romans on the native lines. The assault force was made up of Batavian and Tungrian swordsmen, who quickly cut the front ranks of their opponents down, trampling on their comrades as they tried to retreat. Agricola initiated an outflanking ploy against those at the top of the hill. It is said the Legionnaires took no part in the battle, during which, according to Tacitus, 10,000 tribesmen were killed at the cost of only 360 auxiliaries. In the end, Tacitus declared that "Britain was completely conquered."[238]

Before he left Scotland, Agricola initiated an extensive program of military road building and the construction of further forts with which to secure his conquests. The lines of military communications of supply with the south were particularly well-fortified. In southeastern Caledonia, in what is now Dumfriesshire and the Kirkcudbright area, further forts were built, securing Roman control over the area.

Agricola was recalled to Rome by Domitian in 84 A.D. and was replaced in Britain by a series of governors who decided not to build upon his success in Scotland. The fortress at Inchtuthil was dismantled before it was completed, and fortifications at Gask Ridge in Perthshire were abandoned within a few years of Agricola's recall. It seems likely the economic costs involved in any attempt to consolidate Roman rule in Scotland were vastly greater than any return the Romans might expect from controlling the area. Consequently, Roman occupation was withdrawn to a line which, in due course, was established as one of the *limites* of the Empire. The concept of the *limites* was that of "defensible" frontiers. In the case of Britain, that frontier became Hadrian's Wall, although there was a short-lived attempt in 142 A.D. to push the *limes* (singular of *limites*) to the Antonine Wall.

---

[237] *Mons Graupius AD 83* by D.B. Campbell (2010). Oxford.
[238] Tacitus, *The Life of Cnæus Julius Agricola*, 21-22.

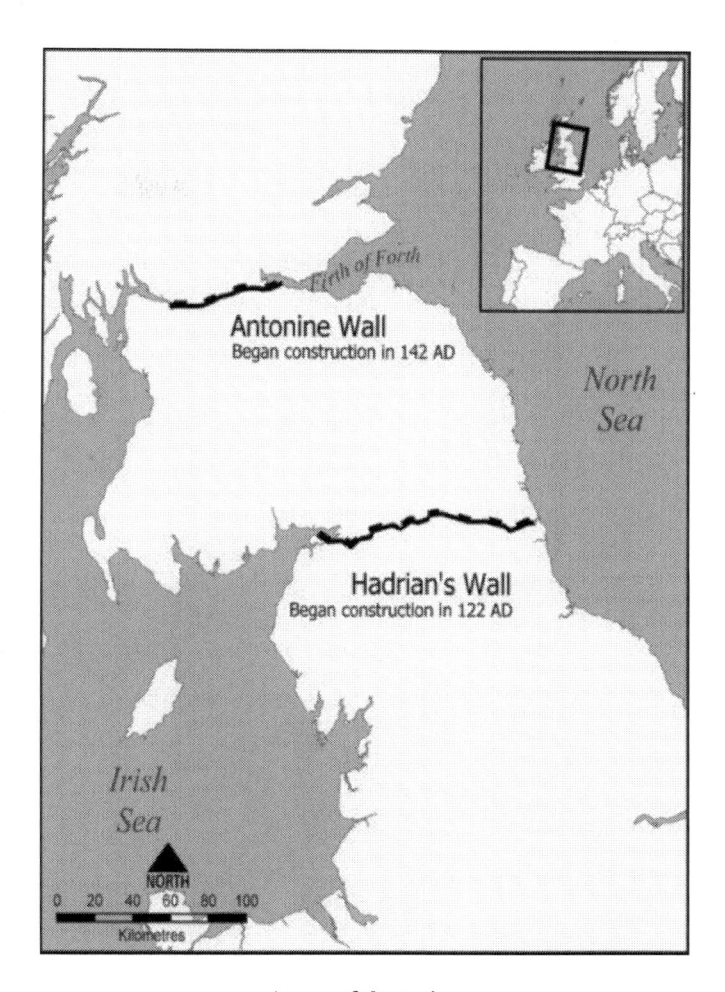

A map of the region

Construction of Hadrian's Wall began in 122 at Newcastle (*Pons Aelius*) and went all the way to Bowness-on-Solway. The line ran parallel to the old Stanegate military road but was as much as two miles north of it in places. This was a strategic decision, for the Stanegate, being a road, ran through valleys and other flat areas for ease of movement, but a wall is at its strongest when it's atop a commanding position that inhibits attackers and allows defenders to see farther. By moving slightly to the north, the wall could be positioned on the hills to the north of the valleys through which the Stanegate ran, and the portion of the wall at the center of the island could take advantage of a series of rough crags, which at times have sheer, north-facing cliffs.

Much of the barrier was 10 feet thick and made of stone bonded with puddled clay, though in other places, the wall is only 7 feet thick. While the thinner portion of the wall seems unduly weak, it must be remembered that the Caledonians did not have any siege equipment, so even though the wall would have been easy enough for a well-equipped Roman army to pierce, it must have seemed formidable to the Caledonian tribes. In fact, it seems the entire wall was originally intended to be 10 feet thick, but a portion of it was made thinner in order to decrease costs and speed up construction time. Evidence for this can be seen in some architectural details, such as at Milecastle 48 at Poltross Burn, where the fortlet (small fort) was constructed in such a way as to accommodate a thicker wall but ended up having only the thinner wall connected to it. The two portions are known to modern researchers as the Broad Wall and the Narrow Wall.

Most of the stone is limestone, the most common type of stone found in the region. The facing stones were roughly squared in order to fit better into regular courses, but no attempt was made at fine dressing. Stones in the wall's interior were rougher, essentially comprising a rubble fill with a large amount of clay.

No portion of Hadrian's Wall has survived to its top, so reconstruction of the wall is theoretical, but atop the wall was probably a protected walkway with crenellations, toothlike slabs of stone at regular intervals with bare spaces in between, a pattern familiar on medieval castles. Evidence for this comes from similar walls from other parts of the empire, as well as the Rudge Cup, a bowl dating from around 150 that shows a stylized depiction of the wall.

The Rudge Cup

The wall stretched westwards 80 Roman miles to Bowness-on-Solway, 15.5 miles (25 km) west of the modern city of Carlisle, which in Roman times was called Luguvalium. Between the

River Irthing and Bowness-on-Solway, the wall was made of turf and timber instead of stone, but the towers continued to be of stone. West of Bowness-on-Solway, the wall stopped, but the milecastles and towers continued in their regular pattern for at least another 26 miles (42 km) along the coast. Doubtless this was to watch for sea raiders, like the later Saxon Shore forts along the southeast coast of Britannia.

Remains of the wall at Milecastle 39

In front of the wall was a ditch, placed several paces to the north of the wall so as not to cause erosion of the wall itself, and it was cut along standard Roman military lines in a steep V shape about 30-40 feet wide at the top and almost 10 feet deep. The excavated earth wasn't used to make a rampart (as was common with an earthen defense system) but was instead formed into a broad mound to the north of the ditch, higher at the south end than the north but with all parts clearly visible from the top of the wall. This ancient tactic, known as a *glacis*, created a clear "killing zone" where attackers could find no cover.

At times, the wall was able to take advantage of natural features to make some portions all but impregnable. In the central portion are numerous crags that rise steeply up from the surrounding ground. The wall goes right up and over them, and one section several miles long actually follows a sheer cliff. Moreover, the wall was strengthened at regular intervals by towers and forts and backed by a broad ditch on the south side called the *Vallum*, which is discussed further below.

Running between and parallel to the wall and the *Vallum* was the Military Way, a replacement for the Stanegate. It ran along the entire length of the wall from the Tyne to Solway Firth and had branch roads leading to forts and settlements. It was similar to many Roman roads, being 18-20 Roman feet wide (18-19.5 modern feet), and had a gravel foundation with curb stones to resist erosion. Atop the foundation was a layer of small basalt stones, and atop this was a surface of fine gravel. This major addition to the wall came at the time of the reoccupation after the abandonment of the Antonine Wall in the late second century.

The material required for building Hadrian's Wall is staggering. Some 1.5 million tons of stone, much of it dressed, was required to build the wall, turrets, milecastles, and forts. This required 15,500 tons of lime and 53,500 pounds of sand for mortar, plus 3,000 tons of water to mix it. Another 198,500 tons of clay was needed for the core. The building work was done by the legions and auxiliary units themselves, which was a common practice that both saved money and stationed soldiers at a vulnerable location until it could be fortified. Much of a Roman legionnaire's life was spent building, not fighting, and thousands of inscriptions have come down from the Roman world of one legion or another proclaiming they had built a fort or a bridge or a stretch of road. Inscriptions show that three legions—the *XX Valeria Victrix* from Chesters, the *II Augusta* from Caerleon, and the *VI Victrix pia fidelis* from York—worked on the wall, along with detachments from the navy (*classis Britannia*) and various auxiliary units. For example, a fragmentary inscription from Milecastle 50 reads, "From the Second Legion Augusta, the Seventh Cohort under the charge of. . ." Sadly, the name of the soldier/overseer has been lost to history.

Men often brought construction skills from their civilian life into practice when they joined the army, so carpenters, stonemasons, tile makers, potters, thatchers, and other such professions were valued when searching for recruits. On top of that, local civilians or civilian work crews may have been brought in from elsewhere to help, but there is no direct evidence for this. The building of the wall was overseen by the Governor of Britannia, Aulus Platorius Nepos, who replaced Falco in 122, and several inscriptions found along the wall mention his name.

In addition to the wall itself, the wall was strengthened by a small fort every Roman mile (.9 of a modern mile). Called milecastles by modern archaeologists and guidebooks, these were square constructions of 194 squared feet. It is unclear how tall they stood, but they certainly were taller than the wall itself in order to give the soldiers extra visibility and range of fire. These were fortified gateways that also allowed traffic to flow north and south. Some archaeologists theorize that only military traffic was allowed through the milecastles, with civilian traffic limited to the main forts in order to better control it.

A picture of the ruins of Milecastle 37

The fact that Hadrian's Wall was pierced every mile by a gate, and a few more times by the main forts, brings up a question that archaeologists have been debating for generations. If the wall was meant to keep the northern tribes out, why did the builders put in so many gates? And if the purpose of the wall was to control traffic like many contemporary archaeologists believe, then why are there ditches in front of the milecastle gates? It's possible there were temporary, removable bridges of wood that the sentries could pull back when they felt threatened, or perhaps the milecastle gates were only for foot traffic and the ditches prevented chariots or carts from coming through. Large-scale traders would have carts, so perhaps they were directed to the main forts where an officer or official with greater authority than a simple soldier could deal with them.

Romans did not make great use of fortifications, as their strategy traditionally depended on beating the enemy in the field through greater discipline and training, so what Hadrian's Wall did was to channel traffic to a few select areas that were easily controlled and provide a means to watch for enemies approaching from the north. Of course, a concerted attack by a large group of northern tribesmen could easily breach a stretch of wall, but the alert would be sounded, and troops could converge from the forts to either side in order to deal with them. Also, the northerners would already be weakened by the initial defense and be without their cavalry and chariots, putting them at a disadvantage.

The entire defensive system was completed before Hadrian's death, a testament to Roman ingenuity and resourcefulness and a project that cemented Hadrian's reputation as one of the empire's great builders.

Hadrian's successor, Antoninus Pius (ruled 138-161), pushed the frontier north and established a defensive line between the Firth of Forth and the Firth of Clyde in 142. The so-called Antonine Wall was a turf rampart with a stone foundation and a wide, deep ditch in front. The rampart was about 10 feet high and 16.5 feet thick and was constructed of turf blocks, a sturdy material that was easy to handle. As with Hadrian's Wall, there was a series of forts and fortlets at regular intervals along its length that numbered at least 28, although the precise number is by no means certain. A road called the Military Way running just south of the wall provided access between them. The construction of this wall took 12 years, a length of time that shows that it wasn't a priority considering that the more ambitious Hadrian's Wall only took a fraction of the time to build.

The Antonine Wall was not the northernmost fortification of the Romans. The army established several forts further out into Caledonia in order to protect trade routes. In addition, Roman marching camps – hastily built fortified camps constructed while a legion was on the march – are more numerous here than in any other border region of the empire. In the 1st century A.D., the historian Josephus wrote that once a legion entered enemy lands, it would "first construct their camp". This could be used as shelter for the night or as a safe base for scouting and local operations. They'd be surrounded by a ditch, with the excavated earth being used to build a rampart behind, and this rampart would be protected by a series of sharp wooden stakes (*pila muralia*). Each soldier would carry two of these as part of his kit. Historians differ as to how these stakes were used; some say they were driven into the ground with the points up in order to act as a barrier, while others say three would be lashed together to make large caltrops. There was an opening that acted as a gate, with a ditch a bit ahead of it to stop cavalry charges. Sometimes the rampart would curve out to make a protected entryway.

Several campaigns into Caledonia occurred in order to subdue the northern tribes. The largest was by Septimius Severus (ruled 193-211) in 209, when he sent a force of tens of thousands of men against the Maeatae and Caledonii. He slaughtered the local inhabitants but suffered tremendous losses himself, which compelled him to repair and strengthen Hadrian's Wall. So many inscriptions were found mentioning his building works that for many years the general scholarly belief was that he had built the wall, not Hadrian.

A bust of Severus

The chronicler Cassius Dio wrote that Severus, "desiring to subjugate the whole of it, invaded Caledonia. But as he advanced through the country he experienced countless hardships in cutting down the forests, levelling the heights, filling up the swamps, and bridging the rivers; but he fought no battle and beheld no enemy in battle array. The enemy purposely put sheep and cattle in front of the soldiers for them to seize, in order that they might be lured on still further until they were worn out; for in fact the water caused great suffering to the Romans, and when they became scattered, they would be attacked. Then, unable to walk, they would be slain by their own men, in order to avoid capture, so that a full fifty thousand died. But Severus did not desist until he approached the extremity of the island."

Severus suddenly took ill in 211, so the campaign was canceled. It's a matter of conjecture whether he would have been able to conquer Scotland, but he certainly seemed to have the will, ordering his men to massacre all the Caledonians they found. He appeared to have taken their defiance as a personal affront. This campaign was also unusual in Roman military history since it was done through steady marches by a single large force that built temporary camps every 10 or 12 miles. Usually, the Romans built a web of fortified points connected by roads in order to outmaneuver the enemy while having a safe place to rest. Looking at a map of the prime agricultural land in the region, it can be seen that the route through Caledonia cut right through it and that a day's march radius from each camp covered virtually all good farmland in the whole region. It appears Severus was conducting a scorched earth campaign, destroying all crops and seed in the area to starve the locals into submission. A lack of seed for planting in the next year would mean scarcity for the following year or years.

While the Antonine Wall had the advantage of being half the length of Hadrian's Wall (40 Roman miles as opposed to 80 Roman miles), it lengthened the lines of supply without any great economic reward, so the wall was abandoned eight years after it was finished and the troops pulled back to Hadrian's Wall in 162. In 208, Septimius Severus moved the troops back to the Antonine Wall and repaired it, but once again, it was abandoned after only a few years in favor of Hadrian's Wall. In both cases, it was unclear why the move north was made because there never seemed to be a real attempt to take Caledonia for the empire. Perhaps it was simply a military move to make it easier to launch attacks on the hostile tribes, and once these enemies were punished, it was decided that they move back to the better fortified and supplied wall of Hadrian.

Ultimately, the Roman attempts to incorporate Scotland into the empire lasted right up until the end of the 3rd century A.D. Agricola's campaign, however, ultimately established the limit of Roman power in Britain, and most Roman efforts afterwards were concentrated not on expansion but on consolidating what they could control.

Londinium

By the time Agricola left Britain, it was an imperial province with a substantial military garrison comprising three legions: the II Augusta (stationed at Caerleon), the XX Valeria Victrix (stationed at Deva, now Chester), and the VI Victrix at Eburacum (stationed at what is now York). In addition, there were probably as many as 75 auxiliary units based predominantly in Wales and the north. Despite the wealth these garrisons brought to the areas in which they were based, they remained less Romanized than in the southern part of the island.

Local government was modeled on the cantonal system the Romans had developed in Gaul.

There were, by the end of the 1st century A.D., 16 distinct civitates, or civic communities. These were the Brigantes, with a capital at Aldborough; the Parisii, whose capital was Brough on Humber; the Silures, based in Caerwent; the Iceni at Caistor by Norwich; the Cantiaci at Canterbury; the Carvetii Durotiges at Dorchester; Dorset; the Dumnoni at Exeter; the Corieltauvi at Leicester; the Catuvellauni at Verulamium; the Atrbates at Silchester; the Belgae at Winchester; and the Cornovii at Wroxeter. In addition to these, there were three separate Roman coloniae at Colchester, Lincoln, and Glevum, now Gloucester. A fourth was added in the 3rd century A.D. at York. Londinium, the provincial capital, had an indeterminate status. The civitates were necessarily large and were further subdivided into as many as 70 lesser urban centers that served the countryside away from the main towns. None of the towns were particularly well-endowed with public buildings, though they were quite large for the time. In the 1st century A.D., there were no defences for the towns, though these were added in later years (why is unclear). The whole province was ruled from Londinium until the 3rd century A.D., when rule was divided between Londinium and York.

This essentially federal structure was run by a combination of different groups. There was no civil service—as the term would be understood today—in the empire at this time. The most senior office holders served periods of varying lengths as administrators in the provinces at specific periods in their careers. They progressed through a series of posts designed to give them military and administrative experience so that anyone reaching the highest levels of government had experience in all levels of the work undertaken in governing the empire. More minor officials were often seconded from the army. The emperor was the head of the whole system, and in him resided the power of imperator and commander-in-chief, though in theory, all of his power was granted at the discretion of the Senate. In practice, it was his control of the army that was the basis of his power.

Provinces like Britain that had substantial military garrisons were kept under the direct control of the emperor. In Britain, any governors appointed were the personal choices of the emperor and were invariably men that he thought he could trust. Governors in Britain were also expected to add to the appointing emperor's prestige through military success. The earliest governors of Britain were drawn from ex-consuls usually at the apex of their political careers who had proven to be skilled administrators. Consequently, in the early days of the Roman conquest, power was given to the emperor's personal representative rather than to institutions. As Roman rule was consolidated in the 1st century A.D., the scale of bureaucracy increased, and the subdivision of Britain is a classic example of how the role of the governor had been reduced and that of administrators had increased.

Before the conquest, the countryside was farmed extensively, and this remained the province's mainstay. Estimates suggest that 90% of the population lived on the land and continued to inhabit traditional farmsteads. About 1% of sites became villas, some of which were built almost immediately after the invasion of 43 A.D. and continued throughout the period of occupation.

Though they were small compared to those of the Mediterranean region, the existence of refined mosaics is evidence of the emergence of a wealthy and sophisticated native aristocracy embracing Roman culture. Britain's mineral deposits—especially gold, silver, and lead—continued to be exploited, and local craft-based production was encouraged by the Romans.

While Britain expanded its mining activities, food production, and manufactured goods, it did not really become a major supplier of anything vital to the Empire. It did, however, become even wealthier than it had been before the invasion, and the population enjoyed greatly increased standards of living. Moreover, the land was subjected to the normal asset stripping that came with a Roman conquest, especially in the earliest days following the invasion, when valuables were removed by the army and traders tried to cash in. There is no way of estimating the quantity of bullion taken from Britain as booty, but given the proliferation of gold and silver coinage and the presence of gold artefacts in Iron Age Britain, it must have been considerable.

The gold found in 1990 in Snettisham in Norfolk, for example, was enough to have paid a unit of Roman auxiliaries for an entire year, and that was from a minor, British site that dated back to before the Roman invasion. Metal resources were quickly exploited, and the Romans were mining lead and silver in the Mendips from 49 A.D. onward. Further mines were in operation soon after in Derbyshire, Yorkshire, and Wales. Gold mining was centered at Dolaucothi in South Wales, and by 75 A.D., the Romans were producing significant amounts of the precious metal. Copper, too, was mined from the earliest years after the invasion, though strangely, given the association of Britain with tin, there is little evidence of Roman exploitation of that metal. Iron was mined throughout the island, and the Romans simply took over existing workings, particularly in Sussex. The iron mined there was primarily used by the Roman fleet based at Boulogne.

The wealth taken by traders is a little easier to assess. Raw materials had been a lure for traders for many years, and the opportunity to expand this trade and those presented by access to native tribes as potential markets for goods was seized upon by many traders and merchants. The money brought into the country by the troops was certainly a factor in increasing trade. By the time of Agricola's departure, a full 10% of the Roman army was stationed in Britain, and the combined spending power of those troops was a major injection into the British economy. Initially, such an influx of cash would have destabilized the local economies which had been under the control of local chiefs, operating on a small scale. The deficit in goods at a time when buyers were available would have caused inflation and resulted in traders diverting goods to Britain to take advantage of the profits to be gained there. This unique set of circumstances is thought to explain the very rapid development of Londinium. As early as 50 A.D., the city had become the main center for overseas traders.

Roman goods spread rapidly and Samian wares, for example, can be found on a vast majority of indigenous sites from as early as 70 A.D. Whether the native products were eclipsed or whether they continued to be produced and sold in some kind of native parallel economy is not clear. After the conquest, Roman coinage spread throughout the island, though slowly at first. Shortages of coins and vast fluctuations in supply suggest that administrative decisions rather than economic necessity governed the supply of money. Initially, the Celtic system of barter and indebtedness seems to have been maintained for a considerable time as Roman coinage gradually became the foremost medium of exchange and trade.

After the conquest, art and culture developed as a hybrid of Celtic and classical Roman features. Various religions, so numerous in the Mediterranean world, spread to Britain in the wake of the polyglot army and its many administrators. Celtic gods continued to be worshipped, but they took on new forms, and the use of Romano-Celtic styles of temples and architecture increased, as did the adoption of Latin epigraphy on altars and dedications. The whole process of amalgamation was speeded up by the habit of Roman soldiers identifying local Celtic gods with members of the Roman pantheon. In this way, specific gods became associated with specific regions and civitates.

This coalescence of Celtic and Roman practice is exemplified by changes in British burial practices. Before the invasion, it was customary for the dead to be buried with animals, and often in wet places. This continued under the Romans, but Roman weapons and sculpture gradually began to be buried along with traditional grave goods. One of the more subtle—some might say insidious—ways in which the Romans altered native practice was in the promotion of the use of small religious objects. These are found widely in both military and civil sites of the period. The small clay figures of the gods are representative of deities such as Venus, but they were produced in such a way as to suggest the traditional mother goddess. A further Romanization of a very British tradition related to human heads. Prior to the invasion, the collecting of human heads and their display was common throughout the island. This practice evolved under the Romans into the use of sculptured stone heads and even bronze ones, many of which have been discovered in British rivers.

In art, new materials, mainly stone sculpture and mosaic, supplanted the Iron Age metalwork of the pre-invasion period. While the mosaics were not always the most exquisite, they did exhibit a specific innovatory blend of Celtic and Roman themes. These developments accelerated a process that had begun early on in the conquest, that of the change from a tribal society to one integrated into the Empire. The process was slow, but the spread of everyday items that exhibited Romano-British styles—as opposed to the localised designs that had been the hallmark of pre-invasion native society—certainly helped to reinforce the concept of one people under Rome.

Following the initial period of rapid importation of goods from the rest of the empire, Britain's economy gradually settled down, and industries established in the wake of the conquest thrived, taking an increasingly large share of the market. Roman pottery was replaced by high-quality local products, but in contrast to the situation before the Romans came, the products were now sold and distributed throughout the island rather than made available only in the immediate vicinity of their production.

With this new trade came improvements in communications systems. The improvements were both the result and the cause of increased trade and led to the positioning of centers of trade on navigable rivers to reduce costs. Roman military roads were always well-built, but the exploitation of Britain's rivers cut haulage costs in half, further stimulating trade. All in all, the early years of the Roman occupation proved beneficial to the local Britons and the Empire as well.

Unlike the planned cities the Romans deliberately founded in some parts of the country, Londinium emerged independently from the system of colonial rule and settlement. As a result, it was not founded near a large native settlement the Romans wanted to dominate, or in a position from which it could govern one of the provincial regions. Rather, it emerged at a transport intersection, growing through private endeavor until the authorities recognized its significance and chose to make use of this in governing the province.

Like many colonial Roman cities, Londinium was established in a raised position close to a river. The River Thames provided many of the things that a town needed, and of which Rome's urban planners were very aware; it was a source of water for drinking, cleaning and growing food, and it could also carry away sewage, a process now considered vital but which would often go neglected in British cities after the fall of Rome. Of course, it also provided a transport link in a time when travel was slow and often difficult. In antiquity, water transport was by far the easiest and most cost efficient way of transporting both bulk goods and people over long distances. Thus, a river terrace on the Thames' north bank and sand banks on the south side of the river provided ground on which to found the city.

For all of those reasons, the Thames proved instrumental in the rise of Londinium. As a transport link, it allowed both news and trade to flow in and out of the city. It was wide enough to carry a great deal of traffic, and Londinium soon developed long stretches of wharfs catering to this trade.

While this didn't make the city unique among settlements in Britain, its proximity to the continent did. It was a short haul from Europe to southeast England and so to the mouth of the Thames. With the easy journey from there upriver to London, it was the safest, most reliable way to bring goods into this growing imperial province. As a result, Londinium became Britain's central connection not just to the rest of the Empire but to its neighbors beyond the borders of Rome.

The ability to cross the Thames further cemented Londinium's position as a transport hub. Within years of the Roman invasion, a bridge had been built across the river, close to the location of the modern London Bridge. Between the key road connection this provided and the river connection of the Thames itself, it became an important center for travel and trade. Businessmen arrived to provide services to the soldiers and administrators serving the area, and soon a thriving city lay on what had previously been empty land. Even in the early days, this city was planned and organized by its residents, even possibly in part by foreign traders wanting a settlement in good order through which to work since Londinium was not an official colony. Growing to 330 acres, it was soon the largest city in Britain, a status it achieved shortly before being burned down in Boudica's native revolt.

Politics may also have played a part in Londinium's location and growth. Lying away from the regional centers and the power of local tribal elites, it was in neutral territory, which made it easier for traders from there to deal with all the different factions still existing within conquered Britain.

Such was Londinium's growth that it quickly attracted official attention. A garrison of troops was based in the city (initially in temporary forts while a more permanent base was built), the procurator quickly moved to the town, and the governor almost certainly did so as well. Thus, by the end of the 1st century B.C., Londinium was the de facto capital of the province of Britannia, if not the official capital. Public buildings were going up to serve the population and provide a sense of Roman civilization, and it was a major center of military, administrative and commercial activities. On a site that had been uninhabited only 60 years before, there now stood a city that would come to dominate England for the next 2,000 years.

The citizens of Londinium paid taxes, along with other Britons, to support the administration governing the province and the troops guarding it. This included a poll tax and an inheritance tax on estates. As a major trade center, Londinium would also have had a lot of customs duties collected - taxes on goods moved from one district of the Empire to another - as well as sales taxes on specific transactions (such as the sale of slaves).

Londinium was a center of production as well as of trade. There were all sorts of craftsmen and manufacturers working in the city, from potters providing everyday necessities to jewelers keeping the rich in style. The members of many professions were formed into guilds, banding together to protect their self-interest by maintaining standards and working together.

The most common manufactured goods were pottery, which were used for storage, kitchenware and eating. Even the dead made use of pottery, which the locals turned into grave goods and cremation containers. Though the army had its own potteries, it also bought ceramics from local manufacturers, helping the industry to develop.

Since pottery was such an essential of daily life, it was usually produced and used locally, and most was in the simple 'grey kitchenware' style. Londinium had small local producers, such as the Sugar Loaf Court potter who served a small neighborhood in the 1st century, but larger industries, such as that producing black burnished pottery in the Thames Estuary, also kept the city supplied.

Some pottery was traded over longer distances. Mortars were produced by specialist manufacturers and imported from elsewhere in Britain or the continent, and amphorae were imported along with the goods they contained, the luxury foods and wines that came from the Mediterranean. High quality goods such as Gaulish samian wares were brought in for the wealthy.

The next most important type of portable goods were metalwork. Much of the metal was recycled, consisting of old and broken items being melted down and recrafted to suit current needs, but Britain also had major sources of lead and iron, and the latter provided a ready source of new material for ironmongers. Furnaces were used to smelt the metal, with the smoke drifting out into the surrounding streets. Large manufacturing firms used slaves as staff, allowing them to produce large volumes of goods at low costs. Manufacturing buildings, then as now, would have been noisy, smelly places to live near.

As well as businesses, forts had their own workshops, and the garrison of Londinium would have been no exception. Armor, weapons, artillery parts and even nails for use in building work were manufactured to ensure that the needs of the military were always met. With its own core of craftsmen and manufacturers, the Roman army never made itself dependent on contracts or private producers; they were their own military-industrial complex.

Metal workers produced luxury items as well as practical ones. In the 1st century, there was a goldsmith close to the likely location of the governor's palace in Londinium.

Manufacturers also contributed to the construction of Londinium, producing bricks and tiles. At least one tile production facility existed in the city, making resources for residents and the surrounding area. These were not products that were shipped far (due to their bulky and fragile nature), so it made sense for the city to produce its own, just as villas apparently ran their own kilns during construction. Some tiles were distinctively marked, especially those used in chimney flues; they might be marked with the tiler's name, a manufacturing mark, or a decorative scene. That said, most tiles were plain, with criss-crossing strips that provided a better grip for the mortar.

All manner of goods flowed through Londinium, including pottery, glass and amphorae of food transported from Gaul, Italy and beyond. Even before the Roman invasion, Britain's economy was based on exporting raw materials such as grain, animals and iron in exchange for manufactured goods from the continent. It seems likely that this pattern continued throughout the Roman occupation. Londinium would therefore have seen goods coming in from the more distant parts of the island and being bought up by merchants. The merchants would then take them away down the river and out across the North Sea to the rest of the Empire. Meanwhile, luxuries such as glassware and jewelry flowed in along with other manufactured items, to be bought primarily by the elite.

These imports included not just enduring luxuries but also perishable foodstuffs from across the empire and particularly the Mediterranean, and care was taken to preserve these once they arrived in the city. A special warehouse built in a pit near Londinium's docks was probably designed to help these foods last. In an age before modern refrigeration methods, preservation was a substantial undertaking in itself, and the warehouse is a sign of the lengths traders and customers would go to for these luxuries.

Though Londinium was built to make use of the River Thames for transport, much of its water supply came from other sources. Wells were dug, and by the 60s chain-driven bucket systems were drawing water at what is now Gresham Street. Iron links dragged wooden buckets up a timber lined well nearly twenty feet deep, powered by a large wooden wheel rotating at the top. This was a more effective method than simple wells for drawing up the vast quantities of water that were needed for the city's industries and public services.

This was soon replaced by one of the most iconic of Roman constructions - an aqueduct system. Bringing in water from outside the town, a system of pipes and sluices controlled the flow of water into tanks on pillars at street corners. Rather than filling the tanks and then stopping, the system kept a constant flow of water moving through, to ensure that the supply was fresh and the pressure on the system at a suitable level to keep it moving without breaking pipes or outlets.

A sewage system was used to carry waste water out of the city and into the river, though it may not have been a sewage system as we would recognize it today. Though impressive underground systems are known to have existed in York and Rome, in Londinium the waste may have been carried away as much by open ditches as by underground pipes. These ditches were not even built for the sole purpose of carrying away sewage - they also carried out the vital task of carrying away excess rainwater and preventing flooding.

After the initial burst of intense activity in the 1st century, trade into and out of Londinium gradually dropped. It was still a major trade center, but as trade and commerce became established elsewhere in the province and trade spread out from that single critical center, activity became a little less intense. This was increasingly notable from the 3rd century onward as changes in military life led to changes in the economy. The British garrisons were more and more made up of men born locally, and they were often the descendants of those who had settled in the area after their own military service. This meant that the army, a major market for foreign luxuries, was no longer as attached to the Mediterranean culture and diet. The troops were also increasingly paid in provisions gathered locally rather than in cash, and this meant that there was less money around to be spent on imports. Indeed, Londinium's decline as an economic powerhouse came along with Britain's gradual detachment from Rome, proof that its economic fate was tied to the empire whose traders had founded it.

The period of the Roman invasions of Britain and the initial conquest of the island was a traumatic one in British history. For the first time, the greater part of the island became part of a world ruled by an alien, Mediterranean culture. It was a time when the outside world stimulated extensive change, though native characteristics continued to play a prominent part in moulding society. The lives of many people changed, but it is clear that some people's lives changed far more than others. Many of the changes were the direct result of the Roman occupation while others evolved to meet the new economic and social situation resulting from the conquest. Society gradually became less and less dominated by tribal divisions, and this coincided with the development of the concept of Britannia as a single place.

This breakdown in the regional system, which was so solidly entrenched in pre-invasion British society, was accompanied by increasing social and economic differentiation as wealth and power became more and more concentrated in the hands of those who most enthusiastically embraced Roman culture and values. This elite became an integral part of a culture that networked with their social and economic equals in other parts of the Roman Empire. Ordinary members of the population became increasingly dependent on this new class. The military installations the Romans installed as part of their pursuit of pacification removed all political power from the natives. As the army settled in Britain, they inevitably became somewhat naturalised, reflecting a mixture of Roman and native characteristics, while remaining highly Romanized. Beyond the frontiers following Agricola's campaign, these tribes remained, for the most part, unaffected by Rome, except when Rome decided to undertake one of its periodic assaults on their territory. Gradually, even these areas fell under Roman influence, if not direct control, and contact with the Romans led to changes within their societies.

In 55 B.C., Britain was a relatively prosperous and populated land and should have been able to ward off the initial attacks of the Romans relatively easily, if only they had unified under a single leader. The reality, however, was that the regionally-based tribes were far too independently minded, the regional economies far too insular, and attitudes and loyalties far too parochial for them to ever seriously consider banding together for a common cause, even if that cause was their own survival. Their whole way of life was based on local groups looking after specific interests, taking advantage of any weakness in their neighbours. It was in this context that the Romans found they could exploit local rivalries, first supporting one local king against another, then changing sides to enable them to gain control over a population that, if they had had to rely on military might alone, would have proven impossible.

Military might, however, was a crucial factor in the Roman success. As in other conquests, the discipline of the Legions, the tactics employed, and the military genius exhibited by some of its commanders meant the Roman army was more than a match for any contemporary foe. Only a unified British defiance would have had any chance of repelling Roman invasions, but that was never a realistic possibility.

The Jewish Wars

After Herod the Great's death, Herod Archelaus now found himself ruler of what had been historic Judea, as well as Samaria and Idumea, but he proved himself such a bad monarch that his subjects, many of whom were anti-Roman, appealed to Augustus to remove him. Augustus accepted the pleas and removed Archelaus in 6 A.D. The other two brothers fared better, with Antipas ruling Galilee until his dismissal by Caligula in 39 A.D. Philip ruled in the northeast until his death.[239]

Judea, Samaria, and Idumea were placed under direct Roman administration.[240] The new Roman province was primarily of importance as a base from which to control both land and coastal routes to the breadbasket of Egypt. It was also a significant bulwark against Parthian excursions. Caesarea was made the capital, and Quirinius became the Legate or Governor responsible for both Syria and Judea. Judea occupied a somewhat ambiguous position in the Roman system as it was neither an Imperial nor a Senatorial Province but had a status as an adjunct or satellite of Syria.[241]

Judea was governed by a prefect, normally a knight of the Equestrian Order, rather than a former consul or praetor of senatorial rank. This may have been because, in relative terms, the tax revenues from this area were small and attracted little interest from the top echelons of Roman society. One of these prefects was Pontius Pilate, who had responsibility for Judea from 26-36 A.D. While the taxes raised may not have been great, they were still bitterly resented by the Jewish population and the 1st levying of the tax under the new system was opposed by the Zealots.[242] The Jews still had a modicum of independence under the new arrangements and were allowed to try offenders under their own laws until 28 A.D. The province of Judea was divided into five districts or conclaves based on Jerusalem, Gadara, Amathus, Jericho and Sepphoris, mirroring earlier administrative systems. Caiaphas was appointed as one of the high priests by Valerius Gratus in 18 A.D., but both of them were removed by the Syrian Legate, Lucius Vitellius, in 36 A.D.

Up until 27 A.D., the province was relatively calm but after 37, Judea attracted the attention of Caligula, who had embarked on a zealous program of enforcing the worship of Roman gods, including himself. He had statues of himself erected throughout the Empire and insisted that he was revered in the same way as other Roman deities.

---

[239] Josephus, *Antiquities*, xvii. 188.
[240] *A History of the Jewish People*. H.H. Ben Sasson (ed.) (1976). Harvard University Press.
[241] P. 247, *A History of the Jewish People*. H.H. Ben Sasson (ed.) (1976). Harvard University Press.
[242] Josephus, *Antiquities*, xviii.

Louis le Grand's picture of a bust of Caligula

Caligula's paranoia in relation to the Governor of Egypt, Flaccus, resulted in him sending Agrippa, the grandson of Herod who had been brought up in Rome and had spent much of his time in the company of Caligula and Claudius, to Egypt. His friendship with the two men who were to become emperors gave him a disproportionate influence in Rome and helped, at least while he was alive, to mitigate Roman attitudes to his people, who were becoming increasingly aggressive in their defiance of Roman attempts to undermine the basic principles of their faith. Having arrived in Egypt to check up on Flaccus and ensure that all subjects were paying due respect to Caligula, Agrippa was openly mocked as the King of the Jews by the Greek population in Alexandria. Flaccus, in an attempt to placate Caligula and reassure him of his loyalty, had statues of the emperor placed in all the city's synagogues.[243] Riots broke out and Caligula removed Flaccus and had him executed.

The incident raised tensions in the whole area, and in 39 A.D., Herod Antipas was accused by

---

[243] Philo f Alexandria, *Flaccus*, vi.43.

Agrippa of fermenting rebellion against Rome. Caligula promptly exiled him and handed over his territory in Galilee to Agrippa. Riots broke out again in Alexandria in 40 A.D. between Greeks and Jews, with the Greeks angered at what they saw as Jewish refusal to honor the emperor. The disorder spread to Jamnia, where Jews tore down an altar. A furious Caligula ordered that a statue of himself be placed in the Temple in Jerusalem. The Governor of Syria at the time, Publius Petronius, was so fearful of the consequences of carrying out this order that he delayed for nearly a year, during which time Agrippa managed to persuade the emperor to reverse his decision.[244]

At this point, Jerusalem was the only city in the Empire that did not have a statue of the Emperor.

In 41 A.D., Agrippa was declared King of Judea by Claudius, to some extent restoring the Herodian dynasty. However, Agrippa's rule was short-lived, as he died in 44 A.D. Claudius took Judea back under direct Roman rule, although Agrippa's son, Agrippa II, was allowed to keep the title of king. He was the seventh and last of the Herodians but never exercised any political power.

In 46 A.D., another insurrection broke out, this time led by two brothers, Jacob and Simon, and it lasted for two years. The Romans put the revolt down with their characteristic cruelty, and both brothers were executed. The reality was, however, that Jewish antipathy towards their Roman masters was now so entrenched that even if attempts had been made to placate the population, in all likelihood the series of revolts that now broke out, beginning with the Great Revolt, could not have been avoided. Rome simply would not accept that part of a province should be allowed to go its own way in terms of adherence to Roman norms, and Jews could and would not accept practices that fundamentally went against their basic beliefs.

Josephus records that the specific incident that provoked the Great Rebellion happened in Caesarea in 66 A.D., when Greek merchants insisted on sacrificing birds in front of a local synagogue.[245] Long standing antagonism between the Greek and Hellenized population and Jews broke into fierce violence which the Roman garrison did nothing to quell. One of the Jewish Temple clerks, Eliezar ben Hanania, in retaliation, refused to pray for the emperor, and protests against Roman taxation quickly became enmeshed with protests about Roman insistence on sacrifices to the emperor and general disaffection with the Hellenized population. There were attacks on Roman citizens and sympathizers, and Roman troops took 17 talents, claiming that amount was owed to the emperor.[246]

---

[244] *Antiquities of the Jews*, 18. PAA.D. – Project on Ancient Cultural Engagement.
https://pace.webhosting.rug.nl/york/york/index.htm
[245] *The Jewish War II*. PAA.D. – Project on Ancient Cultural Engagement.
https://pace.webhosting.rug.nl/york/york/index.htm
[246] Josephus, *Of the War*, II.

The Jews, in mockery of the governor, Florus, who had ordered the theft, handed baskets around to collect money for the "poor" official. Florus did not take this mockery well and ordered troops into Jerusalem to arrest the leaders, after which he had them scourged and crucified. Some of those crucified were Roman citizens who were exempt from crucifixion, and

Florus's actions proved to be the catalyst for nationalist factions to organize themselves and overrun the Roman garrison. The puppet King Agrippa II and his wife Berenice fled the city. Rebels quickly took control of the city and then moved out into the rest of Judea, killing Romans, soldiers and ordinary citizens wherever they found them. All Roman symbols were destroyed, and one of the rebel factions, the Sicarii, surprised the Roman garrison at Masada and took over the fortress.

The Romans now took steps to impose their authority in Judea. Cestius Gallus, the Legate in Syria, led 36,000 troops to restore order. The Romans captured Barbata and Sepphoris, where the Judeans retreated to Atzmon without a fight. They were besieged there and totally defeated. The victorious Romans then went on to take Acre Caesarea and Jaffa, where over 8,000 were massacred. Lydda and Antipatras quickly fell, and Jerusalem was besieged. It is not known why Gallus ordered a retreat to the coast, but this invigorated the rebels, who defeated the Romans at the Battle of Beth Horon. This defeat came as a complete surprise to the Roman hierarchy and came to be seen as one of Rome's worst military losses, as approximately 6,000 Roman troops were killed and thousands more wounded.[247] Most shocking from a Roman perspective was the fact that the Fulminata Legion lost its eagle.

Gallus abandoned his troops and fled back to Syria. The victorious Judeans were made up of numerous factions including Pharisees, Sadducees and Sicarii and taking advantage of this rare moment of unity pushed on to Ashkelon. This proved to be a step too far, and the campaign ended in disaster with over 8,000 Judeans lost to the small Roman garrison holding the town. Within the walls of the city, the Jewish residents were massacred.

The defeat at Ashkelon had lastings effects on Judean strategy. The Jews now decided to concentrate on a defensive war, fortifying and holding key points within the country.[248] At the same time as this change in tactics, the fragile Jewish alliance was breaking apart. After the victory at Beth Horon a Judean Free Government had been formed but the Sicarii tried to take over the city. They failed and were expelled, retreating to their stronghold at Masada to be joined later by a smaller faction led by Simon bar Giora.

Emperor Nero appointed Vespasian to replace the disgraced Gallus, and in 67 A.D. he arrived with his son and an army of over 60,000 men. Vespasian began his campaign in Galilee, where Judean forces were divided into two factions, one loyal to Jerusalem, led by Josephus, and the

---

[247] Josephus, *Of the War*, II.
[248] Josephus, *War of the Jews* II.

other made up of Zealots, comprising mainly poor fishermen and farmers. Vespasian quickly took numerous towns with little resistance, though one or two did provide some ultimately futile opposition. Josephus provided detailed information on a number of these sieges and in particular that of Gischala, a Zealot stronghold. The Zealots abandoned the defense of the town mid siege and made their way to Jerusalem. It took Vespasian only until 68 A.D. to crush all opposition in the north and, according to Josephus, 100,000 Jews were killed or enslaved.[249]

A number of Jews did manage to escape Vespasian's wrath and made their way to Jaffa, where they rebuilt the walls that had been destroyed by Gallus. They also built ships and took to piracy in an attempt to disrupt Roman supply routes. Josephus noted, "They built themselves a great many piratical shops and turned pirate upon the seas near to Syria and Phoenicia and Egypt and made those seas unnavigable to all men."[250]

The Zealots who had escaped the carnage of Galilee made their way to Jerusalem which was quickly cut off from the outside world by the Romans. Within the city the numerous factions rendered the city ungovernable. The Zealots took control of sections of the city while other factions controlled others.

A fierce civil war broke out during which the Zealots and the Sicarii took every opportunity to murder anyone who suggested negotiation with, or surrender to, the Romans. The Zealots proclaimed that the Judean Free Government had made a deal with the Romans to surrender the city and asked for help. Approximately 20,000 heeded the call and assisted the Zealots and the Sicarii to execute various members of the Free Judean Government, including Joseph ben Gurion and Ananus ben Ananus, their leaders. Josephus reported that over 12,000 were killed in this internal conflict. Those Zealots who had gone to Masada were encouraged by the success of their compatriots in Jerusalem and came out of their fortress to pillage Idumea.

While all of this was going on, Vespasian had not been idle. He had systematically taken Judean strongholds in Afeq, Lydda and Javneh, as well as retaking Jaffa. By July 69 A.D. the Romans had retaken Gophna, Akrabta Bet-El, Ephraim and Hebron.

In Rome, events too were moving apace and changing the situation dramatically. In the middle of 68 A.D., Nero was deposed and committed suicide, and his successor Galba was murdered within a few months by Otho leading to a civil war and the Year of the Four Emperors. Vespasian was proclaimed emperor by his troops and hurried back to Rome, leaving his son, Titus, to carry on the campaign in Judea.

Before his departure for Rome, Vespasian had not wanted to besiege Jerusalem just yet. Despite their chronic internecine warfare, the factions holding the city were well-armed and still

---

[249] 'The Population of Western Palestine in the Roman-Byzantine Period' by M. Broshi (1979). *Bulletin of the American Schools of Oriental Research*, 1-10.
[250] Josephus, *War of the Jews* III.

had many troops. Vespasian feared that the casualty rate would be too high.

However, after Vespasian left, his more impetuous son, Titus, decided to besiege Jerusalem, anyway. He began the siege just before Passover in 69 with four legions. He had great initial success and was able to take down the first and second walls near the Jaffa Gate (one of the eight ancient gates of Old Jerusalem, which is unique in that it is at right angles to its adjoining wall), but then the desperate Jews were able to unite and put up stiff resistance. Titus then settled in for a long siege.

He built a wall around the city to prevent food from coming in. Then he launched a sneak attack that took the Antonia Fort (a Herod-built fort on the eastern wall) near the end of July. He leveled it so that he could bring in siege materials against the Temple.

Both John and Simon responded to the desperateness of the situation by executing anyone they deemed a traitor. This caused many people to flee the city during the siege, weakening the defenders even further. It is unlikely that Judea would have been able to maintain its independence forever against Rome at that empire's height of power, but the infighting sped up the process of reconquest, and made the bloodletting and societal damage much worse. Though information about the personalities involved comes from Josephus, who was hostile to his former compatriots, the same pattern of ruthless rule and infighting was recorded in the Bar Kokhba Revolt, decades after Josephus' death.

Titus then sent Josephus to negotiate with the defenders, but this resulted in a sneak attack from them in which Titus himself was nearly captured. In late August, the final assault began. It was at this time that the Temple was destroyed. Josephus claims that Titus did not want to destroy it, but wanted to convert it to a Pagan temple. He blamed its burning on angry Roman soldiers instead. This could, however, have been simply a way to cover Titus' ruthlessness, particularly in light of the fact that Roman soldiers were well aware that breaking discipline in battle and disobeying a general's orders could result in the severest discipline if one survived.

The sack itself was violent and prolonged, lasting for weeks. Many innocent civilians were killed, though some escaped into the tunnels. Simon bar Giora tried this route, but ran out of food and was forced out and captured. The city was finally completely taken by September 7.

Josephus blamed the revolt largely upon dissension between factions of Syrian Greeks and wealthier Jews, as well as the favoritism and tyranny of the previous Roman procurator: "It was in Caesarea that the events took place which led to the final war. This magnificent city was inhabited by two races – the Syrian Greeks, who were heathens, and the Jews. The two parties violently contended for the preeminence. The Jews were the more wealthy; but the Roman soldiery, levied chiefly in Syria, took part with their countrymen. Tumults and bloodshed disturbed the streets. At this time, a procurator named Gessius Florus was appointed, and he, by his barbarities, forced the Jews to begin the war in the twelfth year of the reign of Nero and the seventeenth of the reign of Agrippa.." (Josephus, *The Fall of the Temple of Jerusalem*, par. 4).

According to Josephus, a case of ritual pollution and interreligious conflict sparked off a pre-existing feud in Caesarea, an ancient city built by Herod the Great the previous century on the coast, near what is now Tel Aviv. It was the administrative center of the Roman province of Judea and survived the revolt, albeit as a mostly-non-Jewish city:

> "But the occasion of the war was by no means proportioned to those heavy calamities that it brought upon us. The fatal flame finally broke out from the old feud at Caesarea. The decree of Nero had assigned the magistracy of that city to the Greeks. It happened that the Jews had a synagogue, the ground around which belonged to a Greek. For this spot, the Jews offered a much higher price than it was worth. It was refused, and, to annoy them as much as possible, the owner set up some mean buildings and shops upon it, and so made the approach to the synagogue as narrow and difficult as possible. The more impetuous of the Jewish youth interrupted the workmen. Then the men of greater wealth and influence, and among them John, a publican, collected the large sum of eight talents and sent it as a bribe to Florus, that he might stop the building. He received the money, made great promises, and at once departed for Sebaste from Caesarea. His object was to leave full scope for the riot.
>
> "On the following day, while the Jews were crowding to the synagogue, a citizen of Caesarea outraged them by oversetting an earthen vessel in the way, over which he sacrificed birds, as done by the law in cleansing lepers, and thus he implied that the Jews were a leprous people. The more violent Jews, furious at the insult, attacked the Greeks, who were already in arms. The Jews were worsted, took up the books of the law, and fled to Narbata, about seven miles distant." (Ibid, par. 5-6).

Josephus was highly critical of what he perceived as the fanaticism of the Jewish revolutionaries, of whom he had until recently been part. He was especially harsh toward John of Giscala, Eleazar ben Simon and Simon bar Giora. He may have been influenced by Jewish hostility toward his brother Mathias (who had been under suspicion that he was a collaborator with the Romans) when Mathias was in Jerusalem prior to the siege. Josephus ascribed many atrocities to the revolutionaries and blamed them at least in part for escalating events beyond the point of reconciliation. He cast the Revolt as a situation where outrage was met with reprisal and then further reprisal, with bloody massacres on both sides over what had originally been relatively minor incidents, such as the sacrifice of the birds in Caesarea:

> "And now great calamities and slaughters came on the Jews. On the very same day, two dreadful massacres happened. In Jerusalem, the Jews fell on Netilius and the band of Roman soldiers whom he commanded after they had made terms and had surrendered, and all were killed except the commander himself, who

supplicated for mercy and even agreed to submit to circumcision. On that very day and hour, as though Providence had ordained it, the Greeks in Caesarea rose and slew over 20,000 Jews, and so the city was emptied of its Jewish inhabitants. For Florus caught those who escaped, and sent them to the galleys.

"By this tragedy, the whole nation was driven to madness. The Jews rose and laid waste the villages all around many cites in Syria, and they descended on Gadara, Hippo and Gaulonitus and burnt and destroyed many places. Sebaste and Ashkelon they seized without resistance, and they razed Anthedon and Gaza to the ground.

"When thus the disorder in all Syria had become terrible, Cestius Gallus, the Roman commander at Antioch, marched with an army to Ptolemais and overran all Galilee and invested Jerusalem, expecting that it would be surrendered by means of a powerful party within the walls.

"But the plot was discovered, and the conspirators were flung headlong from the walls, and an attack by Cestius on the north side of the Temple was repulsed with great loss. Seeing the whole country around in arms, and the Jews swarming on all the heights, Cestius withdrew his army by night, leaving 400 of his bravest men to mount guard in the camp and to display their ensigns, that the Jews might be deceived.

"But at break of day it was discovered that the camp was deserted by the army, and the Jews rushed to the assault and slew all the Roman band." (Ibid, par. 10-14).

Josephus was especially critical of extremist bands like the famous Zealots, who attacked any of their own countrymen whom they perceived to be traitors even more vigorously than they did the Romans, and failed to respect previous Jewish religious and political hierarchies: "Large numbers of these evil men stole into the city and grew into a daring faction, who robbed houses openly, and many of the most eminent citizens were murdered by these Zealots, as they were called, from their pretence that they had discovered a conspiracy to betray the city to the Romans. They dismissed many of the Sanhedrin from office, and appointed men of the lowest degree, who would support them in their violence, till the leaders of the people became slaves to their will." (Ibid, par. 23).

Josephus was of the opinion that more Jews were killing each other in what was as much a civil war as a revolt, than they were the Romans or the Romans were killing them: "At length, resistance was provoked, led by Ananus, oldest of the chief priests, a man of great wisdom, and the robber Zealots took refuge in the Temple and fortified it more strongly than before. They appointed as high priest one Phanias, a coarse and clownish rustic, utterly ignorant of the sacerdotal duties, who, when decked in the robes of office, caused great derision. This sport and pastime for the Zealots caused the more religious people to shed tears of grief and shame, and the citizens, unable to endure such insolence, rose in great numbers to avenge the outrage on the sacred rites. Thus, a fierce civil war broke out in which very many were slain." (Ibid, par. 24).

A bust believed to depict Josephus

A bust of Titus

A bust of Vespasian

Despite his relatively pro-Roman stance, Josephus went to great lengths describing the atrocities inflicted during the final assault:

"Thus, the fight continued for three days, till Titus a second time entered the wall. He threw down all the northern part and strongly garrisoned the towers of the south. The strong heights of Sion, the citadel of the Antonia, and the fortified Temple still held out. Titus, eager to save so magnificent a place, resolved to refrain for a few days from the attack, in order that the minds of the besieged might be affected by their woes, and that the slow results of famine might operate. He reviewed his army in full armor and they received their pay in view of the city, the battlements being thronged by spectators during this splendid defiling, who looked on in terror and dismay.

"The famine increased and the misery of the weaker was aggravated by seeing the stronger obtaining food. All natural affection was extinguished, husbands and wives, parents and children snatching the last morsel from each other. Many wretched men were caught by the Romans prowling in the ravines by night to pick up food and these were scourged, tortured and crucified. This was done to terrify the rest, and it went on till there was not wood enough for crosses.

"Terrible crimes were committed in the city. The aged high-priest, Matthias, was accused of holding communication with the enemy. Three of his sons were killed in his presence, and he was executed in sight of the Romans, together with 16 other members of the Sanhedrin. The famine grew so woeful that a woman devoured the body of her own child. At length, after fierce fighting, the Antonia was scaled, and Titus ordered its demolition.

"Titus now promised that the Temple should be spared if the defenders would come forth and fight in any other place, but John and the Zealots refused to surrender it. For several days, the outer cloisters and outer court were attacked with rams, but the immense and compact stones resisted the blows. As many soldiers were slain in seeking to storm the cloisters, Titus ordered the gates to be set on fire. Through that night and the next day, the flames raged through the cloisters. Then, in order to save the Temple itself, he ordered the fire to be quenched. On the tenth of August, the same day of the year on which Nebuchadnezzar destroyed the Temple built by Solomon, the cry was heard that the Temple was on fire. The Jews, with cries of grief and rage, grasped their swords and rushed to take revenge on their enemies or perish in the ruins.

"The slaughter was continued while the fire raged. Soon, no part was left but a small portion of the outer cloisters, where 6,000 people had taken refuge, led by a false prophet who had there promised that God would deliver His people in His Temple. The soldiers set the building on fire and all perished. Titus next spent 18 days in preparations for the attack on the upper city, which was then speedily captured. And now the Romans were not disposed to display any mercy, night alone putting an end to the carnage. During the whole of this siege of Jerusalem, 1,100,000 were slain, and the prisoners numbered 97,000." (Ibid, par. 34-8).

Tacitus wrote about the prelude to the fall of Jerusalem toward the end of his *Histories*, where they break off. In keeping with his belief that the Jews were barbarians with strange customs, he attributed their destruction to their failure to expiate their cultural sins via ritual:

"[5.10] Yet the endurance of the Jews lasted till Gessius Florus was procurator. In his time, the war broke out. Cestius Gallus, legate of Syria, who attempted to crush it, had to fight several battles, generally with ill-success. Cestius dying, either in the course of nature, or from vexation, Vespasian was sent by Nero, and by help of his good fortune, his high reputation, and his excellent subordinates, succeeded within the space of two summers in occupying with his victorious army the whole of the level country and all the cities, except Jerusalem. The following year had been wholly taken up with civil strife, and had passed, as far as the Jews were concerned, in inaction. Peace having been established in Italy, foreign affairs were once more remembered. Our indignation was heightened by the circumstance that the Jews alone had not submitted. At the same time, it was held to be more expedient, in reference to the possible results and contingencies of the new reign that Titus should remain with the army. Accordingly he pitched his camp, as I have related, before the walls of Jerusalem, and displayed his legions in order of battle.

"[5.11] The Jews formed their line close under their walls, whence, if successful, they might venture to advance, and where, if repulsed, they had a refuge at hand. The cavalry with some light infantry was sent to attack them, and fought without any decisive result. Shortly afterwards, the enemy retreated. During the following days, they fought a series of engagements in front of the gates, till they were driven within the walls by continual defeats. The Romans then began to prepare for an assault. It seemed beneath them to await the result of famine. The army demanded the more perilous alternative, some prompted by courage, many by sheer ferocity and greed of gain. Titus himself had Rome with all its wealth and pleasures before his eyes. Jerusalem must fall at once, or it would delay his enjoyment of them. But the commanding situation of the city had been strengthened by enormous works which would have been a thorough defence even for level ground. Two hills of great height were fenced in by walls which had been skilfully obliqued or bent inwards, in such a manner that the flank of an assailant was exposed to missiles. The rock terminated in a precipice; the towers were raised to a height of 60 feet, where the hill lent its aid to the fortifications, where the ground fell, to a height of 120. They had a marvellous appearance, and to a distant spectator, seemed to be of uniform elevation. Within were other walls surrounding the palace, and, rising to a conspicuous height, the tower Antonia, so called by Herod, in honor of Marcus Antonius.

"[5.12] The temple resembled a citadel, and had its own walls, which were more laboriously constructed than the others. Even the colonnades with which it was surrounded formed an admirable outwork. It contained an inexhaustible spring; there were subterranean excavations in the hill, and tanks and cisterns for holding rainwater. The founders of the state had foreseen that frequent wars would result from the singularity of its customs, and so had made every provision against the most protracted siege. After the capture of their city by Pompey, experience and apprehension taught them much. Availing themselves of the sordid policy of the Claudian era to purchase the right of fortification, they raised in time of peace such walls as were suited for war. Their numbers were increased by a vast rabble collected from the overthrow of the other cities. All the most obstinate rebels had escaped into the place, and perpetual seditions were the consequence. There were three generals, and as many armies. Simon held the outer and larger circuit of walls. John, also called Bargioras, occupied the middle city. Eleazar had fortified the temple. John and Simon were strong in numbers and equipment, Eleazar in position. There were continual skirmishes, surprises, and incendiary fires, and a vast quantity of corn was burnt. Before long, John sent some emissaries, who, under pretence of sacrificing, slaughtered Eleazar and his partisans, and gained possession of the temple. The city was thus divided between two factions, till, as the Romans approached, war with the foreigner brought about a reconciliation.

"[5.13] Prodigies had occurred, which this nation, prone to superstition, but hating all religious rites, did not deem it lawful to expiate by offering and sacrifice. There had been seen hosts joining battle in the skies, the fiery gleam of arms, the temple illuminated by a sudden radiance from the clouds. The doors of the inner shrine were suddenly thrown open, and a voice of more than mortal tone was heard to cry that the Gods were departing. At the same instant, there was a mighty stir as of departure. Some few put a fearful meaning on these events, but in most there was a firm persuasion, that in the ancient records of their priests was contained a prediction of how at this very time, the East was to grow powerful, and rulers, coming from Judaea, were to acquire universal empire. These mysterious prophecies had pointed to Vespasian and Titus, but the common people, with the usual blindness of ambition, had interpreted these mighty destinies of themselves, and could not be brought even by disasters to believe the truth. I have heard that the total number of the besieged, of every age and both sexes, amounted to 600,000. All who were able bore arms, and a number, more than proportionate to the population, had the courage to do so. Men and women showed equal resolution, and life seemed more terrible than death, if they were to be forced to leave their country. Such was this city and nation; and Titus Caesar, seeing that the position forbad an assault or any of the more rapid operations of war, determined to proceed by earthworks and covered approaches. The legions had their respective duties assigned to them, and there was a cessation from fighting, till all the inventions, used in ancient warfare, or devised by modern ingenuity for the reduction of cities, were constructed. " (Tacitus, *Histories*, 5.10-13.)

Despite the decisive sack of Jerusalem, the thorough destruction of the Temple (though the Romans were unable, or unwilling, to destroy the massive walls of the Temple Mount, which partly survive to this day), and great loss of life (Josephus claimed a million Jews were killed in the sack of the city, though this seems quite unlikely), the Jewish resistance was far from over. Instead, it moved out to the countryside. Its final spasm would instead come at Masada.

The Siege of Masada proved to be one of the final events of the war, lasting from 73-74 A.D. Its importance lies in the ending, which has become such an iconic element in Jewish history. The mass suicide of the Sicarii defendants is still controversial to this day, with many Jews seeing their actions as an example of heroic resistance to foreign occupation. Masada is consequently regarded as a place of reverence, but others regard the suicides as evidence of an unhealthy extremism and refusal to compromise.

The siege was chronicled in minute detail by Josephus, who had been captured by the Romans during the Siege of Yodfat. He was freed by Vespasian and thereafter chronicled the Roman campaign.[251] Josephus confirmed that the fortress at Masada had been built by the Hasmoneans and strengthened by Herod the Great. The Sicarii, who had taken the fort from the Romans garrisoned there, were led by Eleazar ben Ya'ir.[252] They were joined by those Sicarii expelled

---
[251] P. 186-298. *Flavius Josephus; Selections from His Works* (ed.) A. Wasserstein (1974). New York.
[252] P. 52, 'The Roman Siege Works of Masada, Israel' by I.A. Richmond (1962). *The Journal of Roman Studies*,

from Jerusalem and others who escaped the Roman conquest of the city. In 72 A.D. Lucius Flavius Silva led a force of some 15,000, including 8,000 seasoned troops, to besiege the citadel. The defenders at that time numbered 960. As at Jerusalem, the Romans decided to be patient and built a wall around Masada before beginning the construction of a siege ramp against the western face of the plateau. The whole project involved moving thousands of tons of stones and earth. While the work was backbreaking, the end result was never in doubt, particularly as the defenders did not try to disrupt the progress of the ramp.

The ramp was finally completed in the spring of 73 A.D. A siege tower, complete with a battering ram, was built and slowly moved up the ramp while Roman troops assaulted the wall of the fortress,[253] which was finally breached on April 16, 73 A.D.[254] When the Romans entered the citadel, they found a grim sight. All the buildings except the food stores had been set alight and every single one of the defenders, except for two women and five children, had committed suicide. Josephus wrote, "The Jews hoped that all of their nation beyond the Euphrates would join together with them to raise an insurrection but in the end there were only 960 Zealots who fought the Roman army at Masada."[255]

Josephus contended that the Zealots believed that it was the will of God that they should die and quoted the two women who had hidden with their children in a cistern and who repeated Elazar be Ya'ir's last words to his followers: "Since we long ago resolved never to be servants to the Romans, nor to any other than to God Himself, Who alone is the true and just Lord of mankind, the time is now come that obliges us to make that resolution true in practice. We were the very 1st that revolted and we are the last to fight against them and I cannot but esteem it as a favour that God has granted us that it still is in our power to die bravely and in a state of freedom."[256]

Judaism prohibits suicide, so the defenders drew lots and killed each other in turn so that it was actually only the last man who actually took his own life. The decision not to burn the foodstuffs was to prove that the defenders could have fought but had instead voluntarily chosen death over slavery.

Vol. 52.
[253] P. 52, 'The Roman Siege Works of Masada, Israel' by I.A. Richmond (1962). *The Journal of Roman Studies*, Vol. 52.
[254] 'Capturing a desert fortress; Flavius Silva and the Siege of Masada' by D.B. Campbell (2010). *Ancient Warfare*, 4.2, pp.28-35.
[255] *Flavius Josephus; Selections from His Works* (ed.) A. Wasserstein (1974). New York.
[256] Speech at Masada Jewish Virtual Library. [Online]. Available at: http://www.jewishvirtuallibrary.org/elazar-ben-yair-speech-at-masada

Ricardo Tulio Gandelman's picture of some of the ruins at Masada

An aerial view of the ramp

After Masada was cleared out, Silva left a garrison at the fortress and returned with the bulk of his troops to Caesarea. After Masada had fallen, hostilities between Jewish rebels and the Roman army came to an end in Judea. Communal violence persisted in Egypt between the Jews and Romans, but the siege of Masada proved to be the final major battle in the First Jewish War.

In recent years, there has been some scholarly debate about whether this famous suicide took place and Kenneth Atkinson, for example, claims that there is no archaeological evidence that the defenders did kill each other as tradition has it.[257] Whether true, the Siege of Masada has undoubtedly become for many a symbol of Jewish heroism. Klara Palotai said, "Masada became a symbol for a heroic last stand for the State of Israel and played a major role for Israel in forging national identity."[258]

Masada symbolized the courage of Jewish warriors, and their choice of death over slavery resulted in Masada becoming "the performance space of national heritage."[259] Today, Israelis are less comfortable with glorifying mass suicide, and the whole assessment of the Zealot defenders has resulted in some concluding that far from being patriotic idealists, they were in fact a gang of hardened killers who were the victims of the last Roman operation of the Great Revolt.[260]

---

[257] p. 397, *Making History; Josephus and Historical Method*, Z. Rodgers (ed.) (2007). Brill.
[258] 'The changing meaning of a historical site', by K. Palotai (2002). *Politics of the Performance Space.*
[259] ('The changing meaning of a historical site', by K. Palotai (2002). *Politics of the Performance Space.*

It might be assumed that the overwhelming losses suffered by the Judeans in this revolt would have put an end to Jewish insurrection, but that was far from the case. Inevitably, there was a lengthy period during which a severely chastened population recovered and, by and large, worked within the parameters set by the Roman authorities, but gradually the people did turn once again to attempting to throw off the yoke imposed on them. Indeed, it can be seen in retrospect that the Great Revolt actually only marked the beginning of the Jewish-Roman Wars, which radically impacted both the Roman Empire and the Jews themselves.

The next major conflict became known as the Kitos War and was fought between 115 and 117 A.D. It is sometimes called the rebellion of the diaspora because it involved Jewish communities scattered throughout the Roman world. In 115 A.D., Emperor Trajan was commanding an expedition against the Parthians. Trajan's campaign started off well, and he advanced without any real opposition through Mesopotamia, but Jewish rebels took the opportunity to attack the small Roman garrisons that Trajan left behind as he marched eastwards. Other Jewish revolts in Cyprus, Cyrenaica, and Egypt encouraged the rebels in Judea, and cities with large Jewish populations such as Nisibis, Edessa, Seleucia, and Arbela took advantage of Trajan's preoccupation with the Parthians. Roman garrisons were slaughtered throughout the territories in the rebellion.

In Cyrenaica, the rebels were led by Andreas and destroyed anything that was connected to Rome, including temples and public buildings such as baths and the Caesareum. Orosius claimed that rebel savagery so depopulated the region that it had to be resettled much later by Hadrian: "The Jews waged war on the inhabitants throughout Libya in the most savage fashion, and to such an extent was the country wasted that its cultivators having been slain, its land would have remained utterly depopulated had not the Emperor Hadrian gathered settlers from other places and sent them thither, for the inhabitants had been wiped out."[261]

Cassius Dio also wrote about these Jewish revolts: "Meanwhile the Jews in the region of Cyrene had put one Andreas at their head and were destroying both the Romans and the Greeks. They would cook their flesh, make belts for themselves of their entrails, anoint themselves with their blood and wear their skins for clothing. Many they sawed in two from the head downwards. Others they would give to wild beasts and force still others to fight as gladiators. In all, consequently, two hundred and twenty thousand perished. In Egypt also they performed many similar deeds and in Cyprus under the leadership of Aertemion. There likewise two hundred and forty thousand perished. For this reason no Jew may set foot in that land, but even if one of them is driven upon the island by force of wind he is put to death. Various persons took part in subduing these Jews one being Lusius who was sent by Trajan."[262]

---

[260] 'Ancient battle divides Israel as Masada myth unravels' by P. Cockburn. *The Independent,* 30 March (1997).
[261] Orosius, *Seven Books of History Against the Pagans,* 7.12.6.
[262] Cassius Dio, *Roman History,* V. 68 32.

There is probably some truth in the claims that Cassius Dio's account was exaggerated, but there is little doubt that the Jewish rebels, exasperated by years of repression and encouraged by hopes of freedom from Rome, acted as savagely to the Romans as the Romans had to them in previous years.

In Egypt, the Jews set fire to Alexandria and destroyed temples. They remained on the rampage until they were eventually defeated in 117 A.D. by Marcius Turbo. Similarly, the revolt in Cyprus was put down with great savagery, with all Jews expelled from the island. While these revolts were playing out, a further revolt sprang up in Mesopotamia, and Trajan, realizing the danger of the situation, took steps to deal with the Parthian problem by giving them a king from among their own nobility so he could turn his attention to the insurrection. Trajan undertook a siege of Hatra but suffered from heatstroke and died on his way back to Rome.

Hadrian took the throne in 118 A.D. He quickly subdued Judea, and many Jews were executed after Lydda was taken. Hadrian visited Judea in 130 A.D. and took the decision to rename Jerusalem in his honor as Aelia Capitolina. This rather unwise decision, coupled with his harsh reprisal measures, sowed the seed of the next and final Jewish Roman War, the Bar Kokhba Revolt.

A marble bust of Hadrian

The revolt was led by Simon bar Kokhba and was the last of the three Jewish-Roman Wars, fought between 132 and 136 A.D. The underlying reasons for the revolt were the same as for the previous ones: a desire for independence and disaffection with Roman rule. The specific cause was the building of the new city of Aelia Capitolina over the ruins of Jerusalem, and with it the erection of a temple to Jupiter on the Temple Mount.[263] The Governor at the time, Tineius Rufus, carried out the foundation ceremony in 131 A.D. and managed to offend all Jews by ploughing over land upon which the Temple had once stood.

The Jewish leaders, however, did not act precipitously and planned their revolt carefully so that it was not until 132 A.D. that the insurrection began. Bar Kokhba started the revolt in Modi'in, and from there it spread quickly throughout Judea, cutting off the Roman garrison in Jerusalem. Rufus was still governor, but it is uncertain what happened to him. Regardless, the Judeans inflicted heavy losses on the 10th Legion based in Jerusalem, and the 6th Legion was speedily dispatched to reinforce the city garrison.

The troops protecting Jerusalem now numbered 20,000 but they were unable to bring the rebels to heel, so further troops were sent. Gaius Publicus Marcellus, the Legate of Syria, arrived with the 3rd Legion, and Haterius Nepos, the Governor of Roman Arabia, came with a further legion. Another legion was sent from Egypt but was ambushed by the Judeans and later disbanded.

By the time all the additional forces had arrived in Judea, the troops designated to crush the rebellion numbered over 80,000. This number, though large, was still significantly smaller than the numbers commanded by bar Kokhba. Significant numbers of Jews from the diaspora also returned to Judea to add their weight to the rebellion. Conservative estimates put the number of rebels at over 200,000.

The initial successes of the Judeans took the Romans by surprise. Bar Kokhba used guerrilla tactics to harry the Romans, who gradually changed their tactics and avoided any attempts to bring the rebels to battle and instead concentrated on systematically taking each stronghold in turn through sieges. The Judeans were forced to change their approach and try to defend their bases since not to do so would have cut their supply lines and quickly rendered them ineffective as a fighting force.

Simon bar Kokhba was named as the long awaited Messiah by Rabbi Akiva, and it was he who gave the previously named Simon bar Kosiba the name Simon bar Kokhba, meaning son of the star, a reference to a prophecy relating to the Messiah in the Old Testament. Bar Kokhba took the title Nasi Israel, and he managed to rule over a sizeable part of Judea for just over two years.

The situation from a Roman perspective was becoming extremely serious, with the Judeans minting their own coins and beginning to shape an economy that didn't involve Rome. Hadrian recalled Sextus Julius Severus from Britain and gathered troops from all over the empire. Severus arrived in Judea with an army that doubled the number of troops available, until a third

---

[263] P. 132, 'The Bar Kochba Revolt' by E. Hanan in *The Cambridge History of Judaism Volume 4*, W.D. Davies & L. Finkelstein (general eds), S.T. Katz (ed.). (2006). Cambridge University Press.

of the entire Roman army was now involved in the war against bar Kokhba.

With such a large force, the Romans were now in a position to return to their favored tactic of engaging the rebels in set piece battles. One of the most crucial of these was at Tel Shalem in the Beit She'an valley, and from this point onwards the Judeans steadily lost ground and were confined to the area around the fortress of Betar. The Romans besieged this fort in 135 A.D. According to Jewish tradition, bar Kokhba forfeited divine protection by killing his uncle, but at any rate the fort was captured and razed to the ground after a short siege.

Jewish sources say that the Romans "went on killing until their horses were submerged in blood to their nostrils."[264] Indeed, the Romans were no less brutal in their treatment of any other Jewish leaders of the revolt. Eight members of the Sanhedrin were executed after being tortured. Akiva was flayed with iron combs, Ishmael, another rabbi, had the skin of his head pulled off slowly, and yet another, Hananiah ben Teradion, was wrapped in a scroll of the Law and burned to death slowly with wet brushwood used to prolong his agony.[265] It is not known what happened to bar Kokhba - various legends ascribe different endings ranging from dying of natural causes in exile, dying of a snakebite at the siege of Betar, and being beheaded on the orders of the Sanhedrin to placate Hadrian.

The Romans indulged in an orgy of recriminations that lasted well into 136 A.D., by which all remaining vestiges of the rebellion had been put down. Cassius Dio put Judean losses at nearly 600,000, and he wrote that over 1,000 towns and villages were totally destroyed. It is no exaggeration to suggest that what took place was something akin to genocide. Romans also suffered huge losses, according to Cassius Dio: "Many Romans perished in this war. Therefore, Hadrian, in writing to the Senate did not employ the opening phrase commonly affected by the emperors; If you are in health, it is well; I and the army are in health."[266] Several legions were so reduced in numbers that they were disbanded, and the whole episode had a profound effect on Rome.

In the wake of the violence, Hadrian took steps to root out Jewish nationalism. He prohibited the Torah law and the Jewish calendar and executed numerous scholars. The sacred scroll was burned on the Temple Mount, and he installed statues of himself and Jupiter in the former Temple sanctuary. Even the name Judea was erased from all maps and documents and replaced by the name Syria Palaestina.[267] Jews were forbidden from entering Aelia Capitolina except on the day of Tisha B'Av, when they were allowed to commemorate their defeat at the hands of the Romans.

---

[264] *Ta'anit*, 4.5.
[265] *The Ten Martyrs Jewish Encyclopaedia* by I. Singer and I. Broyde. [Online]. Available at: http://www.jewishencyclopedia.com/articles/10447-martyrs-the-ten
[266] Cassius Dio, *Roman History*, V.
[267] P. 334, *A history of the Jewish People* by H.H. Ben Sasson (1976). Harvard University Press.

The majority of the Jewish population by the end of the three wars had either been killed, exiled, or sold into slavery, and the Jewish religion was brutally suppressed. The Jews were now a small minority in Judea, so much so that the massive losses have led many to date the beginning of the diaspora from the end of the revolt. Judea would not become a center of Jewish religion, culture or political life again until the 20th century, even as small groups of Jews did continue to return throughout the centuries and the Talmud was completed in the 5th century. The Romans effectively ended the Judean state, and there would not be another Jewish state in the region until the birth of Israel in 1948.

The origins of Judea and Israel are still shrouded in myth. Though the most recent archaeological evidence does suggest that sometime in the 10th century B.C. there was a Jewish kingdom in the region, it was no doubt much smaller than that portrayed in the Bible, and the great stories of wars and heroes can be seen as no more than fables. Nonetheless, by the time that archaeological evidence provided far more reliable evidence for the Jewish kingdoms of Judea and Israel, the myths had become considered established facts and shaped that indomitable sense of independence that ultimately led to the Jews pitting themselves against one of the mightiest empires the world has ever seen. The constant and unrelenting determination for independence shown by such a relatively small and powerless group has to be admired, as does their refusal to compromise on their core beliefs. There can be little doubt that those core beliefs, and that obstinate and indomitable spirit, played a key part in the survival of the Jews as a distinct ethnic and religious group in the centuries following their forcible exclusion from the lands they believed had been given to them by God. There were many occasions when the Jews as such a separate group could have been subsumed by greater powers, including the Babylonians, the Egyptians, and the Greeks. The greatest threat of all came from the Romans, but even history's most famous empire proved unable to totally extinguish this small nation.

The Romanization of Gaul

Key to Roman success in Gaul was the system of provinces that Augustus improved based on the earlier Republican models. Until the end of the 3rd century A.D., the province was the basic administrative unit of the Roman Empire. Senatorial provinces, as opposed to Imperial provinces initiated by Augustus, were governed by politicians of senatorial rank. Augustus's innovation, the Imperial province, came about after he had acquired Egypt and decided that he wanted to keep it as a personal fiefdom.

An ancient statue of Augustus

In Egypt's case, and that of later Imperial provinces, the governors were always drawn from the equestrian class. The term *provincial* in Latin had a meaning something akin to the term justification or set of responsibilities and basically was related to the tasks assigned to a governor who held what was known as *imperium*, or the right to command. To begin with, therefore, governors often held a military command as part of their duties.[268]

As was normal for any Roman magistracy under the Republic, appointments to a governorship were for one year and were normally handed out to Consuls and Praetors the year after they completed their year in office in Rome. How a province was treated largely depended on the circumstances under which an area had come under Roman rule.[269] In some instances, the territory was totally subjugated, and treated as *deditio,* in which case the population was more often than not abused and milked for whatever the Romans could extract from them. This more harsh treatment was usually meted out where the Romans perceived that those they had conquered had either put up an unnecessarily stiff resistance, or were still seen as a danger. Once

---

[268] P. 564, *The Administration of the Empire, Cambridge Ancient History Vol. 9* by J. Richardson (1994). Cambridge University Press.
[269] P. 179, *The Administration of Provinces, A Companion to the Roman Empire* by C. Ando (2010). Blackwell.

a territory had been formally annexed, a province was created.

The first of these was Sicily in 214 B.C., closely followed by Sardinia and Corsica. As the number of provinces grew, there were not enough individuals who met the strict qualification requirements to undertake the governance roles and the Senate resorted to extending the period that a governor could serve beyond the normal one year. In some instances the Senate resorted to appointing powerful men rather than ex-magisterial post holders, the most obvious example of which was Pompey.[270] This practice of prorogation, extending the time an individual could govern a province, was totally against the fundamental principle of Republican Rome that was itself built on the concept of annual magistracies. Although unintended, this allowed individuals to amass huge fortunes and centralise power into a few hands and, thus, paved the way for the future Imperial system.

The third element in Rome's success in pacifying its conquered territories, and which went hand in hand with military superiority and sound administration, was the conscious Romanization of those areas it incorporated into the Empire. The term "Romanization," sometimes called "Latinisation," is a catch-all phrase that describes the process through which indigenous populations were incorporated into the Empire through the acquisition of cultural characteristics that made them appear to be Romans.

The Romans arguably did not have any single unitary culture and often absorbed the customs of those they had conquered. In that sense, therefore, the process of Romanization cannot be seen as entirely one way. The exchange of ideas and styles between Rome and its provinces led to what can be described as a metropolitan mix which was a feature throughout the Roman world. Romanization was most obviously manifested in the use of Latin, specifically Vulgar Latin, all across the empire and certainly no noblemen or merchant could hope to rise very far without a grasp of the language. However, other aspects of Romanization included art and architecture, town planning, and the worship of the Roman Pantheon, though this did not necessarily mean that the local gods were totally replaced. The net result of Romanization was not, therefore, homogeneity, since local traditions were blended with those of Rome to create hybrids. In this way in Gaul, a Romano-Celtic religion was created, as was a Gallo-Roman style of sculpture.

While the manifestations of Romanization were, in consequence, different in the various parts of the empire, there is no doubt that Rome consciously promoted specific aspects of its own culture to integrate the local populations and to create circumstances which allowed for easier governance, and hence exploitation, of a province. The foundation of Lugdunum, modern day Lyon, in Gallia Celtica was a prime example of the program of creating provincial centers that could promote loyalty to the state through, among other things, the worship of Roman gods and through the priesthood being composed almost entirely of members of the local elite. Public buildings and the education of the local aristocrats also played their parts in this process of

---

[270] P. 626, *The Constitution of the Roman Republic* by A. Lintott (2000). Oxford University Press.

binding the locals to Rome.[271] In addition to these planned efforts to civilize these barbarians, as the Romans put it, other factors aided the process. The Roman policy of moving troops throughout the Empire brought new ideas and new goods to a province and the mix of people further necessitated the use of Latin as the lingua franca. The Roman obsession with roads, in addition to helping secure a province militarily, also brought with them increased trade and communication with other parts of the Empire, all of which resulted in even more cultural exchange.

The elites, in particular, of newly conquered people often went to great lengths to integrate themselves as fully as possible with their new masters. In Gaul, as in other parts of the empire, the ultimate ambition for so many of these aspirant nobles and merchants was the acquisition of Roman citizenship. Throughout Gaul new citizens often flaunted their new status by building Roman style villas or endowing temples to Roman gods, and this constant copying of things Roman was one of the major factors in the Romanization, or more accurately, the acculturation, of Gaul. However, the Romans rarely left anything to chance and hostage taking also played an important part in securing loyalty, especially in the early days of Roman rule in a province. The children of the local elite were often taken to Rome itself to be raised and educated.[272]

Acculturation was a top down process. The more rural populations were usually the last to succumb. One way of reaching into the hinterlands was by the creation of *coloniae*. In Gaul's case, the numbers were significant. These *coloniae* were usually populated with retired soldiers, often from the Italian peninsula, and they inevitably brought with them Latin, along with their Roman customs and laws. Livy claims that he identified over 400 of these towns that were accorded the status of *colonia*, and he went on to write, "During the Empire, colonia were showcases of Roman culture and examples of the Roman way of life. The native population of the provinces could see how they were expected to live."[273]

Given their importance in the Romanization process and the benefits that it brought to individuals within them, it is no surprise that the promotion of a town to the status of *Colonia civium Romanorum* was greatly desired.[274] At the beginning of Augustus' reign it is estimated that about three quarters of a million Italians lived in Rome's provinces.[275] Augustus settled around 100,000 Italians in Gaul over a 10 year period at the end of the 1st century B.C.

Recent scholarship has identified even more nuanced ways in which the Romans achieved their acculturation objectives. One of these was through what Millet describes as a non-interventionist model.[276] The suggestion he put forward was that native elites were encouraged to increase their

---
[271] Tacitus, *Agricola*, 21.
[272] P.130, *The Romanization of Central Spain. Complexity, Diversity and Change in a Provincial Hinterland* by L.A. Curchin (2004). London, Routledge.
[273] Livy, *History of Rome*, I.11.
[274] 'Colonia', Livius.org (2018). [Online]. Retrieved from: http://www.livius.org/articles/concept/colonia/
[275] P. 263, *Italian Manpower 225B.C. –A.D.14* by P.A. Brunt (1987). Oxford, Oxford University Press.
[276] P. 35, 'Romanization: historical issues and archaeological interpretation' by M. Millet: in T. Blagg and M. Millet,

status and social standing through direct association with the Romans. To that end they were encouraged to dress, speak and live in houses that mirrored their conquerors. The process even involved what was eaten and how it was served. However, Mattingly[277] calls into question this view, and previous interpretations of Romanization. He argued that very clear differences existed between provinces which he believed could be seen in the different economies, religious practices and identities of different provinces. His arguments do not weaken, but rather strengthen the concept of acculturation being a process whereby indigenous and Roman cultures merged and examples of this can be found throughout the Roman world. It did not render a province less Romanized because accommodations with local traditions had been found.[278]

The Roman approach to their conquered territories can be summed up in the phrase *Pax Romana*,[279] the "Roman Peace." Historically speaking, the period of the Pax Romana lasted from the beginning of Augustus's reign in approximately 30 B.C. until the death of Marcus Aurelius in 180 A.D. At its height, Rome ruled over a third of the world's population, approximately 70 million people.[280] The first written reference to the *Pax Romana* was by Seneca the Younger in 55 A.D.[281] It is, of course, a misnomer because in the period in question there were numerous wars, uprisings, and insurrections, but the concept and the ideas behind this notion of the benefits of Roman rule are what matter in the context of understanding how Rome so successfully, in most cases, came to Romanize even the most belligerent tribes and foes. And Gaul certainly comes into that category.

Augustus's genius lay not in totally avoiding external wars or military adventures but in creating a group of the most powerful military and military figures who coalesced around him as the one main ruler. In creating this group, he effectively eliminated the potential for civil wars. To this end, Augustus was aware of the importance of religious ritual in conveying ideas and imprinting them on the minds of the people. He closed the Gates of Janus three times in all, and by so doing he indicated that Rome was at peace. The first ceremony was in 29 B.C., the second came in 25 B.C., and the final time is assumed to have been in 13 B.C., at the time of the commissioning of the Ara Pacis.[282]

Augustus's idea was to make peace the norm in the Roman world, a not inconsiderable challenge given that the Romans regarded war as the usual state of affairs and peace to be only

---

The Early Roman Empire in the West (1990). Oxford, Oxbow Books.

[277] P. 13, 'Being Roman: Expressing Identity in a provincial setting' by D. J. Mattingly in *Journal of Roman Archaeology* (2004) Vol.17, pp. 5-25.

[278] P. 324, 'Necessary Comparisons: A Post-Colonial approach to Religious Syncretism in the Roman Provinces' by J. Webster in *World Archaeology* (1997) Vol.28, No 3.

[279] The term Pax Augusta is sometimes used instead of the more familiar term Pax Romana, out of respect for the Emperor who initiated it.

[280] 'Pax Romana' Encyclopaedia Britannica [Online]. Retrieved: https://www.britannica.com/event/Pax-Romana.

[281] P. 25, *Hegemonic Peace and Empire: The Pax Romana* by A. Parchami (2009). Routledge.

[282] 'The Procession of the Ara Pacis' by I. Scott Ryberg (1949). *Memoirs of the American Academy in Rome* 19, pp.79-101.

an interlude between one war and the next. Yet it was this success in changing hearts and minds that played a major part in controlling the conquered territories. As part of his strategy to sell the idea of peace, Augustus re-introduced the *Ligis Seculares*, or Secular Games. These games had been traditional in Republican Rome but had not been held since 148 B.C. The concept was that the Romans celebrated the end of one *saeculum* and the beginning of the next, and were spaced out in 100 year intervals, as this was assumed to be the maximum length of a human life. The festivities lasted for three days and three nights and included theatrical performances and sacrifices in addition to the normal sporting and gladiatorial events.

By reintroducing them, Augustus was reinforcing his key message that he was not about the new but about restoring the traditional, and in choosing this particular festival, he signaled a "new" beginning of a return to the "old ways." According to Roman mythology, the games had begun when a Sabine named Lesius prayed for a cure for his desperately ill children and was told by the gods to commit a sacrifice on the Campus Martius to Dis Pater, coincidentally the Roman god that the Gauls equated to their major deity. Some ancient writers claimed that the games were first celebrated in 509 B.C., but the only recorded instances were in 248 B.C. and 148 B.C. Augustus was a shrewd judge of the Roman public and knew that aside from their martial abilities, their other great talent was celebrating. He used that desire for ever more elaborate entertainment as a way of imparting his message. He cemented the idea of a new age with peace by building the Ara Pacis, or Peace Altar, and dedicating it on the July 4, 13 B.C., on the same day as the games began. The altar was built on the Campus Martius.

Augustus mentioned the altar in his *Res Gestae Divi Augusti*: "When I returned from Spain and Gaul, having successfully accomplished deeds in those provinces, the Senate voted to consecrate the Altar of August Peace. In the Campus Martius on which it ordered the magistrates and priests and Vestal Virgins to offer annual sacrifices."[283]

His plan was new to Rome in the sense of dedicating an altar in such a prominent place in Rome to the abstract concept of peace and was in marked contrast to the many celebrations of war and victories. The altar's design emphasized the benefits of peace, so images of fertile fields and an abundance of wealth and food dominated the friezes. Augustus was the lead celebrant in the procession, and there could be no doubt in any Roman's mind that he was portraying himself as the champion of peace.

The altar can be seen as a representation of all the practices of Roman state religion, incorporating the pragmatic, the elegant, and the entertaining in a display of cohesion and authority. By championing peace in this way, using Roman predilection for tradition and ritual, Augustus promoted a powerful and very effective campaign of political messaging. His efforts were successful in changing the Roman mindset and enabled the *Pax Romana* to be successfully introduced as a policy that was totally embedded within the concept of Romanization.

---

[283] *Res Gestae Divi Augusti*, 12.

The Senate decreed that an inscription recording the games should be set up in the Tarentum, a site on the Campus Martius that still survives and provides details of some of the events. From this inscription it is known that Augustus personally took part in proceedings during the nighttime on his own, and he was accompanied by Agrippa for those held during daylight hours. After the sacrifices, a song composed by Horace, the *Carmen Saeculare*, was sung by a choir of young boys and girls. Theatrical productions of Latin and Greek plays were put on after every major sacrifice, and other events included chariot races and hunting expeditions. Further *Ludi*[284] were held in 88 A.D. and in 148 A.D., and these subsequent holdings of the games (and in the reigns of two of the five "Good Emperors") demonstrate the consistency of policy in this period. The format of the later events mirrored those held by Augustus in all major details.

The benefits of peace, in economic and security terms, through these tactics became accepted as the target rather than the previous preoccupation with honor and booty associated with war. Emperors who followed Augustus, by and large, adopted the same policy and, indeed, the last five Emperors of the *Pax Romana* are collectively known as the "Five Good Emperors." The five were Nerva, Trajan, Hadrian, Antoninus Pius, and Marcus Aurelius. The periods of their reigns, between 96 A.D. and 180 A.D., brought a significant expansion of the empire, but even more importantly, the empire was consolidated. Defenses were strengthened and a more or less uniform provincial system administered the local areas under Roman control, all of which facilitated the Romanization of Gaul. This internal tranquility and protracted period of good government was a major factor in the process of assimilating the four provinces of Transalpine Gaul into the empire.

Edward Gibbon, the most famous historian to write about the Roman Empire, was particularly glowing in his assessment of this period: "If a man were called upon to fix that period in the history of the world during which the condition of the human race was most happy and prosperous, he would, without hesitation, name that which elapsed from the death of Domitian to the accession of Commodus."[285]

Matthew Arnold, the English poet, was equally glowing about Marcus Aurelius, claiming that he lived and acted "in a state of society modern by its essential characteristics in an epoch akin to our own, in a brilliant center of civilisation."[286]

Whether or not this period was as tranquil and prosperous as these writers suggest, there is no doubt that the *Pax Romana* was promulgated as a very tangible benefit of Roman rule. Similarly, there is ample evidence that the increased trade and the wealth that this generated led many conquered peoples to accept Roman rule rather more readily than if they had been subjected to deteriorating economic conditions or constant warfare. All five of the Good Emperors embarked

---

[284] Latin for public game.
[285] *The History of the Decline and Fall of the Roman Empire* by E. Gibbon (1776).
[286] *Marcus Aurelius*, by M. Arnold (2015). University of Adelaide.

on ambitious building programs throughout the empire, and the internal stability facilitated the building of impressive public structures which, in turn, enhanced the lives of the Empires' citizens. With the completion of the numerous aqueducts that provided plentiful supplies of water came the ability to build bath houses, and the building of amphitheaters allowed for Roman pastimes such as gladiatorial contests to be conducted. All of these projects directly and positively impinged on the everyday lives of Gauls and bound them even more closely to Rome.

The sense of civic pride as towns grew into cities, accompanied by the increased standard of living that was made possible by the *Pax Romana*, was crucial in Rome's success in taming the various regions of Gaul. However, all good things come to an end, and this particular "Golden Age" is generally accepted to have ended with the death of Marcus Aurelius. He was already experiencing real difficulties in preventing the increasingly belligerent Germanic tribes from breaching the frontiers of the empire and only succeeded in preventing large scale encroachments thanks to his own military and political acumen. Upon his death and the rise of emperors who possessed significantly less ability, the pressures on the empire became too great, and gradual decline of Rome began.

The 3rd century A.D. ushered in a period of extreme internal disorder fanned by external pressures. In the period from 235-285 A.D., there were no fewer than 20 emperors, with the majority either falling in battle or being assassinated. In 260 A.D., Marcus Cassianius Latinius Postumus, a Gaul, led an insurrection against Gallienus and seized power and established himself as the new emperor in Gaul. He controlled Britain and Spain for a short period as well. Gallienus responded and attacked Gaul, but the conflict was inconclusive and Postumus set up the capital of the Gallic Empire at Augusta Treverorum, with its own Senate. He never attempted to march on Rome, and his new empire lasted until 274 A.D., when Tetricus was defeated by Emperor Aurelion.

The Battle of Chalons-sur-Marne marked the end of this period of Gallic separation from Rome, but it was the forerunner of things to come. The following years saw major invasions of Gaul by Franks, Vandals, and Burgundians, and by the time the western part of the Roman Empire had fallen in 476 A.D., Gaul had fallen into the hands of the invaders. In 481 A.D., the transformation was complete when Clovis became King of the Franks, drove the Visigoths into Spain, and defeated the Germans and Burgundians. He left a consolidated kingdom that was both Roman and Germanic.[287]

It can be argued that Rome, as an emerging power, was always destined to become involved in Gaul. Its proximity to Italy, the place of the "barbarian Gaul" in the psyche of the Roman population, and Rome's newly acquired territories in Spain after the conclusion of the Punic Wars made such involvement inevitable. Once Cisalpine Gaul had been pacified, Rome's need to consider its position in relation to Transalpine Gaul undoubtedly became a priority, and the first

---

[287] *SPQR* by M. Beard (2015). Liverlight.

direct military intervention came in the area of modern day southern France that the Romans called Gallia Narbonensis.

The term Gallia Narbonensis comes from the Latin for Gaul of Narbonne, which was the principal settlement of the province located in modern day Languedoc and Provence. It was sometimes also known as Provincia Nostra, or Our Province, and is the origin of the modern term Provence, because it was the first Roman province north of the Alps and Gallia Transalpina, Transalpine Gaul, to distinguish it from Cisalpine Gaul in northern Italy. It was made a province in 118 B.C. and included the whole of what is now the French Mediterranean coastline, with the Cevennes and Alps to the north and west, and the Iberian provinces to the south west.

The Romans began significant trading in this region from the mid-2nd century B.C., particularly with the Greek colony of Massalia, which by this time was already a well-established and wealthy port. Massalia allied itself with the Romans in order to secure itself from the nearby Aquitani, Carthaginians, and the numerous other potential predators who threatened its existence. In return for defending the city, Massalia ceded to Rome a strip of land that was used to build a land route to Iberia. The Massalians had little compunction in handing over territory since their main preoccupation was trade, but the decision ultimately proved problematic for them, bringing, as it did, Roman armies to their doorstep.

It was on this strip of land that the settlement of Narbo or Narbonne was constructed. While the settlement was being built, the Romans also embarked on the building of the Via Domitia to connect Gaul to Iberia. At the same time they constructed the Via Aquitania which ran through Tolosa (modern day Toulouse) to Burdigala, in modern day Bordeaux. Narbonne became an important trading center through the building of these roads as trade increasingly developed due to the considerably easier travel that they enabled. The region had become a province in 121 B.C., initially named Gallia Transalpina, but it was the construction and development of Narbo, later Narbonne, which truly cemented Roman rule in the region.

The pacification of the region was not without its difficulties. In the earliest days Quintus Fabius Maximus had to defeat incursions from the Allobroges and the Arverni, but once having decisively defeated these tribes, the security of Gallia Narbonensis was secured. Once that was complete, the importance of Narbonensis in terms of the development of the empire cannot be overstated. Not only was it a wealthy area in terms of resources, manpower, and as a trading partner, it was geographically positioned to help both in the consolidation of existing areas of Roman control and as a base for future expansion to the north. The land route to the Iberian provinces was crucial in enabling Rome to exploit fully its new acquisitions, and it was part of the defensive buffer long desired by Romans against the possibility of attacks into Italy from the Gauls. The control of the vital trade routes along the Rhone Valley was yet another factor in enabling Rome to maximize the economic advantages given by control of the routes to Massalia.

As such a key position, it was inevitable that the province would be embroiled in the internal power struggles of Rome. Julius Caesar became its governor and exploited its wealth to further his own political ambitions. Eventually, he also used it as a base for his ultimately successful annexation of the other areas of Gaul. The Gallic Wars that Caesar embarked upon have often been characterized as being fundamentally about Caesar's need to acquire his own source of personal wealth and his need to match the achievements of his bitter rival, Pompey the Great, for ultimate control of Rome. Whether those were the main motivations of Caesar, the ostensible reasons for Roman intervention in Gallia Comata were the incursions by the Helvetii into areas of Narbonensis in an attempt to reach the Atlantic seaboard.

From 58-50 B.C., Caesar undertook no fewer than eight campaigns during which, by his estimates, he took 800 towns and defeated 300 separate tribes. There has been considerable debate about the size of the tribal armies that Caesar confronted, and there is no way of knowing for certain how many warriors were under arms at any time. However, based on the population, figures of up to half a million warriors would not be totally unfeasible. Similarly, it is uncertain how many Gauls died in the eight years of the Gallic Wars, but some estimates suggest that perhaps a third of the total population died, and possibly a third were sold into slavery at the conclusion of the fighting. Vercingetorix's scorched earth policy added to the devastation suffered by the Gallic population, but the main culprit was Caesar's policy of ruthless suppression of any opposition to his rule. Caesar justified the ferocity of his campaigns by referring constantly to the threat that the Gauls still posed to Rome's security and by reminding Romans of the sack of the city by Gauls hundreds of years earlier.

Many of the figures relating to casualties are based on Caesar's own accounts in his *Gallic Wars*, and as he had a vested interest in exaggerating his own successes, his figures have to be viewed with extreme caution. Notwithstanding that, it is clear that the wars ravaged Gaul and losses were considerable both in terms of military casualties, those taken into slavery, and the damage done to towns and villages. More unbiased estimates suggest that over one million Gauls died or were enslaved in the Wars. Despite the brutality that Caesar demonstrated throughout his campaigns in Gaul, once the Wars were successfully concluded, his main concern was to pacify the local populations as quickly and effectively as possible so that the newly acquired territories could yield up their wealth for his cause. The policy of Romanization was applied systematically and many erstwhile enemies soon became good friends who provided troops and much needed finance to assist Caesar in the Civil War that erupted between himself and Pompey. In keeping with tried and tested approaches, Caesar promoted the building of new towns with structures built of brick and stone, incorporating all the major features of Roman civilisation: bath houses, temples and amphitheaters.

It was during the Civil War against Pompey that Caesar became responsible for placing the final piece in the Narbonensis jigsaw when he besieged and captured Massilia. In 49 B.C., Lucius Domitius Ahenobarbus had become proconsul of Gaul and was ordered to take control of Massilia as a means of curbing Caesar. Caesar was en route to the Iberian Peninsula when he found the city barred against him by supporters of Ahenobarbus. Caesar reacted quickly and began a siege of the city using three newly raised legions, coincidentally the same three that nearly 60 years later would be annihilated in the Teutoburg Forest in Germany.

With the siege underway, Ahenobarbus arrived to conduct the defense of the city. Massilia, as a major port, relied on naval power, but Caesar's fleet defeated the Massiliots and enforced a punitive blockade. Caesar left the conduct of the siege to his legatus, Gaius Trebonius, who was particularly adept at siege warfare and used the full panoply of Roman siege weapons, towers, catapults and testudo rams in the engagement. At sea, overconfidence resulted in a relief force managing to sail through to the city and bring reinforcements for Ahenobarbus, but a further naval victory for Caesar in early September resulted in the reimposition of the blockade. The fate of the city now rested on whether the city's defenses could withstand Caesar's attacks long enough for the besiegers to become disillusioned or weakened to such an extent that the capture of Massilia became impractical.

Caesar was determined to take the city and had a 30 foot tower built right underneath the city walls. Despite all the efforts of the Massiliots to destroy it and kill those working on it, the tower gradually grew in size. This structure was quite extraordinary in its complexity and consisted of brick walls five feet thick with six separate stories. As the construction proceeded, each completed story was covered with a fire resistant roof which rested on the supporting walls. Protective screens were then hung on the eaves which were hoisted by screws one storey at a time and the work on the next one then began. This process was carried out six times until the structure was completed.[288]

The defenders tried everything they could against the siege work, including burning pitch, but to no avail. Caesar's forces were able to mine underneath the city walls, at which point the Massiliots agreed to a truce that Caesar believed to be the precursor to surrender. However, the defenders used the truce to destroy the siege works.[289] This was, from Caesar's viewpoint, a monstrous violation of the truce. Dio, on the other hand, suggests that the destruction of the siege engines occurred because Caesar's troops violated the truce[290] rather than the other way around.

No matter who did what and when, the city was not able to maintain its defense against the far superior forces at Caesar's command and eventually surrendered. Caesar was relatively lenient on the city despite his contention that the defenders had broken the terms of the truce. Lucius Ahenobarbus escaped to Thessaly and while Caesar confiscated most of the city's territories, the city itself was allowed a nominal autonomy that was little comfort for the defeated Massiliots. With the conquest of the city, however, the province of Narbonensis was established and all those living in the region were now under Roman rule. The process of Romanization accelerated,

---

[288] Julius Caesar, *Gallic Wars*, Book II, 8.9.
[289] Julius Caesar, *Gallic Wars*, Book II,.14.
[290] Cassius Dio, *Roman History*, 41.25.

and Narbonensis in short order became a truly Roman province.

Gallia Lugdunensis was the name given to the province that was formed from the lands taken by Caesar and formerly known as Gallia Celtica. The region is best described as a cultural area that incorporated parts of modern day Switzerland, France, Luxembourg, and the west bank of the Rhine. Caesar was the first Roman to classify the unconquered areas of Gaul into three regions that he referred to as Belgica, Aquitania, and Celtica. He was also the one to coin the term "Gauls" for the inhabitants, though they called themselves Celts. The territory of these central Celts was bordered by the Seine and Marne in the northeast, and the Garonne in the southwest, with these rivers providing the physical borders between Celtica and Belgica and Aquitania respectively.

Caesar brought the region under Roman control during the Gallic Wars, and the area was quickly settled and Romanized. It was subsequently enhanced by building works during the *Pax Romana*. The Colonia Copia Claudia Augusta Lugdunum, modern day Lyon, was founded in 43 B.C. by Lucius Munatius Plancus and became the capital of the province that came to bear its name. Lucius was a Roman senator and is famous in history for managing to successfully weave his way through the intricate and dangerous politics of the latter years of the Republic and the early years of the Principate. He fought as a senior officer under Caesar in the Gallic Wars and in the wars against Pompey.

When his mentor was assassinated in 44 B.C., Plancus was proconsul of Gallia Comata, and he became involved in intrigue with Cicero about the potential defection of Senatorial troops to Antony, who at the time was besieging Brutus in Mutina. He persuaded the Senate that Lepidus was preventing him going to Brutus's assistance but that he remained loyal to them. His intrigues were ultimately rewarded with a Consulship, along with Lepidus in 42 B.C., but once again he chose the right side at the right time when he abandoned Antony and switched his support to Octavian. According to Suetonius, it was Plancus who suggested that Octavian take the title Augustus.[291] Plancus's tomb, unlike those of so many other prominent Romans, has survived in Gaeta, but apart from his renown for his political acumen, his real legacy lies in the foundation of both Lugdunum and Augusta Raurica.

Augustus reorganized the area as an Imperial province known as Gallia Lugdunensis. He took off some parts of what had been part of Celtica and gave the lands between the Loire and the Garonne to the new province of Aquitania, as well as some more central areas to Germania Superior. There is some doubt as to when exactly the new province was created, but it is generally agreed that it was either somewhere between 27 and 25 B.C. or 16 and 13 B.C. since these dates coincided with visits by Augustus to the area.

From their earliest beginnings, Lugunensis as a province and Lugdunum as a city were

---

[291] Suetonius, *Twelve Caesars: Life of Augustus*, 7.

extremely important to the empire. The city itself was strategically positioned both for trade and as a military base. For 300 years after its foundation it was without a doubt the most important city in Gaul. Two emperors, Claudius and Caracalla, were born there. Claudius was born at Lugdunum during the consulship of Julius Antonius and Fabius Africanus, on August 1, 10 B.C., the very day when the first altar was dedicated to Augustus the God. [292]

The city was founded as part of Rome's very conscious policy of pacification through Romanization, which involved setting up settlements populated by retired veterans who then became instrumental in spreading the Latin language, as well as providing garrisons to ensure the locals stayed in line. The city had a relatively large population right from its inception, and it is generally accepted that it began with a population in excess of several thousand. The fact that four aqueducts were built within a couple of years of its foundation suggests that the city grew remarkably quickly. By the end of Augustus's reign it had a large, cosmopolitan population and was the commercial and financial heart of Gaul. A mint was established there in 15 B.C., and it continued to produce coins for the next three centuries.

In the province of Lugdunensis the native people were the Allobroges who had provided the excuse for Caesar to launch his campaign into Gallia Comata. Lugdunum was not the only such settlement in the province - others included Vienne, Noviodunum, and Augusta Raurica - but it was by far the most important. It was visited by Augustus himself on at least three occasions, and Agrippa, Drusus, Tiberius, Germanicus, Caligula and Nero also all spent time there. At its height the city had a population of approximately 200,000.

The site of Roman Lugdunum was on the remains of earlier Celtic settlements, and given its important geographic location this is unsurprising. The origin of the name Lugdunum is somewhat clouded in mystery, but it seems to be linked to the Celtic term *dunum* which means a hill or citadel and suggests a link to the earlier Celtic settlement. The "lug" part of the name is less easily explained. There have been various suggestions linking it to the Celtic god Lugh, but there is no archaeological evidence of any worship of this deity in the area. Another suggestion is that it derives from the Latin word for light, *lux*, and other candidates include the word *lougos*, or raven.[293]

Regardless of its name, the city proved to be the ideal base for Augustus, well served as it was by a complex system of Roman roads that reached most parts of Gaul, for his planned invasion of Germania. In addition to the aqueducts that were built to supply the rapidly expanding city with water beginning in 20 B.C. and the impressive range of monuments built to emphasize the city's status, Lugdunum was famous for its theaters. The oldest theater in all of Gaul was built in the city in around 16 B.C. by Augustus's decree and was expanded from its original capacity of 4,500 to over 10,000 during the reign of Hadrian.

---

[292] Suetonius, *Twelve Caesars: Life of Claudius*, 2.
[293] *En sorvolant la Gaule (Looking at Gaul)* by C. Goudineau (2007). Babelio.

In 19 A.D., the Amphitheater of the Three Gauls was built, and it was later enlarged in the middle of the 2nd century A.D. This theater was part of a larger federal sanctuary dedicated to the cult of Rome and Augustus and was used by the 60 Gallic tribes when they gathered at Lugdunum, especially for the games held in honor of the Imperial cult. It was situated at the bottom of the hill, now known as La Croix-Rousse, at what was at that time the confluence of the Rivers Rhone and Saone. An existing inscription reads, "For the safety of Tiberius Caesar Augustus. Julius Rufus, citizen of the city of Santons, priest of Rome and of Augustus, his son and grandson built this amphitheater and its podium at their own expense."

The Amphitheater of the Three Gauls

The ruins of one of the aqueducts

The inscription reveals much about the new order in this part of Gaul. The builders of the theater came from an old Gallic family who had become Roman citizens shortly after the end of the Gallic Wars. They built other monuments in the city, including the Arch of Germanicus. This family was not originally from Gallia Celtica but Gallia Aquitania, and their removal to Lugdunum provides evidence of the city's growing importance in Gaul and the abandonment of older Celtic settlements in favor of newer Roman towns. As this suggests, Lugdunum became a diverse mixture of communities, including traders, sailors, wine growers, and artisans such as potter and artists. Within each separate community there was a well-defined hierarchy with boards representing specific professions and providing a structure to the whole commercial structure. Some of these communities were so organized and cohesive that they had their own cemeteries.[294]

From its foundation, Lugdunum held the status of *optimo iure*, which gave its citizens all the political and civic benefits of the Romans. However, those benefits came at a price since they

---

[294] P. 181, *Lugdunum: Naissance d'une capital (Lugdunum: Birth of a Capital)* (ed.) A. Desbat (2005). Catalogue d'exposition, Musée de la Civilisation gallo-romaine de Lyon.

were more heavily taxed than their counterparts within Italy.[295] In terms of administration, the city mirrored Rome and was governed by magistrates and a senate. The magistrates were divided into three separate categories, *quaestor, aedile* and *duumviri*, and in general an ambitious magistrate would start as a *quaestor* and work his way through to the top position, the *duumviri*. As in Rome, the various magistracies took on specific responsibilities. The *aediles*, for example, took care of road maintenance and the upkeep of all the public buildings. The *quaestors* and *duumviri* were more directly involved in tax gathering, while the *duumviri* also had judicial functions and took charge of elections.

In addition to a very well-run administrative system, strong trading links, and an advantageous geographical position, Lugdunum had one further advantage: it was the seat of the legate of Roman Gaul, which, in effect, made it the capital of the whole of Gaul. As the capital, the center of the Imperial cult was based there, as well as the various amphitheaters and temples to house the cult and those who came to honor the emperor. In the same vein, the Imperial priesthood was also based in Lugdunum, and since the priesthood of the Imperial cult was the highest federal administrative office to which any Gallic Roman could aspire, the city attracted the most ambitious and talented Gallic aristocrats.

In the city, the Ara Augusti was erected by all the Gallic states. This was a very large altar upon which were inscribed the names of all 60 Gallic states that sent representatives to Lugdunum each year to honor the emperor. Each state was represented on the altar by a figurine, and it is thought that some of these figures were statues while others were reliefs. In addition, there was a massive statue of Augustus placed in the middle of the 60 other figures.[296] It is known that the annual celebration began in 12 B.C.:

Lugdunum inevitably played a role in major events during the rest of Rome's history, and it was crucial for Roman politics. When Rome was badly damaged during the Great Fire of Rome in the reign of Nero, Lugdunum sent four million sesterces to help the victims. Their generosity did not go unrewarded, because only a year later Lugdunum suffered its own massively destructive fire and Nero sent the same sum back to assist in the rebuilding. Nero's generosity was in turn repaid about a year later in 68 A.D., when Vindex, the legatus of Gallia Lugdunensis, led a revolt against Nero but Lugdunum remained loyal to the emperor.

As luck would have it, Nero committed suicide and his successor Galba was so incensed by Lugdunum's loyalty to Nero that he punished the city with increased taxes. Fortunately for Lugdunum, Galba's reign was extremely brief, and after the Year of the Four Emperors, it found itself back in favor. Lugdunum remained the most important city in Gaul until well into the 4th century A.D. and then became an important regional city following the collapse of the empire.

---

[295] P.955, *History of Lyon :The origins to today Lyon,* by A. Pelletier (2007). Publishing Art and History Lyon.
[296] Strabo, *Geography*, Vol. I.

Gallia Belgica was located in the northeastern region of Gaul and comprised modern day Belgium, Luxembourg and parts of the Netherlands. Caesar's success in Gallia Celtica quickly brought him up against the Belgae, and in a series of hard won victories he succeeded in defeating what he described as the most dangerous of the Gallic groups. Caesar was wary of meeting the Belgae in open conflict and instead adopted tactics involving skirmishes, using his cavalry and smaller units of tribesmen. He only risked larger scale battle when he managed to isolate individual tribes. This piecemeal strategy proved effective and, along with his more lenient treatment of those who submitted to his authority, resulted in a much quicker conquest of Belgica than might have been anticipated.

Following Caesar's victory in the Gallic Wars, Belgica became a province in 50 B.C. and was officially confirmed as such by Augustus in 22 B.C. The province was named after the main tribe of the region, the Belgae, but other major tribes included the Treveri, Mediomatrici, Sequani, and a number of other smaller groups. The southern border of the new province was formed by the Rivers Marne and Seine, just as they had prior to Caesar's victory. Caesar wrote that the Belgae were descended from Germanic peoples from the eastern bank of the Rhine but provided no evidence to confirm his claim. Historians now believe the Belgae were descendants of one of the Celtic tribes.[297]

Augustus restructured the provinces of Gaul, and in 22 B.C. Marcus Agrippa split the whole of Gallia Comata into the three major provinces on the basis of what he saw as differences in language, race, and traditions. Gallia Belgica was, under his plan, meant to reflect a perceived mixture of Celtic and Germanic peoples.[298] Reims was made the capital, but this was later moved to Trier, though the exact date of the relocation is unknown. Reims was founded by the Gauls around 80 B.C. and was known as Durocorteron, or "place of the round tower." It was built as the capital of the Remi tribe, which allied with the Romans during the Gallic Wars and remained loyal to Rome throughout the fighting and subsequent insurrections. This brought them into favor with the Romans, who elevated their capital to the status of capital of the new province of Belgica. At its height it had a population of somewhere between 50,000 and 100,000 people.[299]

Reims remained a very settled and prosperous city throughout the early years of the empire, but in due course it was supplanted as Belgica's capital due to restructuring and the emergence of Trier as an important center. Trier was situated in the territory of the Treveri, who were subjugated by Caesar in the Gallic Wars. The city was founded in 16 B.C. as Augusta Treverorum in honor of the emperor and became capital of Belgica following Domitian's reforms in 90 A.D. Its status led to a gradually increasing population, and at its height it approached 100,000. Many of the most famous Roman structures in Trier, such as the Porta

---

[297] Pp. 12-14, *Gallia Belgica* by E.M. Wightman (1985) University of California Press.
[298] *Encyclopedia of the Roman Empire* (Facts on File Library of World History) by M. Bunson (2002). Facts on File: New York.
[299] P. 47, *An historical Geography of France* by X. de Planhol (1994). Cambridge University Press.

Negra gate, date from the later Roman period, but during its time as the capital of the region, it was a major trading center.

Berthold Werner's picture of the remains of the Porta Negra

Today's historians view Agrippa's divisions of Gaul as arbitrary at worst and based on a lack of understanding of the ethnography of the area at worst. Thus, while the division of Gaul Comata into three provinces was administratively more efficient, it did not reflect the reality of the makeup of indigenous populations within Gaul.[300] As with other parts of Gaul, the early emperors employed a conscious program of Romanization, combined with a toleration of certain local customs and traditions to help pacify and control the province.

Within Belgica, four *civitates* were created that were more or less based on existing tribal boundaries, and these civitates in turn were subdivided into smaller units. The *civitates*, named Menapiorum, Nerviorum, Treverorum and Tungrorum, were administered from separate capitals, though these changed over the years. The whole government of the region was administered by a Concilia based in Reims (and then Trier), and, as with all the provinces of Gaul, the Concilia looked to the legatus based in Lugdunum as the ultimate authority. All local nobles were required to take part in the festival in Lugdunum that honored the emperor as described above, and Belgic nobility were no different in this respect from their peers in other areas of Gaul. Belgica, too, gradually adopted Romanized names, and Roman laws and customs inexorably

---

[300] *The Cambridge Ancient History New Ed. Vol 10* ed. A.K. Bowman (1996). Cambridge University Press.

forced out the local ones. Rebellions were minor and sporadic.[301]

The further restructuring of Belgica that occurred in 90 A.D., referred to above in connection with the moving of the province's capital, changed Belgica dramatically. Emperor Domitian reorganized it to separate the militarized zones adjacent to the Rhine from the civilian areas. Northeastern Belgica was split from the rest of the province and renamed Germania Inferior, and subsequently Germania Secunda. The eastern part became Germania Superior and the new Gallia Belgica was expanded southwards to include Cambrai, Arras, Amiens, Reims, Metz, and Trier.

From the very beginning of its status as a province, the Romans considered Belgica to be more advanced economically than most other parts of Gaul, and they considered the tribesmen as good recruits for the auxiliary units that Rome depended upon. As with other parts of Gaul, Roman customs, laws, and ways were absorbed remarkably easily, and this was no doubt in part due to the increased prosperity that the *Pax Romana* brought in its wake.

Gallia Aquitania, like Gallia Comata, can be translated as "Land of the Long Haired Gaul," and as a Roman province it bordered Gallia Lugdunensis, Narbonensis, and Hispania Tarraconesis. Geographically, its boundaries were provided by the Rivers Garonne and Loire, as well as the Pyrenees. The 20 Aquitanian tribes and the 14 Celtic tribes that inhabited the area lived mainly along the Atlantic coast, but significant numbers also lived in the interior on the slopes of the Cemmenus Mountains. The soil along the coast tended to be sandy, and the thin soil was capable of growing millet but little else. However, the coastal region held by the Tarbelli tribe was rich in gold, which could be mined comparatively easily. The interior, more mountainous regions had better soil, so the tribes occupying those areas not only were able to grow a wider variety of crops but had the advantage of silver and iron mines.

The Carduci tribe was also renowned for its linen production. All of these natural advantages combined to make Aquitania an attractive prospect in terms of conquest. Strabo characterized the people as wealthy and legends tell of Aquitani kings driving gold carriages and scattering gold and silver coins to the population.[302]

As in other parts of Gaul, the tribal groups were organized into larger bodies that the Romans called *civitates* and which were used as the basis of their administrative system. Following Caesar's victory in the Gallic Wars, he named the region Aquitania based on its triangular shape rather than the supposed length of its inhabitants' hair. Other suggestions for the origins of the name include the idea that it was somehow connected to the Latin word *aqua* or from a word similar to the modern Basque word Akize.

Sporadic rebellions continued against Roman rule until Agrippa won a decisive victory against the Aquitani in 38 B.C. It was the smallest of the four provinces that were set up in Gaul in the

---

[301] P. 74, *Gallia Belgica* by E.M. Wightman (1985) University of California Press.
[302] Strabo, *Geography*, IV.2.

aftermath of the various wars and was added to by Augustus following consultations with local Gallic chieftains. Agrippa used the results of a census conducted in 27 B.C. to come up with his division of the whole of Gaul, and, as with other parts of Gaul, he tended to overlook any information that contradicted his assessment of local languages and ethnic background.[303] The new province was placed under the command of a praetor, but interestingly no legions were posted to it.

Strabo suggested that there were significant differences between the Aquitani and the other Gauls. He and Caesar both cited differences in language and laws, but Strabo also highlighted what he considered to be significant physical differences. His belief was that the Aquitanians were closer to Iberians than Gauls.[304] Strabo's conclusions were more accurate than Caesar's, and archaeological evidence has confirmed that the Aquitani were indeed more akin to Iberians than Celts. The prevailing language at the time of the Roman conquest was an early form of Basque, and scholars have debated whether this Aquitanian language can be classified as Proto-Basque or as a remnant of the earlier Vaconic language group that had been common in the area. This particular issue might seem of little importance, but Basque is the last surviving non-Indo-European language in Western Europe and has had an effect on French and Spanish. For linguists, its origins are therefore a matter of significant interest.

The boundaries set up under Augustus, despite the mixing of the very different tribes, remained in place until Diocletian's reforms in the later empire period around 293 A.D. The largest settlement in the new province was Burdigala, modern day Bordeaux, and it is believed there was a settlement on this site as early as the 567 B.C. Historians think it was founded by a Celtic tribe, the Bituriges Vivisci, probably of Aquitania origin. The settlement was close to the Atlantic coast in the north of the Aquitaine region and built on a bend in the River Garonne. It was, and still is, divided into two parts, with the right bank to the east and the left bank to the west. The left bank was the most developed part of the town because the river at that side was deep enough to allow the passing of merchants.

The Romans' first real involvement with the town came in 107 B.C. when they tried to defend their allies, the Allobroges. The Romans were defeated at this Battle of Burdigala in 107 B.C., during which their commander Lucius Cassius Longinus was killed, adding to the humiliation. The city finally fell into Roman hands around 60 B.C.

It had been coveted for quite some time because it was a major center for the tin and lead trade that was so vital to Rome. Eventually, following the Gallic Wars, it became the capital of the province of Aquitaine and flourished as a commercial center well into the 4th century A.D.

It might be argued that the most important thing that the Romans brought to Burdigala was the

---

[303] *Encyclopedia of the Roman Empire* (Facts on File Library of World History) by M. Bunson (2002). Facts on File: New York.
[304] Strabo, *Geography*, IV.2.

vine. To this day, it is the center of an immense wine industry.

Gaul as a whole was very far from being the backward land of uncivilized savages depicted by the Romans. It was vastly populated and had a social structure of its own, as well as an organized set of religious beliefs, watched over by a highly educated priesthood. Gaul was never a cohesive nation state or anything remotely like it, but the Gauls did have the capacity, through the Druids, to combine very disparate tribes for short periods of time to achieve particular objectives. Gaul's ultimate weakness was that it did not have the capacity to sustain unity for long enough periods to ward off more organized civilizations.

In Rome, the Gauls came up against the worst possible enemy for them, one that was systematic, patient, and efficient. Of course, the Romans also had the advantage of being unified and led by a military genius in Caesar. Both sides had very able and brave soldiers, as well as capable leaders, but the eventual Roman military success after eight years of fighting is understandable even though the numbers on each side would at first blush suggest that the Roman conquest should have been impossible.

Despite the military defeat, and even allowing for the reduced numbers of the Gallic population due to their losses in the conflict, it can be reasonably argued that the Gauls should have been able to resist the total integration of their culture into that of Rome. The fact that they did not do so is the result of a combination of factors. The first of these were the administrative systems which Rome employed, often based on local ones, a conscious program of Romanization, and a period of internal peace, the *Pax Romana*, that enabled Rome to consolidate its control. Roman roads not only brought all regions into contact, allowing military responses to problems to be swift, but they also brought increased trade and prosperity. Roman settlements, often based on older Gallic *oppida*, brought further wealth and security, as well as veterans and other colonists who spread Latin and Roman culture. The building of major public works enhanced the lives of many Gauls and bound them to the new order.

To be fair, the *Pax Romana* brought an unprecedented period of prosperity, and to share in that prosperity the Gauls had to become Romanized, speak the language, and accept the Roman Pantheon. All of this created an atmosphere in which the elites were only too keen to become Roman. Academics at the Catholic University Eichstatt-Ingolstadt concluded after exhaustive research that Gaul was one of the most Romanized areas of the empire, and the depth of Romanization can be seen in the fact that modern France is still considered to be a "Latin" country.

After the death of Marcus Aurelius, matters changed drastically for the worse. Cassius Dio remarked that after his death, Roman history "now descends from a kingdom of gold to one of iron and rust."[305] The decline of the empire was slow and painful, yet Gaul, despite all the trials

---

[305] Cassius Dio, *Roman History*, 7.1 36.3-4.

and tribulations, continued to be a Romanized province, and Rome's culture stayed in place. The fact that Rome retained its hold on Gaul for over 500 years is a remarkable tribute to the effectiveness of the Romans' attempts to assimilate people who were once among their most legendary enemies.

The Romanization of Hispania

With military pacification completed, the Romans were now in a position to develop Hispania unhampered. The aim of the emperors was the full integration of the peninsula into the empire, and this required a different approach than the oppressive tactics adopted by the Republic. The peninsula underwent a series of territorial reshuffles which eventually saw the emergence of three distinct zones: Tarraconensis, which included an extended Nearer Spain covering most of central Spain, Cantabria, Asturias and Galicia; Baetia, largely Andalusia with a new boundary pushed back from the Tagus to the Guadiana; and Lusitania, a newly formed province that formed the geographic foundations of modern Portugal. In later years, the Balearic Islands and parts of Morocco were also incorporated into the empire and administered from the peninsula.[306]

The provinces in Spain under Augustus became a mixture of Imperial and Senatorial. The Imperial provinces were governed by *legati Augusti pro praetore*, delegates of Augustus with praetorian rank. These officials could be former Consuls or former praetors, but either way they usually had a military background. They were assisted by *legati legionis*, military tribunes and prefects. They also had judicial and administrative power.

In Hispania, the *legatus Augusti* had a legate to assist him with judicial functions. Finances were administered by the Equestrian procurators, but this was quite different from the situation in Senatorial provinces, where they were concerned only with the property of the Princeps and a quaestor was in charge of public finances. Strabo recounts Augustus's changes in his *History of Rome*: "[N]ow, the provinces having been allotted, some to the people and the senate, some to the leader of the Romans, Baetica belongs to the people, and a praetor is sent to it with a quaestor and a legate; they have fixed its boundary to the east near Castulo. The rest is Caesar's and he sends out two legates, a praetorian and a consular. The praetorian, with a legate with him, administers justice to the Lusitanians, who live next to Baetica and extend to the river Durius and its mouth; that is the name they now give to this area. Here there is Augusta Emerita. The rest, the greater part of Spain, is under the consular governor, with a considerable army of three legions and three legates. One of these keeps guard with two legions over all the country beyond the Durius to the north, what used to be called Lusitania and dubbed Callaecia; the northern mountains with the Astures and the Cantabri join on to it. The adjacent coast as far as the Pyrenees is guarded by the second legate with the other legion and the third oversees the inland area. It contains the already mentioned peaceful peoples who have adopted civilised Italian manners and wear the toga, the Celtiberians and those that live on either side of the Iberus down

---

[306] It is this incorporation that formed the basis of Spanish claims to those areas in later years.

to the maritime area. The governor himself winters in the maritime area, especially in Carthago and Tarraco, administering justice. And in summer he goes on circuit inspecting anything that needs reform."[307]

In addition to this administrative effort, the Romans began the process of, as they saw it, civilizing the region and bringing the benefits of Roman rule to the Iberians. A program of urbanization was instigated, and new towns were used to lure recalcitrant Iberians into acquiescence through the granting of privileges. Augustus began the process by encouraging an influx of Roman and Italian culture. 21 colonies were founded, surpassing the numbers of those founded by the Phoenicians, Carthaginians, and Greeks, and the citizens of many of these cities were granted Latin rights, the ultimate reward for accepting Roman rule. The towns came to be linked by a 12,000 mile road network, including the Via Augusta that ran from Cadiz along the coast to the Pyrenees. The main purpose behind these roads was military, but they also contributed hugely to the economic development of the peninsula and the expansion of the Roman way of life.

With the towns came all the usual features of Roman urban living, most notably aqueducts, amphitheaters, temples, baths and administrative buildings. These new structures constantly reinforced the power of Rome, encouraged Iberians to enjoy the fruits of civilization, and induced, possibly seduced, them to become Roman. This policy, and the long period of Roman rule, resulted in Hispania becoming totally Romanized, possibly even more so than Gallia Narbonensis. A very thorough intertwining of Italian and Celtiberian ways of life saw a separation of classes, with the towns and larger communities becoming very Roman while the lower class workers, miners, and peasants were affected only by the Roman language, currency, and service in the army.

The children of the leaders of the tribes were often taken as hostages and educated either in Rome or in Roman households in Iberia. Many of those educated in this way became thoroughly Romanized, and as they grew into adulthood and set up their own households, they became advocates for the Roman way of life. They were often quite zealous in their appreciation of the benefits of Roman rule, and, as with so many converts, were often keen to display their new status as Romans on every occasion they could. As members of the local elites, they had a considerable effect on the whole Romanization process.

Hispania provided troops for the legions who were renowned for their stamina, probably due to their hard upbringing in the Iberian mountains or labor in the fields. The upper classes, too, made their contribution to the empire and produced a number of brilliant intellectuals and writers. Marcus Porcius Latro was an Iberian who taught Ovid. Seneca the Elder and Seneca the Younger were both from the peninsula, as were Pomponius Mela, Lucius Columella, Quintilian the historian, and the satirist Martial. Citizens from Hispania took on more and more positions of

---

[307] Strabo, *Geography*, II.iii.4.20.

power - Cornelius Balbus became Consul, while Hadrian and Trajan became emperors.

After Italy itself, Spain became one of the most productive parts of the empire. Olives, oil, grain and wine were exported to all parts of the Mediterranean. Spanish silver, lead, tin, copper, gold and iron could be found throughout the known world with tin and lead from Spain even finding its way to India. Pliny reckoned that the annual gold output of the Asturias, Galician and Lusitanian mines amounted to 20,000 pounds in weight.[308] In terms of agriculture, the Romans introduced an agrarian pattern of large landed estates known as *latifundia*. These were normally owned and run by Iberians or rich immigrants from Rome. They became a powerful landowning class, and the pattern they established was maintained until very recently and proved to be one of the major obstacles to the modernization of Spanish agriculture.

Despite the many inadequacies of Roman rule, and the fact that the numerous tribes in the north took a long time to enter the fold, the peninsula certainly enjoyed a prolonged period of political stability and commercial prosperity under the first period of the empire that was matched only in the days of Spain's own imperial glory. Peace and civilization bring their own rewards, and, inevitably, Romanization and progressive integration brought improvements in most aspects of life to the vast majority of Iberians. As part of his administrative reforms, Augustus had made provincial governors salaried officials, and this one measure alone had reduced the corruption that had been so widespread in Spain under the Republic. He also introduced reforms such as the levying of a new general tax that distributed the burden of taxation more evenly. The introduction of this tax in 38 B.C. was considered to be of such importance that it was regarded as the dawn of a new era. Even up until the late Middle Ages it was used as the point of departure for calculating dates in Spain instead of Christ's year of birth.

The Roman legions in Iberia were gradually reduced as more and more towns in the Peninsula gained civic emancipation. The numbers of enslaved also decreased over time, and more Iberians achieved tenant farmer status. Intermarriage resulted in the population becoming a mixture of indigenous Iberians and Romans born in Rome, and Romans born in Spain. By the beginning of the 5th century A.D., the population could be more accurately called Hispano-Roman than anything else. This mixed population looked to Rome as the very heart of the civilized world, and many of its greatest figures flocked there, guaranteeing that despite its wealth and prosperity, the Iberian Peninsula remained a satellite of Rome.

One of the most lasting bequests of Rome to the peninsula was the Latin language. No subsequent invasion, no matter how protracted, managed to replace it in Spain once it had been established. The language that came to dominate the peninsula was not the Classical Latin of educated Roman elites but rather the common Latin used by soldiers and peasants of the empire. It came to be known as Vulgar Latin, and its adoption in Spain was no great surprise. The pre-Roman population spoke a vast range of languages and dialects that could not withstand the

---

[308] Pliny the Elder, *The Natural Histories*, III.4.

convenience and effectiveness of a sophisticated language spoken by conquerors, settlers, educators, administrators and magistrates alike. In the new Roman world, traders had to speak the language and the many Iberians drafted into the legions as auxiliaries had to learn it. The Latin spoken in Spain was colored by the vocabulary and habits of pronunciation of the languages it overlaid, but it was a language that over the years evolved into the Romance languages of the peninsula, in much the same way the Latin of Italy became Italian and the Latin of Gaul became French.

The empire's other lasting gift to Spain was Christianity, which reached the Mediterranean coasts in the middle of the 1st century A.D. As might be guessed in the case of new ideas and cultures, Christianity first took root in the cities of the south and east, while in the interior, Christianity found it harder to gain a foothold among the staunchly pagan tribes. As elsewhere in the empire, Christians were subjected to harsh repression in the 2nd and 3rd centuries in particular, but the punishments handed out to Christians were so severe that in the end they had the effect of garnering sympathy from non-Christians and resulted in a greater conversion rate than might otherwise have been the case. During those years, the empire was becoming even more authoritarian, and Christianity came to be seen as the religion of the poor and the victimized. As corruption reemerged, more and more Iberians found themselves poverty stricken and had to resort to selling themselves into slavery. It was a Spaniard, Emperor Theodosius, who made Christianity the official religion of the Empire in 380 A.D. and branded devotees of all other religions as heretics that had to be punished. It was also in Spain that three of the most important Councils that established Christian doctrine were held.[309]

In the late 3rd century A.D., the invasions of the Peninsula by Franks and Suevi devastated Iberia and Roman rule began to crumble. It was the Christian Church that became the symbol of stability in this chaotic and hostile world. As Christianity grew, Spain began to see itself as something distinct from the empire, and the more Roman administration disintegrated, the more the Church took over and filled the vacuum, both in secular and religious life. Thus, even when Roman rule finally collapsed, having been so weakened by years of decay, in one sense, the empire did survive because the Church, modeled on the hierarchical and authoritarian pattern of Rome, outlived and perpetuated the organism that helped to produce it. In the centuries to come, it proved to be Spain's strongest source of continuity.

The end of Roman Spain can be dated to 418 A.D. The Romans invited the Visigoths to help them oust various Alans, Suevi and Vandals that had poured into Spain since 409, and the Visigoths were promised lands in Aquitaine in return for assistance in restoring the three Hispanic provinces to Rome. The Visigoths were successful in their mission, but, instead of returning to Gaul as agreed, they took over control of Hispania themselves. With a population of over 6 million, the Visigoths' mere 200,000 should have been swamped, but they were not and instead established their capital at Toledo. They ruled mostly without problems until the end of

---

[309] The three Councils are the Synod of Elvira, the Synod of Arles, and the Synod of Ancyra.

the 7th century.

The Romans had become involved in Spain not as a result of a direct and planned policy of territorial expansion but rather as an adjunct to its wars against the Carthaginians. Having defeated Carthage in the First Punic War, the main aim of Roman policy in the western Mediterranean was the prevention of its enemy from recovering their power and wealth through the exploitation and annexation of the Iberian Peninsula. It is possible that if the Carthaginians had kept to the treaty that established the Ebro as the border between their two spheres of influence, peace might have been preserved for some time, although it is unlikely that war could have been avoided indefinitely. Regardless, Hannibal was determined to renew the war against Rome and successfully manipulated the Romans into declaring war first.

In retrospect, despite auspicious factors such as the stirrings of the Gauls at the time, the Carthaginians were not ready to take the war to Rome. The net result was that Roman determination to root out their enemies from their holdings in Spain was accomplished by victory in the Second Punic War. In casting the Carthaginians out of Spain, the Romans found themselves in control and began developing Iberia for its own ends. The exploitation of the peninsula under the Republic was brutal to say the least and resulted in constant revolts that initiated further repression in a never ending cycle. It was not until the time of Augustus and the early emperors that Rome employed the carrot as well as the stick and began a policy of Romanizing the population.

This was not a quick fix either, and, indeed, the final military subjugation of the peninsula took another 100 years after Augustus. The widespread use of Latin, the foundation of colonies, and the enhancement of urban centers to include all the refinements of Roman life gradually won over the population, and the provinces of Spain became so integrated into the Roman system that it even produced emperors from among its own people. The later years of the empire saw a return to the oppressive practices that had so alienated the indigenous population in the period under the Republic, and dissatisfaction with Rome eroded its authority to the extent that when Iberia was invaded in the 5th century A.D., Spain no longer saw Rome as its natural protector. The Christian Church had become the one source of continuity and stability.

Nevertheless, by the time it had evaporated, Roman rule had brought immense changes to the Iberian Peninsula, notably the introduction of a new language that forms the basis of modern Spanish today. It changed patterns of landholding to ones that persisted well into the modern era, and it saw the establishment of a Roman Catholic Church that the Spaniards took to heart. The administrative system that the Romans applied also still has ramifications and forms the basis of many of the autonomous regions of the country. Despite the conquest and settlement of much of the peninsula by the Moors in the 8th century A.D., the Roman legacy survived and still plays a part in shaping Spain today.

Online Resources

Other books about Rome by Charles River Editors

Other books about ancient history by Charles River Editors

Further Reading

The conquest of Gaul, by Gaius Julius Caesar, translated by S. A. Handford and revised by Jane F. Gardner

"De Bello Gallico" and Other Commentaries at Project Gutenberg.

Gilliver, Kate. Caesar's Gallic Wars 58–50 B.C. London: Osprey Publishing, 2002.

Goldsworthy, Adrian. Caesar. London, England: Orion Books Ltd, 2007.

Grant, Michael. Julius Caesar. London, England: Weidenfeld and Nicolson, 1969.

Holland, Tom. Rubicon.

Matyszak, Philip. The enemies of Rome.

Wyke, Maria .Caesar: A Life in Western Culture. Chicago: University of Chicago Press, 2008.

Free Books by Charles River Editors

We have brand new titles available for free most days of the week. To see which of our titles are currently free, click on this link.

Discounted Books by Charles River Editors

We have titles at a discount price of just 99 cents everyday. To see which of our titles are currently 99 cents, click on this link.

Printed in Great Britain
by Amazon